JOURNEY
into the LAND
of
TRIALS

The Story of
Davy Crockett's Expedition
to the Alamo

Manley F. Cobia Jr.

Hillsboro Press
PROVIDENCE PUBLISHING CORPORATION
FRANKLIN, TENNESSEE

TENNESSEE HERITAGE LIBRARY

Printed in the United States of America

07   06   05   04   03   1   2   3   4   5

Library of Congress Catalog Card Number: 2002115379

ISBN: 1-57736-268-3

Cover photo of the Alamo by Richard Federici

Cover design by Gary Bozeman

HILLSBORO PRESS
an imprint of
Providence Publishing Corporation
238 Seaboard Lane • Franklin, Tennessee 37067
800-321-5692
www.providencepubcorp.com

Contents

Acknowledgments

W ithout the kindness and assistance of the many librarians and archivists, it would have been impossible to have assembled the information and illustrations necessary to produce this book. Those who helped me in procuring copies of articles, documents, and books included: Jack D. Wood of the Jackson/Madison County Library in Tennessee; Mary Medearis, Magdalene Collums, and Gail Martin of the Southwest Arkansas Regional Archives in the Old Washington Historic State Park, Washington, Arkansas; Lisa Cornelius of the Red River County Library in Clarksville; Joan L. Dobson of the Dallas Public Library; Anne Kendall and Pamela Lynn Palmer of Special Collections at the Ralph W. Steen Library on the campus of the Stephen F. Austin State University; Dianna Scott of the Stern-Hoya House Library and Museum; Lillian Melton of the Nacogdoches Public Library, in Nacogdoches; Virginia Dickerson of the San Augustine Public Library; Jim Nance of San Augustine; Ellen N. Murry of the Star of the Republic Museum in the Washington-on-the-Brazos State Historical Park; Mrs. O. M. Brown of the Chappell Hill Historical Society; John Anderson of the Texas State Library and Archives Commission in Austin; and Martha Utterback, Linda Edwards, Warren Stricker, Sally Koch, Melinda Loomis, and the late Bernice Strong, all of the Daughters of the Republic of Texas Library in San Antonio, Texas.

Special thanks to W. K. McNeil, folklorist of the Ozark Mountain Folk Center in Mountain View, Arkansas, who gave me some helpful suggestions on where to begin looking for information about Crockett in Arkansas; Skipper Steely of Paris, Texas, was gracious enough to invite us to his backyard barbecue and share some of his extensive knowledge of the earliest settlers and tales of Old Miller County; Mrs. Bill Hall of the Red River County Public Library, who responded enthusiastically to my numerous questions concerning the early settlers of Clarksville; Mary Fowler of the Bertha Voger Memorial Library in Honey Grove spent considerable time looking up information in old newspaper clippings and books which dealt with Crockett's sojourn in northeast Texas. Dorothy Gossett Jones, who has written a book about the Gossett family in Texas, provided valuable information, as did Eliza Bishop of the Houston County Historical Commission in the city of Crockett. Ms. Bishop instantly unraveled the mystery of the David Crockett Oak Tree.

I am also grateful to Allison Webster of the University Press of Kentucky in Lexington for her thoughtful suggestions and encouraging words.

Finally, much credit goes to the staff at Providence House Publishers in Franklin, Tennessee, for their professionalism and efficiency.

Introduction

ociety's understanding of historical figures is to a great extent dependent upon the quality of its sources. It was once believed that much of our perception of Davy Crockett came from folklore, but it has been determined that our sources are predominately literary. Even by the time he set out for Texas, Crockett was already a national celebrity. Two books, including a best-selling biography, had been written about him. His autobiography, not yet even two years old, was in its twelfth printing, and a series of publications called the *Davy Crockett Almanacs* had just begun their twenty-two-year run. The fourth book, and perhaps the one most responsible for solidifying the dominant Crockett legend, was the best-selling *Col. Crockett's Exploits and Adventures in Texas, Written by Himself* (hereafter referred to as *Exploits*). Within months of its release, the *Western Monthly Magazine* published a critique wherein the reviewer expressed suspicion that the book was probably a spurious product. Preferring to think of the late David Crockett metaphorically, the reviewer observed, "His private qualities are forgotten and merged into those of his class and age—of whom he is the allegory and personification."[1] Other, more scientific, approaches would be forthcoming.

In 1893, Frederick Jackson Turner introduced his highly persuasive "frontier hypothesis," which refuted the popular belief that American democracy had been forged in the halls of legislation and was instead born in the forests of North America. Emphasizing the impact of the frontier environment upon the individual, Turner's thesis heralded the scholarly triumph for the forces of nature over the Old World institution of heredity. Whereas Turner appreciated the moccasin-clad frontiersman and hailed Andrew Jackson as a model of egalitarianism and individualism, trendsetting Vernon Louis Parrington saw Jacksonian Democracy as a brutish repudiation of Jeffersonian liberalism. Jackson may have exhibited more low class habits than a president of the United States should, but Parrington seemed satisfied that he at least shared none of Crockett's primitive simplicity. Although certain that American thought was grounded in the Jeffersonian tradition of liberalism and rebellion, Parrington dismissed Crockett as a joke.

Arthur M. Schlesinger Jr. took Jacksonian Democracy very seriously but found the Davy Crockett of history to be a "picturesque if somewhat phony frontiersman."[2] Constance Rourke, Walter Blair, and Richard M. Dorson explored various combinations of the Crockett of history and legend. Blair expanded the field of inquiry by identifying six separate Crockett personalities. Accrediting the fictional Crockett as a subject of serious study to the near total "neglect of the historical man,"[3] was to James A. Shackford a fallacious and misguided approach. Observing the scholarly practice of referring to the historical Crockett as "David" and the mythological figure as "Davy," Shackford set out to expropriate for history the "Crockett God made."[4] Blair may have thought the task of demythologization impossible, but Shackford was confident that a disciplined application of critical historiographical techniques would succeed in securing proper recognition for the Crockett of history. Shackford viewed Crockett as the protagonist playing out the ancient story of man venturing into the wilderness. More important, he saw Crockett as not only representative of this nation's "common stock" but as a pioneer who explored America's physical frontier and the "spiritual frontier" of democracy.[5] Not entirely serious, Shackford apologized to those who found the real Crockett less exciting than his imaginary counterparts.

Just prior to the release of Shackford's book in the mid-1950s, Walt Disney Studios premiered its phenomenally popular television mini-series, *Davy Crockett, King of the Wild Frontier*. While attempting to be both entertaining and morally instructive, the studio took the standard theatrical liberties, thereby allowing them to squeeze the last twenty-four years of the hero's life into three episodes. In the existing atmosphere of relative harmony between pop culture and traditional values, the message to America's young was a potent one: Moses had to climb to the mountain top, Crockett was born there. This all proved to be too much for a few outspoken cynics who accused Disney of brainwashing an entire generation of children and purposely manipulating the public's perception of history. Such a man, they charged, never existed. Angry parents denounced these public disclosures as detrimental and socially irresponsible. Even if entirely true, they argued, some truth should remain hidden, if for no other reason than for the sake of America's children. William F. Buckley Jr. predicted that Crockett would survive the assaults of the liberal press. The question was in what form.

Continued reliance on *Exploits* was clearly evident in the work of Rourke and Disney Studios. Both spent considerable effort telling the story of Crockett's journey to Texas and the Alamo. This final phase took up well over a quarter of the main text in Rourke's book, while Disney devoted one-third of their entire program to the Texas segment. For generations of Americans, Crockett's journey to Texas provided a climactic final chapter to the story of a life lived honorably.

That perception of Crockett began to unravel in 1975 when Carmen Perry's translation of a Mexican officer's diary was published. Of the entire book, it was the implications of a single paragraph that caught everyone's attention. Here, in writing, was the testimony of an eyewitness to the execution of seven Alamo defenders, one of whom was identified as David Crockett. Perry received some bad publicity, disagreeable mail, and late night phone calls. Two years later, Daniel Kilgore formulated a composite model of the execution by incorporating additional testimonies. For such a tiny book, Kilgore generated an enormous amount of attention, almost all of it negative. Forgotten in all the controversy, which has ignited more debate than any other topic concerning the Alamo, the story of Crockett's last journey remains essentially untold.

The dramatic discovery of the hero's final moments, as taken from long lost documents, inspired postmodern scholarship to reopen their investigation into the historical Crockett. Two of the

most influential historians who contributed to a more contemporaneous understanding of Crockett were Richard Boyd Hauck and Paul
Andrew Hutton. Basically portraying Crockett as "a perfectly ordinary pioneer who had a brief flirtation with greatness,"[6] the "new
perspectives" represents a sharp break from the image known to
previous generations. Critical research boldly asserted that David
was not born on a mountain top, never wore a coonskin cap, did not
repair the Liberty Bell, and certainly did not die as we had imagined.

Despite the fact that Shackford had produced evidence to the
contrary, America persisted in the belief that Crockett left home for
the specific purpose of joining the fight for freedom in Texas.
Utilizing information previously unavailable, postmodern scholarship was able to do more than merely confirm Shackford's theory.
Their studies revealed that Crockett's motives for going to Texas, and
ultimately, the Alamo, were rather unremarkable. Embittered by
defeat in his campaign for a fourth congressional term, Crockett
departed Tennessee for Texas "to explore the land as well as the
economic prospects, not to fight a war."[7] While "in search of
economic and political opportunity,"[8] Crockett found what he
believed to be the "right path to fame and political fortune in
Texas."[9] Taking the Old San Antonio Road south, Crockett made his
way to the Alamo, where, "determined to live up to his legend,"[10] he
died a "martyr on the altar of Manifest Destiny."[11] Shackford had
discredited *Exploits*, but scholarship now exposed the book for what
it really was, "a call for chauvinistic support of American expansionism."[12]

Historian Margaret J. King studied what she described as the
"Disneyfication" of Crockett, a process by which the studio transformed the frontiersman into "the common man with dignity." She
astutely observed that the verbal accusations made thirty years
earlier amounted to nothing less than a direct challenge to the
popular perception that the historical Crockett was a man of good
character. And to King, this was the "most intriguing, contradictory,
and elusive phase" of the controversy.[13] It constitutes the central
issue of a conflict that has not yet been resolved.

The conclusions reached by postmodern scholarship inspired a
renewed round of comparative analysis by nonacademics. For
example, when historian Richard Shenkman compared the "true Davy

Crockett" with the Crockett from Disneyland, he found the personal qualities of the man who actually went to Texas far less honorable than what the children of the mid-1950s had been led to believe. In his 1988 best-selling book *Legends, Lies, & Cherished Myths of American History*, Shenkman revealed that Crockett, a former "juvenile delinquent" who never learned how to count, was considered to have been an "ignoramus" by his own friends. In Shenkman's final analysis, Crockett "wasn't respectable, and he wasn't the perfect role model for children."[14] Peter Jennings closed the century with the results of his own study, concluding that the real Crockett was nothing more than "a bit of a drunk and a scoundrel. . . ."[15]

In retrospect, the twentieth century saw a sharp decline in the influence of authentic and authoritative tradition. Attempting to establish a new sense of cohesion between the real world and idealized values, western society adopted certain fundamental assumptions. Under the scrutiny of critical analysis, the once true story of the heroic Crockett, as described by history, legend, and myth, has been discredited like Washington's cherry tree misadventure. Deprived of his coonskins and divested of noble qualities, conventional wisdom now argues that the immutable truth about Crockett is that he was devoutly antiauthoritarian, a model of "militant individualism,"[16] and as a peace-loving man dedicated to fighting for human rights, he represents the "spirit of unbridled democracy and bold egalitarianism."[17] Utilizing vocabulary palatable to adherents of the often contentious and seemingly irreconcilable pillars of postmodern liberalism, it is, though less heroic in the classical sense, a spirit synchronized with the prevailing philosophies of our time. While academic scholarship generally concedes that Crockett was a minor hero despite his agglomeration of faults, it is an acknowledgment constructed for reasons which past generations of Americans never would have thought possible.

As with many romantic tales emanating from a golden age, Crockett's story remains viable, if only because of an inert suspicion that at the very core of the legend lies a kernel of truth. Despite its near complete lack of reverence for historical accuracy, *Exploits* might be a melodramatic, though not an entirely inappropriate, title for a book chronicling Crockett's expedition to Texas. For his own study, Shackford concentrated only upon those elements of Crockett's last journey which he could document, but, of course, real people do not cease to exist where the trail of documentation ends. While any attempt to construct a historical accounting of Crockett's journey of no return, involving the necessary speculation about various possibilities, could only result in a rendition revealing few similarities to the book which carries the above title, there is certainly no need to offer any apologies here. The evaluations of Crockett's conduct during his final months, as offered by the "new perspectives," are simply not realistic. The tangible and circumstantial evidence supports an entirely different appraisal of the man who actually went to Texas.

1

A Republic in Sequence

Democracy in the Age of Heroes

It is conceivable that from a distance, early frontiersmen might have looked out upon nature in all its beauty and majesty, and experienced something analogous to what we might imagine Adam may have felt. Life in Eden was idyllic. There was no history, no sense of time, no need for laws. But outside the gates of Eden, nature was essentially an unrelenting cycle of horrific events. For hunters, killing was a way of life. To the political animal, nature was a place which was out of control.

It was in the atmosphere of revolution that Thomas Jefferson gave Jean-Jacques Rousseau's pronouncement that man is born in a natural state of freedom a political application. The optimistic Jeffersonians cautiously adopted Rousseau's faith in the natural goodness of the common man but did not subscribe to the philosopher's doctrine that the simplistic, independent, primitive man was psychologically more content than his complex, interdependent, civilized descendant. Yet, both Rousseauian naturalism and Jeffersonian agrarianism have their foundation in the mythology of the Garden of Eden.

America's founders were men of republican principles. The political lines of demarcation were drawn when Jefferson formed the Democratic-Republican Party to counter the Federalists, an assortment of aristocrats whom he had labeled as monarchists. The Democratic-Republicans were accused by the Federalists of favoring mob rule. Assailed as an intellectual, the impaler of

1

butterflies, inventor of gadgets useful only to the idle, Jefferson was portrayed as a philosopher, a contemplator of the abstract, in effect, a man who was not likely to get much of anything done. He was, in the opinion of his opponents, a very different kind of man than George Washington.

Often coupled with the phrase "the rise of the common man," Jacksonian Democracy, a social revolution spawned by the phenomenal popularity of Major General Andrew Jackson, was in full swing by 1828. Just as his supporters hailed Jackson as the political successor to Jefferson, Jacksonian Democracy emerged out of the Jeffersonian brand. One does not normally picture your stereotypical Jacksonian in the quiet of his cabin library reading post-classical Neoplatonic literature, though it no doubt happened. Presidential incumbent John Quincy Adams, a man of considerable education, intellect, and political experience, was overqualified compared to Jackson. While Jefferson considered Jackson unqualified for the presidency, some even believed he lacked the intellectual capacity to understand political theory. But when the electorate compared Adams, the man of thoughts and words, with Jackson, the man of common sense and action, the president appeared artificial, contrived, and generally lacking in every quality they admired in the general.

The school of American metaphysics may have proclaimed that America needed to discover an identity all its own, democratic in scope, and universally sweeping, but it was Jefferson who displayed the best sense of direction by looking west. Albert Pike would abandon Harvard for the open spaces west of the Mississippi River to perceive the exhilaration of unlimited freedom from all behavioral constraints, ceremony, and pretentiousness. This sense of freedom, a perception theologian Reinhold Niebuhr would later assert to be an experience known only to humans, was understood by some as the ultimate expression of independence from political despotism. In theory, it was this estrangement which propelled the individual beyond the stifling confines of social class to where all responsibility rested with him alone, thereby making the "self-made man" a possibility. And so, it was perceived that democracy in its purest or perhaps most primitive form was to be played out in the forests and plains of the west.

While the Jackson Administration applauded the July Revolution of 1830, the French aristocracy again feared for their lives. In May 1831, Alexis de Tocqueville and Gustave de Beaumont arrived in New York City to begin their study of American society. Nine months later, Tocqueville had accumulated the information he needed to write his classic work, *Democracy in America*. During their stay in Michigan, Tocqueville, an avid hunter fascinated by the prospect of experiencing the kind of freedom found in a primitive setting, informed some local residents of his ambition to take a leisurely excursion through the woods. They thought he was out of his mind.

Near the conclusion of their tour of America in December, the Frenchmen cruised down the Mississippi River on a steamboat where they met Sam Houston. Suitably attired in his buckskin leggings, moccasins, and Indian-styled hunting shirt, Houston, a citizen of the Cherokee Nation, would be about as close to Rousseau's "noble savage" as Tocqueville could hope to meet. Upon enquiring how such a man could have earned the respect of the populace, they were invariably told it was because "having come from the people," he had raised himself to success "by his own exertions." Houston may have been the product of an "unfortunate characteristic of popular sovereignty,"[1] but a week earlier in Memphis, Tocqueville was told a shocking story which convinced him of the extent to which democracy is capable of conferring dignity. In his diary, he wrote:

> Two years ago the inhabitants of the district of which Memphis is the capital sent to the House of Representatives in Congress an individual named David Crockett, who has had no education, can read with difficulty, has no property, no fixed residence, but passes his life hunting, selling his game to live, and dwelling continuously in the woods. His competitor, a man of wealth and talent, failed.[2]

Tocqueville characterized Crockett's habit of "electioneering," that is, conversing with individual voters, as a practice which would "disgust distinguished men." But then, real gentlemen knew that hunting was a sport, not a way of life. In Crockett, here was a man with limited social contact who could ridicule his opponents for their economic prosperity and openly brag about his lack of education as though it were an accomplishment, even to the point of claiming that reading and writing were unnatural acts.

Born in the sparsely populated hill country of what eventually became eastern Tennessee, Crockett's upbringing was noted for its shortage of social and economic advantages. As an introspective fifteen-year-old who wanted to make something of his life, David realized he had a major problem. Not only uneducated in the most rudimentary functions of arithmetic, he was, by his own admission, illiterate and ignorant of the first letter of the alphabet.[3] On his own initiative, he made arrangements to rectify this condition.[4] Though Crockett still entered the lower rungs of community leadership severely disadvantaged, he would compensate by taking full advantage of the anti-intellectual atmosphere cultivated in the emerging democracy, portraying himself as a self-made man whose talents were naturally derived.[5] Although Tocqueville acknowledged that the common man in America seemed "adequate for the ordinary conduct of society, despite their petty passions, their incomplete education, their vulgar manners," he was less certain as to how well they would perform in a time of crisis.[6] While assured that Crockett and his constituency were an anomaly in American life, Tocqueville concluded such phenomenon was exactly what could be expected when "the right of suffrage is universal."[7]

IN HIS OWN IMAGE

By the time Daniel Boone died in 1820, the eastern states were already beginning to look upon the west with a little nostalgia. Just prior to Boone's death, artist James Otto Lewis painted the legendary Kentuckian dressed in buckskin leggings, fringed hunting shirt, and moccasins. Lewis's portrait gave stage performer Noah Ludlow a fairly good idea as to what a real frontiersman should look like. In 1822, Ludlow first sang "The Hunters of Kentucky," a song about Jackson's "half-horse, half-alligator" volunteers, appropriately, on a New Orleans stage. After a rousing reception, Ludlow soon began touring the United States billed as the "Old Kentucky Hunter" to packed theaters everywhere. No one in the audiences seemed to notice, or care, that the singer, having been unable to locate a beaver hat like the one Boone held in his hand for the Lewis portrait, had opted for a coonskin cap. Publicly credited for the decimation of the British ranks at New Orleans, Jackson's Tennessee Volunteers were viewed as being of the same stock as Kentuckians.

While the Jackson campaign was using "The Hunters of Kentucky" as their election campaign song, a young actor named James H. Hackett made an offer of three hundred dollars for the best original play featuring an American as the principal character. The winning script was submitted by James K. Paulding. The play was "The Lion of the West, or, A Trip to Washington," later to be retitled, "The Kentuckian, or, A Trip to New York." Months before the first curtain was set to rise on opening night in New York City on April 25, 1831, rumor spread that the play's central figure was a caricature of Congressman Crockett.

The main character in the play was a Kentuckian named Nimrod Wildfire. Historically, Nimrod was the founder of the Babylonian kingdom. In both Babylonian and Hebrew tradition, Nimrod was portrayed as a great hunter. Possessing the mythological traits of strength, honesty, and bravery, the rambunctious Wildfire was a hunter, a colonel in the militia, and, as it just so happened, a candidate for Congress. And like the man in whose images he was identified, Wildfire was also a master storyteller and hero of the tall tale.

In this two-act play, Wildfire visits his cousin in the big city and clashes with an array of personalities belonging to various social classes. The play was basically a farce on differing aspects of British and American cultures with Wildfire and the would-be aristocracy representing the extremes. Confident and in command back home, but overbearing and awkward in society, Wildfire closed the play by confessing that culturally he was a sorry excuse for a "white man." Although audiences appreciated the fact that Wildfire possessed some truly noble qualities, they also sensed that he would never reach his potential.

Eighteen thirty-three saw the publication of two best-selling biographies, one of which was an update of Daniel Boone. The other biography was *The Life and Adventures of Colonel David Crockett of West Tennessee*. Plagiarizing pertinent dialogue from the play, the author of *The Life and Adventures* attributed the words, with appropriate modifications, to Crockett. It was precisely this aspect of

Crockett's image, that of a wild man, a Wildfire turned loose on society, which was susceptible to distortion and manipulation by his political adversaries. During the summer of 1833, the "notorious Davy Crockett" was the talk of the resort town of Saratoga Springs.[8]

Returned to the House of Representatives by popular demand, Crockett was back in the nation's capital when the Twenty-third Congress convened in 1833. By coincidence, Hackett, having returned to the United States following warm receptions and supportive reviews in England, was scheduled to premier his popular play in Washington. Benjamin Perley Poore was present in a packed theater when, at seven o'clock sharp, Congressman Crockett, escorted by the theater manager to a reserved seat in the front row, made his grand entrance. While the band played "Crockett's Victory March," a popular song of the day, the entire theater spontaneously erupted into applause and cheering, which, as Poore recalled, "made the very house shake with hurrahs for Colonel Crockett. . . ."[9] Once the crowd settled down, the curtain rose, and the now very popular Hackett came on stage dressed in his hunting outfit as the even more popular Wildfire. Hackett stepped to the front of the stage and bowed to an appreciative audience. He then respectfully bowed to Colonel Crockett. In what Poore described as "no small amusement and gratification"[10] to the audience, Crockett rose from his seat and bowed to Colonel Wildfire. In one brief instant, Crockett proved to the audience he was exactly what Wildfire aspired to be.

Even before returning to Washington in 1833, Crockett had already decided that he must produce an autobiography to correct an image problem that he was responsible for encouraging. For example, during his second campaign for the Tennessee State Legislature in 1823 against the respected Dr. William Butler, Crockett used the strategy of accentuating the differences between himself and society. On one occasion, as Crockett was mingling in a crowd, he called out to Butler who happened to be walking by. Surprised and unable to spot Crockett immediately, Butler replied, "D———n it, Crockett, is that you?" "Be sure it is," replied the hunter, "but I don't want it understood that I have come electioneering. I have just crept out of the cane, to see what discoveries I could make among the white folks."[11]

Crockett spent practically the entire introduction of his autobiography denouncing *The Life and Adventures* as a fraudulent work.

Portrait of David Crockett painted by Chester Harding in Boston on May 4, 1834. Long-term loan to the National Portrait Gallery, Smithsonian Institution; future bequest of Ms. Katharine Bradford.

It was his experience that a multitude of people, disabled by a grossly warped preconceived image, had "expressed the most profound astonishment at finding me in human shape, and with the countenance, appearance, and common feelings of a human being."[12] Crockett concluded by stating that even before the reader finishes, they will agree with a laugh, that his autobiography represents the "exact image of its Author. . . ."[13]

Soliciting advance orders for the upcoming autobiography from the publisher, Edward Carey and Abraham Hart of Philadelphia, one Boston distributor assured their customers that this book had been written by Crockett "with his own hand." Though not exactly written *all* by himself, *A Narrative of the Life of David Crockett of the State of Tennessee, Written by Himself* was released in February 1834. Sales of the *Narrative* quickly eclipsed the unauthorized publication.

Typical of any autobiography, Crockett presented himself in the way he wanted his readers to see him. Countering the perception that he was a wild man who comes out of the woods every now and then to see what is going on, Crockett attempted to portray himself as the most distinguished hunter of the west and a self-made gentleman. Unlike *The Life and Adventures*, the language found in the *Narrative* does not appear to be forced, as if the author was making a conscious effort to convince the reader he was an authentic westerner. The conspicuous absence of the "half-horse, half-alligator" rhetoric must, as Shackford so aptly pointed out, be credited to Crockett.

To help invigorate his new balanced image and support the sales of his autobiography, Crockett toured several eastern cities. In addition to personal appearances, a second book published by Carey and Hart titled *An Account of Col. Crockett's Tour to the North and Down East* would reinforce the desired balanced image. Over the next year or so, Crockett would have at least five portraits or sketches made. The first four images portrayed him in the attire of a gentleman. The last painting featured him as a hunter in his native habitat. Aspiring, with feigned disinterest, to the possibility of one day becoming president of the United States, Crockett needed to convince the voters that like Jackson, he too was the master of two worlds. And it was because of this desire for balance that Crockett could bow to Nimrod Wildfire, the stage hero who had conquered the wilderness, and sought to master his new environment.

A CRISIS OF GOVERNMENT

Crockett and the Democrats repeatedly clashed over a number of issues, most important of which was his Land Bill. Unable to procure sufficient backing from his own party, Crockett was eventually forced to look elsewhere for support. The Whig Party, the very name of which recalled the republican vigor of the revolution and patriotic resistance to tyranny, was not really much of an organization. The common bond which drew these men together was the fact they were all opposed to President Jackson.

Martin Van Buren came to Washington with a well-established reputation for being evasive, noncommittal, secretive, and a master manipulator. A devout Jeffersonian who abhorred Federalism, Van Buren revived a deeply fractured Democratic Party, gave it a sense of purpose and direction, and demanded allegiance from members. For public consumption Van Buren pretended to be innocuous, but the fact was that where politics was concerned, he was far from harmless and he had the track record to prove it. Dubbed the "little magician" and the "little red fox," Van Buren's notoriety as a schemer would reach such proportions, he would be blamed for just about everything from high society scandals to economic depressions. Although both were champions of the common people, Van Buren had no confidence in the ability of Crockett's backwoods constituents to contribute to social progress. Crockett detested Van Buren and his politics.

Crockett officially broke with the Democrats during his second term. Speaking before the House of Representatives in 1831, Crockett told his fellow constituents, "I am yet a Jackson man in principles," he said, "but General Jackson is not; he has become a Van Buren man."[14] Not long after that speech, Jackson wrote from the White House to a friend in Tennessee about the upcoming elections, "I trust for the honor of the state, your Congressional District will not disgrace themselves longer by sending that profligate man Crockett back to Congress."[15] When Crockett returned to Congress two years later, the war against the administration had escalated into a national crisis.

In the spring of 1834, an unprecedented move by the Senate sent the nation's capital into turmoil. It was claimed the president had seized control of the government's money, defied Congress, the Supreme Court, and some said, shown total disrespect for the Constitution. On March 28, the Senate passed a resolution accusing the president of having assumed powers not conferred upon his office by the Constitution. Jackson counterattacked and literally redefined the presidency. Jackson convincingly asserted that the president of the United States, unlike the legislators in the House and the Senate, was the direct representative of all the people and was therefore responsible to them, not Congress.

Whereas the president's claims were certainly innovative, his conduct was seen by many as alarming. When a number of the nation's most intelligent men looked at the life cycle of republics, as described by the ancient historian Polybius, they found disturbing parallels between the United States of 1834 and the last days of the Roman Republic. Many had concluded the nation was in the final stages of a rapid descent into tyranny. Crockett was one of those who accepted the reign of "Andrew the first King" as proof that their nation's "republican liberties," as bequeathed by the Founding Fathers, had seen their better days.[16] "It appears as if Jackson can do anything he pleases," Crockett wrote to a friend, "and the people will say he is right."[17] After all, had not history taught that the citizens of Rome were ready to relinquish their republican liberties to Caesar? U.S. Supreme Court Justice Joseph Story, acknowledged throughout the English-speaking world as a preeminent legal scholar, echoed the words used by Thucydides to describe tyranny under Pericles when he wrote, "Though we live under the form of a republic we are in fact under the absolute rule of a single man."[18]

Despite the public displays of power, Crockett believed that poor health and old age had rendered the president susceptible to the suggestions of unscrupulous manipulators. While the Democratic Party more or less operated in the open, there was another group composed of men closest to the president which did not. Opponents of the administration charged that this group, known as the "Kitchen Cabinet," had neither the authorization of the Constitution nor the consent of the people and was therefore operating illegitimately as a secret extension of the government. In one letter, Crockett divulged the name of this elite group's central figure, Vice President

This disparaging cartoon of President Jackson appeared during the presidential campaign of 1832. Courtesy of the Library of Congress.

Vice President Martin Van Buren, shown here in 1836, was almost single handedly responsible for reviving and restructuring the Democratic Party after the disastrous 1824 election. Unlike the majority of the Founders, Van Buren believed in the two party system. To Van Buren, restructuring the Democratic Party required the purging of anyone who demonstrated an appreciation for Federalist ideas. Courtesy of the Library of Congress.

Van Buren, whom he described as "a perfect Scoundral."[19]

Politically, Jackson may very well have been the most powerful president this nation has ever had. As Jacksonian scholar Robert Remini wrote, "No one, not Washington, Jefferson, or Franklin, ever held the American people in such near-total submission."[20] In Van Buren, Crockett saw the most thoroughly corrupt individual, skillfully manipulating the old general who was oblivious to the fact he was no longer in command. Crockett had no doubt that Jackson's purpose for launching his Bank War was so he could access government funds in order to secure Van Buren's election in 1836.

When citizens cast their ballots, they do so with the understanding that the outcome may not be to their liking. It is by this acceptance that the electorate gives their consent to the outcome, and hence, to the process. For those who wish to withdraw their consent, there are two options; the first is revolt, and the second would be to immigrate to another country. And this brings us to the original reason why Crockett contemplated leaving the United States.

Writing to Charles Schultz on Christmas Day in 1834, Crockett revealed his contingency plans should Van Buren win the election. Two days later, in a letter to John Ash, he reiterated his intentions:

> . . . I am not Certain that the people will object to being transfered by Jackson over to that Political Judeas little Van If so I have Sworn for the last four years that If Vanburen is our next President I will

leave the united States I will not live under his kingdom and I See no chance to beat him.[21]

Clearly, Crockett's original premise for leaving the country had nothing to do with his losing an election, but rather with his disapproval of the political direction the nation was taking.

Convinced that Jackson had already arranged for Van Buren's nomination as the Democratic candidate at the upcoming convention in Baltimore, a group of disenchanted Tennesseans, who did not particularly agree with Jackson's choice, held their own little convention in a Washington hotel room in the spring of 1835. When Jackson learned of the meeting, he was outraged! Writing to James K. Polk in a letter marked "private," Jackson stated that if he were only given the opportunity, he would have Tennessee "erect upon her republican legs again, and Mr. Bell, Davy Crockett and Co., hurled as they ought, from the confidence of the people"within six weeks.[22] Jackson continued his tirade against these defectors, which included the Speaker of the House John Bell, by asserting that eternal banishment from the confidence of the people of Tennessee would be too lenient a punishment for them. Writing at length on this same subject to Felix Grundy, Jackson referred to these men as "apostates," and "hypocritical demagogues."[23] Before the summer was over, Crockett would find a convenient excuse not to wait until the presidential election to make his move.

THE LAST CAMPAIGN

As the party of the common people, the Democrats seemed only willing to field men of education to oppose the virtually uneducated Crockett. The latest challenger was an attorney by the name of Adam Huntsman, also known as "Peg Leg," because he wore a wooden stump in place of the leg he lost in the Creek Indian War. During the Congressional sessions, the Jackson political machine had worked overtime to prevent passage of Crockett's Land Bill. When the Twenty-third Congress adjourned in 1835, Crockett had to return home once again and explain why his legislation had not passed. Consequently, Huntsman, who had never lost an election, entered the campaign confident of the outcome.

Writing in the summer to his book publishers Carey and Hart, an equally confident Crockett boasted about how well the campaign was going. Crockett also related how he told the voters of his plans to write another book, tentatively titled *The Second Fall of Adam*. Crockett then revealed his alternate plan, as reconstructed by Shackford, "if I don't beat my competitor I will [go to Texes?]. . . ."[24] In closing, he promised to write them again in four weeks to let them know the results of the election.

The *Jackson Truth Teller* reported in July that both candidates were generating plenty of interest in the race by "speechifying the people." Crockett was reportedly collecting material for his new book, while the resourceful Huntsman predicted that he would soon have Crockett "up a tree." The article also reported the campaign was proceeding "with perfect harmony and good humor" between the candidates.[25] "Stump speaking" in west Tennessee referred to candidates traveling together giving speeches before crowds in the towns and villages throughout the district. These occasions culminated in dancing and drinking, the whiskey often being provided by the candidates. Huntsman, who disapproved of this practice, not only called Crockett a "whiskey man" but even accused him of "electioneering."

On the courthouse lawn in Madison County there stands a plaque which states that following his defeat for reelection in 1831, Crockett told a crowd from the courthouse steps, "You can go to hell, but I am going to Texas."[26] The plaque goes on to read that he went to Texas and was killed at the Alamo. Crockett did lose his bid for reelection in 1831, but the plaque is in error as to the year of departure. Nonetheless, this comment is invariably pointed to in support of the belief that Crockett, overwhelmed by feelings of rejection, departed Tennessee a sore loser.

A few west Tennessee historians share the opinion that Madison County was not the only place where Crockett made this remark about hell and Texas. There is a tradition in Gibson County that he said the same thing to a crowd in Trenton.[27] There are also stories which strongly suggest Crockett included this ultimatum in his campaign speeches prior to election day. Presented in the form of a proposal, Crockett told the people in his ultimate campaign version that if they would reelect him, he would do the best he could for them. If they decided against him, then they knew where they could all go, and he would go to Texas. This being the case, his post-election statement does not necessarily have to be seen as a bitter reaction to the decision of a capricious electorate. In fact, there is a very good possibility Crockett's proposition to the voters actually evolved over a period of time.

Merchant James Mallory remembered hearing what might have been an early version of the congressman's campaign promise during a visit to the town of Dover. Evidently, the customary tree stump from upon which the speaker was to address his audience was in short supply, so Crockett borrowed a box from Mallory's store. Mallory remembered hearing Crockett tell the crowd, "If I am not elected, I'll either go to hell or to Texas."[28]

At some point during the campaign, Crockett evidently announced that in the event of his defeat, "Huntsman could go to hell and he would go to Texas." William Alexander Ridgway recalled being present at one of those speeches during that last campaign when he heard Crockett deny ever having made such a statement. Ridgway then heard Crockett remark in Huntsman's presence, "Now, Huntsman I never said that. I said you may go to Congress and I will go to Texas."[29]

Before departing the town where they made their last scheduled speech, both Huntsman and Crockett heard that a large crowd was gathering in Dresden where they had already spoken but intended to pass through on their way home. Crockett arrived in Dresden first and took to the stump immediately. In the course of his impromptu speech, Huntsman rode into town. Probably not surprised, but irritated nonetheless, Huntsman pushed his way through the crowd to the very front. Seeing that Huntsman had succeeded in stealing much of the crowd's attention, Crockett countered this unwanted influence by acknowledging his opponent's presence. Pretending to be astonished at the sight of his opponent, Crockett was heard to exclaim, "Adam Huntsman, I believe if I were to go to hell, that you would follow me there."[30] This comment would suggest the Dresden crowd was already familiar with an earlier form of his election ultimatum.

Matilda Fields, Crockett's daughter, recalled the day her father came home with the news of the election results. She remembered him telling her mother, Elizabeth, "Well, Bet, I am beat, and I'm off for Texas."[31] As promised, Crockett wrote again to Carey and Hart, if only to inform them of his defeat. He mentioned in the letter he had been informed by very reliable sources that voters in Jackson were paid off to vote against him. In the postscript, Crockett stated he had no regrets as to his course of action.[32] It was a hard-fought campaign, but Matilda later reflected on how her father handled his setback. "I don't think father cared much for his defeat," she recalled, "he wanted to go to Texas anyhow."[33]

As the repercussions of Jackson's removal of the government's deposits from the Second Bank of the United States began to ripple throughout the nation, real estate in the west became more attractive. So why choose Texas? Starting over for Crockett offered none of the romantic allure associated with returning to nature. By the summer of 1835, Mexican Texas was advertised as bigger, richer, and more beautiful than any other place on earth. Here was a place where prosperity was said to be unavoidable. Terms for acquiring land were so good in Texas there was no need for Crockett's Land Bill. Although the political future of Texas was yet to be determined, Crockett knew it would be a future without Jackson and Van Buren.

2

The Journey Begins

A Time for Leaving

Beginning in June 1836, the *New York Herald* printed the first of six installments of the recently discovered journal of Mexican Colonel Juan Nepomuceno Almonte. It was about this time that Carey and Hart claimed to have come into possession of a journal Crockett kept from his departure until his final entry, ominously dated March 5. The journal was said to have been recovered at the San Jacinto Battlefield by a Charles T. Beale, who discovered the item in a trunk belonging to Major General Manuel Fernández Castrillón. Beale sent the journal to a certain Alex J. Dumas, Esq., of New Orleans, who then forwarded it to none other than Carey and Hart.

It was more than mere coincidence that the explanation given by Carey and Hart describing how Crockett's journal made its way to Philadelphia paralleled the story provided by the *Herald* as to how they obtained Almonte's writings. There, however, the similarities end. Carey and Hart's motives for publishing the Crockett diary were purely monetary. They knew from the very beginning that Charles T. Beale and Alex J. Dumas did not exist. Virtually no one in, or out of, Philadelphia knew of the existence of Crockett's journal until its public appearance as a commercial product.

To create Crockett's journal, Carey and Hart recruited the talents of playwright Richard Penn Smith. Required to produce rapidly and with little reliable information to go on, the real author of *Exploits* had to resort to his imagination. Within months, the nonexistent journal became an instant best seller and continued to generate brisk sales for the next ten years. Thereafter, the book would, through numerous publishers and under various titles, enjoy an extended life by repeatedly being combined with the *Narrative* and *Tour* books, thus encompassing in a single volume Crockett's complete life story as "Written by Himself." Ironically, *Exploits* would be Smith's most popular work, one for which he would never openly receive due credit during his lifetime. Despite the fact that while Carey and Hart's hoax would be exposed in an 1839 Philadelphia magazine edited by none other than Edgar Allan Poe, and three years later in another magazine, wherein Poe himself would not only refer to the book as a fraudulent work but even identify Smith as the real author, *Exploits* continued to command respect as the genuine article for over the next one hundred years. Unlike Constance Rourke, who maintained in her 1934 book, *Davy Crockett*, that *Exploits* may have had a "basis in fact,"[1] Shackford chose not to cross that often ambiguous line separating the legendary from the historical.

Traditionally, the hero's adventure is often initiated by circumstances beyond his control. In Crockett's case, his last adventure is inaugurated by political defeat. *Exploits* began with the completion of Crockett's last campaign, followed by his announcement of defeat. In fact, Crockett's letters of July 8 and August 11 to Carey and Hart not only form the basis for chapters one and two respectively, but they appear almost in their entirety. In book form, however, Crockett's words have a new look featuring standardized spelling, punctuation, and capitalization. For the most part, Smith made little effort to even attempt to mimic Crockett's style of writing. As to precisely why he was going to Texas, Smith explained that the purpose of Crockett's journey was to "give the Texians a helping hand on the high road to freedom."[2] According to Smith, Crockett was never really serious about abandoning his country. He planned to return to the United States once political normalcy was restored. For Smith's readers, Crockett was always an American citizen.

Having had in their possession two authentic Crockett letters, Carey and Hart were able to drape the beginning of *Exploits* with a veil of legitimacy. But rather than rely on legend, or the interpretations of other historians, Shackford referred directly to the opening segment of Crockett's letter to his brother-in-law, George Patton, written on the eve of his departure for Texas. Below is the extent to which Crockett wrote about his trip to Texas:

> Dear Brother
> I have Concluded to drop you a line the whole Connection is well and I am on the eve of Starting to the Texes—on to morrow morning mySelf Abner Burgin and Lindsy K Tinkle & our Nephew William Patton from the Lowar Country this will make our Company we will go through Arkinsaw and I want to explore the Texes well before I return . . .[3]

Shackford noted that Crockett neglected to mention anything about joining the Texas Revolution. He therefore concluded that contrary to popular perception, Crockett "had no idea at this time of going to Texas to join the Texan forces and to fight for Texas independence." His intention, Shackford said, was to "explore the country" in preparation for "one more move west to one more new frontier."[4]

Stanley J. Folmsbee, Richard Boyd Hauck, Paul Andrew Hutton, and other scholars have augmented Shackford's interpretation of Crockett's motives for going to Texas. Resentful of his defeat in the recent election and the fact that the economic prosperity he sought had thus far eluded him, Crockett decided he would go to Texas to examine its potential for new opportunities. Historian Jeff Long, who strongly disputed the belief that the Tennessean had any interest in fighting in the revolution or defending liberty, best summarized the postmodern view of Crockett's motives by simply stating, "He went for himself."[5] Following Hauck's lead, Long added a little psychodrama by claiming Crockett also wanted to chase down his runaway legend.[6]

Is it possible Crockett could have been uninformed as to what was happening in Texas? It was a widely known fact throughout the United States that Mexico was embroiled in revolution. As of yet, no historian has argued that Crockett was unaware, blissfully or otherwise, of the escalating tensions in Texas. Aware of Shackford's work, historian Walter Lord stated, referring to Crockett, "the Texas revolution was going full blast, but it was not for him."[7] Almost forty years later, historian William C. Davis reiterated Lord's observation.

"Surely he knew of the growing uproar out there, and that the colonists were virtually in rebellion now, but that was their fight, not his."[8] Therefore, the generally accepted theory, as originally advanced by Shackford, is that Crockett's letter of October 31 serves as testimony to the fact he had no thoughts about, nor did he have any interest in, joining anybody's revolution. This conclusion, as drawn from his failure to mention any such inclinations, is derived from placing far too much emphasis on this one letter.

Judging from the salutation and the opening lines, it is evident this could not have been Crockett's first communication with Patton. Crockett was informing Patton, for the first time, the exact date of his departure and who was going with him. He was not writing to announce his intentions to go to Texas. This would have been inappropriate here, for the way these lines about Texas were written it would seem that Patton was already aware of Crockett's long-term plans.

Crockett's long-term contingency plans were probably in the making for well over a year. There is good reason to believe he talked with one man in particular who was more knowledgeable on the subject of Texas than most. On April 23, 1834, two days prior to

This photograph of the old Crockett cabin near Rutherford, Tennessee, was taken circa 1932. Courtesy of the Daughters of the Republic of Texas Library.

embarking upon his tour of the northeastern cities, Crockett social-
ized with his friend Sam Houston[9] who had already been living in
Texas for two years. Looking at two letters written from Washington,
dated the twentieth and twenty-fourth, it is obvious that the future of
Texas preoccupied Houston's thoughts.[10]

Houston made it explicitly clear in these two letters that he had
given up on the idea of the United States acquiring Texas.
Convinced the status quo could not continue indefinitely, it was
Houston's firm belief that within three years Texas would become a
sovereign political state and would forever remain separated from
Mexico. Furthermore, it was his opinion that nothing could alter
what he believed was the natural course of events. But until the
proper moment, Houston intended to publicly endorse the Mexican
Constitution of 1824.

We can only speculate about the topics of discussion that came
up between Houston and Crockett. Houston was a man consumed by
an unequaled passion for Texas. We might imagine that Crockett, who
was already interested in Texas, may have done plenty of listening.
Being as close to Jackson as he was, Houston could not have
approved of Crockett's political allegiances, but nevertheless did not
allow such differences to affect their friendship. By Christmas of that
same year, Crockett was writing to friends about his intention to move
to Texas should Van Buren ascend to the presidency.

There is reason to believe that Crockett may not have discussed
with his family all the uncertainties involved in a move to Texas.
Years later, his youngest daughter, Matilda, was quoted as saying,
"We did not know that he intended going into the army until he wrote
mother a letter after he got to Texas."[11] But if Crockett did not
discuss the unstable political climate in Texas with his immediate
family, he may have discussed it with at least one close friend.

Samuel C. Reid Jr. served under Ben McCulloch's command
during the war between the United States and Mexico and wrote a
book about McCulloch's Texas Rangers. According to Reid, Crockett
and McCulloch were hunting companions who definitely discussed
more than just going to Texas to hunt buffalo in the fall of 1835. In
fact, Crockett, who not only had plans to join the Texian army, was
supposedly already forming his own company of volunteers when
McCulloch agreed to join him.[12] Reid was, however, mistakenly

under the impression that both were aware the war had already started. Instead, Crockett and McCulloch probably discussed plans to form a company in the expectation that a revolution was imminent. This version of Crockett's intention to join the revolutionary army, originally committed to print only eleven years after the Alamo, can hardly be considered a recent development in the building of Crockett's legend.

It would appear their plans were put on hold when McCulloch had to postpone his departure to Texas. Basically, the plan was to go to Texas first, find a good location for a homestead, return to Tennessee, then move the family. Besides, who could predict when the long expected revolution would finally begin? Next month? Next year? In fact, that is precisely the most significant fragment of information missing in his letter to Patton. Crockett made no mention of the latest events in Texas, specifically the arrival of Mexican troops on Texas soil in September or the skirmish at Gonzales, which had taken place thirty days earlier on October 1. The most reasonable explanation for the absence of such significant information is that he was simply not yet aware these events had occurred. By the time Crockett had written to Patton, Texas was just beginning its descent into chaos. Based on what he believed to be true about the capabilities of the common people to deal with large scale crisis situations, such a descent would not have surprised Tocqueville. And based on what he knew about Crockett, Tocqueville would not have expected much from him either. If Crockett was not thinking about war the day he left home, the coming days would give him an unexpected opportunity to demonstrate just how receptive he actually was to the idea of taking part in a revolution. Looking forward to starting his journey, Crockett might very well have anticipated that future events in Texas would mark the most momentous episode in his lifetime.

ONE NOVEMBER MORNING

Crockett continued to generate national news throughout August. Released upon the public during the summer election campaign, *The Life of Martin Van Buren, Hair-apparent to the "Government,"*

and the Appointed Successor of General Jackson, By David Crockett,
can be viewed as a vicious assault against its subject. Other than
permitting the use of his name, this pretentious work was produced
without Crockett's participation, an apparent fact that did not go
entirely unnoticed. The *Charleston Courier*, a Democrat newspaper
in the aristocratic South Carolina city, published a scathing review
of the book in their August 17 issue, which read in part, "Col.
Crockett certainly never could have written it, for it exhibits a
general cast of style, vigor of thought, and ingenious force of argument, beyond one of the Colonel's literary and intellectual
calibre." Shackford theorized that the real publisher, Carey and
Hart, marketed the book under a pseudonym. If correct, then the
publishers may have displayed some sense by distancing themselves from their own product. The public, however, displayed the
most sense by ignoring the book.

By mid-August, names of the congressional election's winners
and losers were beginning to appear in newspapers across the
country. The *Arkansas Gazette* published the election results from
west Tennessee on August 25: "A. Huntsman is elected to Congress
from the 12th district of Tennessee, beating the buffoon, Davy
Crockett, by about 300 majority." Unable to do anything about the
outcome, the *Arkansas Advocate* took issue with the *Gazette's* charac-
terization of Crockett. The *Advocate* responded three days later with
this simple little story:

> We learn from one of the Tennessee papers, that while Col Crocket,
> a few days ago, was addressing the people in Wesley, a pert political
> opponent, with the view of confounding him, handed him a coon
> skin asking him if it was good fur. The speaker, instead of flying into
> a passion, deliberately took the skin, blew it, examined it, and
> turning to the owner, dryly remarked: "No, sir, 'tis not good fur; my
> dogs wouldn't run such a coon, nor bark at a man that was fool
> enough to carry such a skin." The poor fellow, slank away, and has
> not been heard of since.

Unable to conceal their elation, the *Charleston Courier* took
particular pleasure in making known their reaction to the recent
news from Tennessee in their August 31 edition:

Singular.—Col. Davy Crockett, hitherto regarded as the *Nimerod of the West,* has been beaten for Congress by a *Mr. Huntsman.* The Colonel has lately suffered himself to be made a *lion,* or some other wild beast, *tamed,* if not caged, for public shew—and it is no wonder that he should have yielded to the prowess of a *Huntsman, when again let loose in his native wilds.* We fear that *"Go ahead"* will be no longer either the Colonel's motto or destiny.

Democrat newspapers across the country focused on Crockett's anticipated exodus as the day of his impending departure for Texas approached. One such example appeared in a Louisiana newspaper, which was reprinted in the *Arkansas Gazette* on October 6: "We learn through a letter from a friend that Davy Crockett, convinced by his recent defeat that the people of the U.S. are not qualified for self-government, has determined to set out for Texas. There is something like spirit in this. If all those federalists who concur in opinion with Crockett, would put out with him for Texas, what a breaking up there would be among the mushroom aristocracy of the western villages."

Another example of fidgety anticipation turned up in the October 15 edition of the *New York Sun* when they announced, "Colonel Crockett is going to migrate to Texas." The paper suggested that "Davy" should take the editor of the *New York Herald* with him.[13]

President Jackson's October 31 letter to Andrew J. Hutchings was predominantly personal, save for a section on Tennessee politics. Still brooding over what he referred to as that "miserable caucus" of "Crockett and Co.," Jackson was unwilling to let go of his enemies even though it had been more than ten weeks since the elections.[14] News of Crockett's defeat surely must have been known to him by that time. It was purely coincidental Crockett would also be writing that same day. In contrast, most notably missing in his last letter from Tennessee is the anti-administration rhetoric which so dominated the contents of previous letters.

Crockett's departure for Texas had been delayed by some business on his wife's side of the family. As coexecutor of his deceased father-in-law's estate, Crockett was required to make a court appearance in the last week of October. In addition to Burgin, Tinkle, Patton, and McCulloch, Henry Skidmore was also scheduled to leave with Crockett but was unable to make the departure date.[15] Both

McCulloch and Skidmore intended to leave sometime afterwards and catch up with the group later. McCulloch planned to rendezvous with "old Davy" in Nacogdoches, a Texas metropolis where they would dine on buffalo meat for Christmas.[16]

Richard Penn Smith did not write for those who knew Crockett; he wrote for those who yearned to know what happened during the last days of a famous man who lived and died in a faraway region of the world they would probably never see. Nor did Smith write for those few who saw him off that November morning. They told a somewhat different story than the one which came out of Philadelphia. This small group did not witness the departure of a hero, off to meet his greatest challenge, but that of a father and husband. Matilda remembered the last time she saw her father, and her expectation that she would see him again: "I remember distinctly the morning he started on his journey to Texas. He was dressed in his hunting suit, wearing a coonskin cap, and carried a fine rifle presented to him by friends in Philadelphia . . . He seemed very confident the morning he went away that he would soon have us all to join him in Texas."[17]

An apocryphal, yet plausible, version of this departure was described in an old newspaper clipping. According to this rendition, an unmistakable sense of apprehension permeated the cabin as the moment of separation approached. David hugged and kissed his children and their mother several times. Elizabeth tearfully hugged her husband one last time and said, "God bless you, dear, and keep you." As David reached the edge of the field, he turned and paused for one last look at the family assembled in front of the cabin. With one last good-bye, he turned then disappeared into the woods. As if mesmerized by the moment, the family just stood in front of their cabin, staring silently into the trees. Somehow certain their lives had now changed forever, Elizabeth quietly commented, possibly without forethought, that they were never going to see him again.[18]

THE CELESTIAL SIGN

Due to its reputation as the harbinger of events to come, the early 1830s brought the typical speculation about the approach of Halley's Comet. Hoping to soothe the apprehensions of the people and at the same time avert a global catastrophe, the one man capable of performing Olympian feats was summoned forth. In 1832, newspapers across the country carried the following announcement: "Appointment By The President.—David Crockett, of Tennessee, to stand on the Allegheny mountains and catch the Comet, on its approach to the earth, and wring off its tail, to keep it from burning up the world!"[19] Rourke did not miss the metaphysical implications that Halley's Comet appearance in the night sky over west Tennessee coincided with Crockett's departure for Texas.

Despite Shackford's efforts to permanently invalidate *Exploits*, historians continued to find the book's depiction of Crockett traveling from home to Little Rock by boat entirely plausible well into the 1990s. Rourke expanded upon *Exploits* slightly, noting that Crockett first went down the Obion River, then disembarked and made the lonely trek through the woods to Mills Point on the Mississippi River, where he boarded a steamboat.[20] Neither Shackford, Folmsbee, or Anna Grace Catron even attempted to guess Crockett's mode of travel when he left home. Ironically, Walter Lord concluded that Crockett began his journey by boat down the Mississippi River on November 1.[21] However, the purchase of a horse for William Patton, as mentioned in Crockett's letter of October 31, would definitely suggest that the little group, of which *Exploits* makes no mention of, intended to travel by land. In fact, upon reading a copy of the alleged autobiography, David's youngest son, Robert Patton Crockett, confidently concluded that the portion of the book dealing with his father's trip to Texas was a forgery. While complimenting the author's writing ability, Robert specifically cited as incorrect the book's depiction of his father's boarding a boat at Mills Point. Robert stated that his father definitely left home on horseback.[22] Historian Skipper Steely has pointed out that during this segment of the journey Crockett traveled briefly with a wagon caravan comprised of a religious sect seeking their own version of earthly paradise in the Red River region.[23]

Rourke basically reinforced the presumption established in *Exploits* that Crockett was well aware the revolution in Texas was underway when he left home, and that he was going there expressly for the purpose of joining the war effort. As to how Crockett saw his role in the revolution, Rourke infused a little mystery into the story.

Ready to depart for Texas, she had Crockett comment, "There's something about this which makes me feel I must be in it."[24] One might infer from this that his journey was not planned out well in advance but was a spur of the moment decision. Not knowing what may lie ahead is, of course, an integral component of the hero's journey. But writing long after Smith, Rourke had a distinct advantage. Looking beyond the revolution, Rourke's Crockett was able to foresee Texas becoming part of the United States. Almost as an afterthought, Crockett realized that Texas could offer him and his family a home for the future, and in this way he remained just as much an American citizen as he was in *Exploits*.

It is possible the script writers at Disney Studios were uncomfortable with the fact that Crockett made no mention of joining the revolution in his letter of October 31, a letter they must have been familiar with since the opening segment was reprinted in Rourke's book. Perhaps, too, they may have preferred a less mystical, more tangible explanation for how Crockett came to the decision to go to Texas. What they came up with was definitely in line with the social values of their times.

To demonstrate how Crockett might have reached this decision, Disney invented a scene which took place during a cruise on a Mississippi steamboat. One evening, Crockett's longtime friend, Georgie Russel, casually mentioned that they had not yet decided on their destination. Meditating on that very question, Crockett pulled out a copy of the latest edition of the *Memphis Courier*, and, without saying a word, handed it to Georgie. One look at the headline, *Santa Anna Invades Texas!* and Georgie, intuitively perceiving what Davy had been contemplating, erupted and vigorously protested against the very idea of going to Texas when there were so many other places to explore. Georgie insisted that just because a few settlers were in trouble, fighting for their rights against an entire army, was hardly any reason to go running off to Texas. At this point in Disney's film version, Crockett calmly interjected a little piece of information he thought his good friend might find relevant to the discussion—that the settlers in trouble just happened to be "Americans." Of course, even as he was speaking, Georgie began to realize he was making the quintessential moral argument for going to Texas.[25] So, according to the "Disneyfied" version, not only was Crockett's decision to go to

Texas made after leaving home, but it was directly influenced by learning that the revolution had started. Obviously drawn to where "Americans" were fighting for liberty, Disney's Crockett came across as a man brimming with patriotic devotion.

The news that hostilities in Texas had started may have first entered Tennessee through Memphis via New Orleans. Traveling overland through west Tennessee, the first place Crockett and his three companions could have expected to receive any news from the outside world would have been in a town like Jackson. Sam Houston's letter of October 5, appealing to American citizens to come to Texas and join the fight against tyranny, had already appeared in the *Arkansas Gazette* as early as October 27. Since at least two Kentucky newspapers reproduced the letter during the first week of November,[26] the electrifying news from Texas must have been circulating throughout west Tennessee. When Crockett arrived in Jackson, volunteers were already beginning to assemble.

Named after the president, Jackson was the county seat of Madison County and the administration's political stronghold in west Tennessee. This was where the Democratic Party, desperately seeking to avoid an embarrassing repeat of what happened two years earlier when Crockett won the county, weighed in with full force. Using funds provided by the Union Bank, officers of the institution paid voters twenty-five dollars each to cast their ballots for Huntsman. Speaking from the steps of the Madison County Courthouse, Crockett must have taken particular pleasure informing the crowd that he was now in the early stages of carrying out his campaign promise.

Inexperienced, aspiring soldiers are always in need of leaders and since Crockett, one of the most popular men in Tennessee—a civic leader, former volunteer with war experience, and duly elected colonel in the state militia—just happened to be there at the right moment, they naturally looked to him. There was no question in Jackson as to how receptive Crockett was to the idea of joining the revolution. As one eyewitness wrote a few days later, "Col. Crockett went on some time ago at the head of 30 men well armed and equipped."[27] Only fifty miles into his journey, and Crockett's name had suddenly become inextricably bound to the Texas Revolution.

Riding twenty-five miles south to Bolivar, Crockett spent the night at the residence of Dr. Calvin Jones. Jones wrote of the crowds that had spontaneously lined the streets and how "every eye was strained to catch a glance of him," but then crossed it out. In its place, he wrote of these same people with "every very hand extended either in curiosity or regard." Crockett had left public office, and was now leaving home, with the respect of many who had voted against him. Jones also commented about the aggressive young men experiencing their newly discovered premonitions of glory. But Crockett's presence somehow lent credibility to a scene which Jones thought was otherwise lacking in legitimacy. As a witness to the sincerity of the moment, Jones commented that the "occasion proved him to be more of a Lion than I had supposed." With a cosmic omen streaking across the skies above and volunteers going off to war, Jones observed there was a surreal quality about the whole occasion. Crockett was given a hero's send-off in Bolivar, as if he were in the doctor's words, a "passing comet, never to be seen again."[28]

Sixty miles to the west of Bolivar lay the Mississippi River. There was more than one way to get to Texas, but Crockett decided to follow his original itinerary which would take him through Arkansas. After spending the night in Bolivar, Crockett and his group took the main road the following morning to a city where he had given many speeches back in the days when it was still in his congressional district. Some of those who started out with Crockett from Jackson may have begun to lose interest. Others may have simply decided to take a different route. Sometime early in the second week of November, Crockett and a group greatly diminished in number turned up in Memphis.

LAST NIGHT ON THE TOWN

General James Winchester thought of the Mississippi River as the "American Nile," and at the point where the Wolf River empties into the great waterway he envisioned a great city. By the time journalist James D. Davis arrived in the late 1820s, Memphis was in the process of building a reputation for being a disease ridden mud puddle. Of course, the city survived and Davis eventually became known as the "father of Memphis history." On occasion, when Davis's work has been compared with information contained in official documents, the comparison has been somewhat disconcerting. Part of Davis's problem may have been the obvious difficulties one encounters when attempting to transfer from memory to paper events that were as much as thirty years old. Another problem, and a far more serious one from the historian's point of view, is that Davis has been accused of being more concerned with writing a good story rather than writing history. Although *Exploits* made no mention of a stop in Memphis, Davis did.

While Memphis was certainly more of a western town than a southern one, the western drinking establishment with its swinging doors, long bar, and gambling tables had not yet begun to appear on the scene. As the saloon's forerunner, the tavern enjoyed a reputation as a meeting place for respectable citizens. Functionally democratic, the tavern attracted and served the notables, the anonymous, and the not so eloquent. In *Exploits*, Crockett was depicted as a man who frequently discovered in normal, everyday situations a reason to get "liquored." Such a portrayal was not necessarily considered to be socially irresponsible in 1836.

There were several respectable spots in Memphis where one could buy a drink and Crockett must have hit them all on his last stop. According to Davis, an account of Crockett's last visit to Memphis was prepared by a Colonel William T. Avery; however, nothing was mentioned in that account about the evening's activities. Since Avery neglected to report on Crockett's last night on the town, Davis proposed to fill the void. This time, Davis wrote as an eyewitness.

In true western style, Davis did not bother himself with exact dates or, in this particular account, any date at all. He only stated that having arrived early in the day, Crockett checked into the City Hotel and spent most of the daylight hours in the streets talking with old friends. Suspecting something had to be in the works with Crockett around, Davis headed uptown shortly after nightfall. The sixteen-year-old found Crockett and about twelve others, including two close friends Gus Young and Robert Lawrence, the latter being president of the city's only bank, conversing in the street outside the Union Hotel. He was just in time, too, for shortly after joining the group, the subject of drinking came up. Someone quickly pointed out that the Union Hotel just happened to have a bar, so in they went. As best as Davis could remember, the hotel was run by a man named Jeffries who, he said, later moved to Little Rock where he prospered in the same line of work. Once inside though, it became obvious that the facilities were not designed to handle a crowd of their size. It was decided, just as the barkeeper was ready to begin serving drinks, they should all go to Hart's Saloon over on Market Street.

Hart's Saloon was a sizeable establishment. Besides being a tavern, it also functioned as a drug store and bakery. As for the taproom, Hart's had class. Davis considered it to be the best drinking establishment in Memphis.

James D. Davis was one of a small group of friends who remembered Crockett's last visit to Memphis. Courtesy of the Memphis-Shelby County Library.

The establishment's proprietor, Royal G. Hart, while having a high opinion of himself as a poet also had some annoying habits, like requiring his customers to pay after each drink. Assuming the role of spokesman for the group, Gus Young took the initiative by ordering the first round. Everything was going along just fine until Hart asked for payment. Gus cheerfully assured Hart that he would be paid for all of the drinks—tomorrow. Prepared for situations such as this, Hart proudly pointed with confidence to a recently hung sign, which, he not only felt revealed a justifiable business policy, but an exquisite example of his poetic abilities.

> Since man to man is so unjust,
> Tis hard to tell what man to trust.
> I've trusted many—to my sorrow—
> So pay to-day, and I'll trust to-morrow.[29]

Failing to appreciate the sign's artistic merits and feeling thoroughly insulted, Gus lost no time as he moved to physically reprimand Hart! Several in the group quickly intervened, with

Crockett telling Gus to calm down and that he would pay for the drinks himself. Responding in unison, several others immediately voiced their objection, each insisting they would pay for the drinks. Speaking with a sense of final authority, Gus denied these volunteers the privilege of paying for the bill. He then turned to Colonel Toddy Dixon, a future mayor of Memphis, and asked for a five-dollar loan.

Now that Hart had his money, things started to calm down. Dixon, in seeking to revive the original spirit of the evening, called out for another round. Asserting his apparent leadership, Gus countered by decreeing everyone should now abandon Hart's and report to McCool's place. Hart suddenly became very apologetic when he heard this. As everyone was filing out, Hart tried to explain that it was all a misunderstanding; it was only business.

With everyone gone to McCool's, Hart was left to try and figure out what had gone wrong. Taking another look at the object of contention, Hart noticed that while he was occupied with the business at hand, someone had scribbled a few words on his sign. "Then go to hell, you damned fool. We'll go and drink with Neil McCool."[30] Hart promptly tore the sign off the wall and angrily ripped it into shreds. Unable to rid his mind of those last words, Hart later accused Davis of ruining his sign. Davis said he never responded to the accusation.

When Gus came up with the idea of vacating Hart's Saloon in favor of McCool's, he may not have taken into consideration the fact that Neil McCool also had a quirk of his own. Whereas Hart was overly concerned with prompt payments, McCool was irrationally preoccupied with neatness. Meticulous in his personal appearance, he was an immaculate dresser, always certain that every hair was in place. This fanaticism tended to spill over into his work habits.

According to Davis, McCool's place was not in the same class as Hart's. Plain looking in its appearance, Davis simply described it as a grocery store. McCool's was however, the largest store of its kind in Memphis and had the widest selection of goods. Still, there was nothing really extraordinary about the place, save its exceptional tidiness. McCool had every item arranged in a neat and orderly manner. As for the store's unadorned look, McCool had set about correcting that inadequacy the day before by spreading a delicate oil cloth over his counter. Davis said McCool was so apprehensive about his new cloth getting smudged that he would not even permit a gentleman to place his hat upon it. The dominant mood of the place was hardly conducive to celebrations, but this crowd was thirsting for a good time.

Practically next door to Hart's, it did not take the crowd long to get to McCool's. Davis said several in the crowd, which by this time had been augmented by curious fun seekers, picked "old Davy up, and carried him on their shoulders," right into McCool's. The crowd then proceeded to place him on the counter, feet first! With Crockett standing on the counter, the crowd demanded a speech and he did not disappoint them. It was a short speech, and Davis was confident he remembered it verbatim. "My friends, I suppose you are all aware that I was recently a candidate for Congress in an adjoining District. I told the voters that if they would elect me I would serve them to the best of my ability; but if they did not, they might go to hell, and I would go to Texas. I am on my way now."[31] Crockett then leaped off the counter as the crowd enthusiastically shouted their approval.

With the opening ceremonies concluded, it was now time for everyone to get down to some celebrating. Despite the promise of a profitable evening, McCool was not in an obliging mood. While Crockett held center stage, McCool managed to redirect his anger by grinding down on lumps of sugar. All he could think about was that since Crockett's filthy footwear had come into contact with his fine cloth, it no longer looked so fine!

By coincidence, Gus Young, whom McCool took to be the gang leader, just happened to be standing right across from him. Bearing down even harder on his sugar crusher, McCool, without diverting his eyes from his activity, addressed Mr. Young by name in a low but stern voice saying, "such treatment is intolerable."[32] Little did McCool know, but Mr. Young was not the right person to direct such a comment.

Objects were thrown, and a brief scuffle ensued. After vaulting the bar in a fit of rage, six of Young's most loyal friends were able to physically restrain McCool. Hardly considered the type to use vulgar language, McCool proved himself to be surprisingly fluent. Eventually, he was able to compose himself so he could order everyone out of his place. It did not matter that no one had paid for their drinks. He just wanted them out.

Back in the streets, the nucleus of the group convened to plot their next move. Crockett recommended going home, saying it just was not their night for merrymaking unless they were looking for a fight. To quote Davis, "although he [Crockett] was in hunt of a fight, he did not want it on this side of the Mississippi river. . . ."[33] The majority felt that it would be ill-mannered of them to permit him to leave Memphis on a sour note.

So, it was decided to hit Old Jo Cooper's place next. As a wholesaler, Cooper had the largest stock and the best quality liquor for miles around. Sharing with McCool some of the same idiosyncrasies then associated with bachelors, Cooper was not usually considered to be charitable with his stock of liquor. As it turned out, Cooper was very charitable that night. His vast assortment of liquor came free of charge. Crockett entertained them with more speeches. All of the participants remained in the finest of humor throughout the remainder of the evening which ended without further incident.

3

Across the American Nile

TO THE OTHER SIDE

D uring his research, Shackford uncovered numerous facts and documents which are crucial in reconstructing Crockett's expedition to Texas. Having come across the Davis account, Shackford had to settle with simply picking up the story in Memphis. But if Shackford, Folmsbee, and Catron set the scholarly tone as to how to view Crockett from a new perspective, Walter Lord's book *A Time to Stand* was particularly significant in the telling of the Alamo story. His book was the first account intended for popular consumption that deviated from the traditional storybook format. The heroes of the Alamo were heroes whose flaws were made visible. Crockett was one case in point.

Walter Lord saw Crockett as a charismatic figure with good instincts, a man whose realm of influence reached all the way to the doorstep of civilization. While acknowledging that Crockett had an amiable personality, Lord judged him to have been a "simple man" of "little depth," as naive as they come.[1] He surmised that at forty-nine, Crockett must have viewed this journey as his last shot at success and nothing must be allowed to interfere. Concurring with Shackford and Folmsbee that following his night of carousing in Memphis, Lord reported Crockett then boarded a steamboat bound for Little Rock and subsequently conducted himself in a manner expected of your stereotypical "good ole boy." "More drinking and parties at every place the steamboat touched along the Mississippi," Lord wrote.[2] But that was not exactly what happened.

A small group of friends followed Crockett from the City Hotel in downtown Memphis to the Catfish Bay ferry landing. Once again, James D. Davis was present. Writing about the event decades later, Davis assured readers his recollection of how Crockett looked that day was "as vivid as if it were yesterday."

> He wore that same veritable coon-skin cap and hunting shirt, bearing upon his shoulder his ever faithful rifle. No other equipments, save his shot-pouch and powder-horn, do I remember seeing. I witnessed the last parting salutations between him and those few devoted friends. He stepped into the boat. The chain untied from the stob, and thrown with a rattle by old Limus into the bow of the boat, it pushed away from shore, and floating lazily down the little Wolf, out into the big river, and rowed across to the other side, bearing that remarkable man away from his State and kindred forever.[3]

Taken at face value, Davis seems to be saying that Limus simply ferried Crockett across the river and dropped him off on the Arkansas side. If this is in fact what actually happened, Crockett and his friends would not have been dropped off in a barren wilderness.

Between 1824 and 1836, Congress set aside several hundred thousand dollars for the construction of roads in the Arkansas Territory. The purpose of these roads was to expedite the movement of military personnel and equipment in the event of a national emergency. The first road to be constructed extended from the western banks of the Mississippi River, almost directly across from Memphis, to Little Rock and beyond. This road was completed in 1828. Certainly as a former congressman Crockett would have been well acquainted with the existence of these roads and the main purpose for which they were then being used: the transfer of the eastern Indian tribes to the western territories. The present day Highway 40 closely follows the path of the original military road for approximately 135 miles into Little Rock.

Acquired by the United States as part of the Louisiana Purchase, Arkansas officially became a U.S. Territory in 1819. Two years later, Little Rock was designated the territorial capital. The day after Crockett left home, the town of Little Rock, a community consisting

After selling the Advocate, *the largely self-educated Albert Pike devoted himself to the study of law. Pike became a successful attorney, judge, and was admitted to practice before the Supreme Court. Pike served as a captain during the war with Mexico in 1846, and briefly as a Confederate brigadier general. He translated Latin and French law books, the Indian* Rig-Veda, *while gaining renown as a poet. For more than a quarter century, Pike was the grand commander of the Supreme Council of the A & A Scottish Rite, Southern Jurisdiction. When he died in 1891, Pike was acknowledged as the highest ranking Mason in the world. Courtesy of the Arkansas Historical Commission.*

of several brick structures and having already grown to almost one thousand residents, was incorporated into a city.

That same month, one local newspaper reported, "Our streets are almost constantly thronged with emigrants, passing through our city, for the Red river country. . . ." A separate article reported that having caught "Texas fever," four Little Rock residents had just departed for that distant land.[4] Brothers Jesse and William Badgett, bound for Texas, had already departed Little Rock a week earlier. With statehood not far off and a war looming on its southern border, there was a great deal for Little Rock residents to read about.

In November 1834, an English scientist named George William Featherstonhaugh passed through Little Rock and was astounded to find a community of that size could support "no less than three cheap newspapers which are not read but devoured by everybody."[5] Typical of that day, Little Rock newspapers were issued on a weekly basis. Anything concerning national politics was always viewed with great interest as the political war between the Democrats and Whigs being waged stateside had predictably spread into Arkansas. American newspapers of the early 1830s were not the least embarrassed about slanting their reports and generally made every effort to flaunt their political affiliation.

The first newspaper to be published in Arkansas, and only the second west of the Mississippi River, was the *Arkansas Gazette*. Originally from New York, the paper's founder William E. Woodruff had worked for several years in the newspaper business in Tennessee prior to relocating to Little Rock in 1821. Under his auspices, the *Gazette* became the most prominent newspaper in the territory. The *Gazette* would claim to be the oldest newspaper in existence west of the Mississippi until October 1991, when it ceased publication after being sold to the *Arkansas Democrat*.

As an alternative to the Democratic *Gazette*, the *Arkansas Advocate* began circulation in 1830. Founded for the purpose of espousing the viewpoints of the Whig Party, the *Advocate's* orientation was strictly political. The name most frequently associated with the *Advocate* was that of Albert Pike, a virtual renaissance man of the frontier. Pike's association with the *Advocate* began in 1832 when he contributed a series of columns, which, admittedly were less than perfectly aboveboard, were extremely effective against the

Democrats. Horace Greeley was sufficiently impressed with the quality of these articles and had them reprinted in the *New York Tribune*. The following year, Pike was hired as an assistant editor at the *Advocate*. After serving as editor for a little over a year, Pike bought the *Advocate* in 1835. Believing the new fashionable democracy to be the mutated offspring of what he called the "Jeffersonian heresies, aggravated by Jacksonian degeneration,"[6] Pike was a natural for the paper's political orientation. One of Pike's favorite targets was Van Buren.

A third paper, the *Little Rock Times*, produced by Jefferson Smith and John H. Reed, tended to unofficially side with the *Gazette* against the *Advocate*. In the weekly exchange of accusations and counter accusations, Pike often seemed to be the most resourceful, cleverly combining insults with humor. Pike once claimed that a dog had been bitten by the editor of a competing newspaper. In a follow-up article, Pike reported the dog had died. Another example of Pike's wit appeared in his November 6 issue of 1835. "The editor of a friendly paper over the river, says that we make up mouths at him, we remind him of Davy Crockett. Why? Because we are grinning at a' coon?" Six days later, the real Crockett showed up in Little Rock.

A GRAND ENTRY

In the spring of 1955, the United States was still feeling the effects of Walt Disney's *Davy Crockett* marketing campaign. Anticipating a scheduled visit to Little Rock by Fess Parker, the *Arkansas Gazette* commenced a sixteen-part series on Crockett geared especially for children. It was only appropriate the paper should feature an article about Crockett's visit to Little Rock for their older, more mature readers. Margaret Smith Ross of the Arkansas History Commission was quite possibly the only person in America at the time who knew that Crockett did not reach Little Rock via steamboat. While Shackford was able to verify through copies of an old Baltimore newspaper that Crockett really did visit Little Rock, Ross had access to documents indigenous to the Arkansas capital that perhaps few historians outside the city even knew existed. In her article for the *Gazette*, she used these documents as well as internal evidence from *Exploits* to demonstrate that the book purporting to be an authentic journal could not possibly be anything but fraudulent. Ross may also have been the only historian in 1955 who knew Crockett was in a hurry to get to Texas and why.[7]

It seemed wherever Crockett went anxious crowds congregated, frequently teeming with foolish speculations that this implausible specimen of humanity would appear before them in a form other than human, such as a "wild man of the woods, clothed in a hunting shirt and covered with hair" or some "hideous monster."[8] Although some of the more demanding crowds were invariably disappointed, Crockett always proved himself to be quite human in form. When Hackett brought his *Lion of the West* show to the western city of Cincinnati in 1833, local critics detected clues in the Wildfire character which suggested the play had been contrived solely for the purpose of ridiculing westerners. Crockett, however, felt it safe to be seen in his hunting attire now that he was back in the west. After all, he was the real hunter/legislator, not Wildfire. On Thursday, November 12, Crockett rode into Little Rock, an authentic frontier city. Typically, the curious gathered to see so that they too could believe.

Clothes neither make the man as the old saying goes, nor do they make the hunter. Spotting a deer about five miles outside the Little Rock city limits, Crockett grabbed a Pennsylvania/Kentucky rifle and reached into his possibles bag. The Pennsylvania/Kentucky long rifle, an advanced weapon for its time, was a wonderfully fine example of craftsmanship. A .40-caliber flintlock rifle was quite capable of bringing down medium-size game such as deer. Vastly superior to the smooth bore musket, the high velocity/low trajectory flintlock had an effective range of approximately two hundred yards.

Becoming skilled in the use of a flintlock required a great deal of practice and experience. Despite its capability, there were any number of factors originating both from within and without, which could compromise the accuracy of a shot. In addition to proper breathing, the flintlock user had to learn to concentrate totally on the target and ignore the sparks, tiny fragments of super heated steel splintering off uncomfortably close to the eyes. This can be particularly intimidating to the novice. Ammunition, like the black powder used in these rifles, was often self-made and not always consistent in quality. Parasitic drag resulting from a rifle ball's poor aerodynamic contour might also suppress downrange velocity. The only external certainty lies within nature itself. Through experience, the marksman knows his weapon's capability, and that at some point the omnipresent force of gravity will bend the rifle ball's linear flight path into a parabolic curve. If the rifleman misses his target, he knows who is to blame. In the real world, predators fail most of the time.

Bracing his fully primed weapon against his shoulder and with full faith that the laws of nature remain in place, the rifleman takes aim. The trigger is pulled and the hammer slams forward against the frizzen, which ignites the powder in the pan. Sparks from the pan burst through the touch hole igniting the main charge. The rifle ball is sent hurtling down range toward its target exiting the muzzle at approximately eighteen hundred feet per

William Woodruff was almost forty years of age when Crockett arrived in Little Rock. By that time, the native New Yorker had created the most powerful newspaper in the Arkansas Territory. Well mannered and reserved in his personal demeanor, Woodruff was an aggressive editor who did not permit his pro-Texas sympathies to distort his biased perception of Crockett. Courtesy of the Arkansas Historical Commission.

second. At the sound of a rifle shot, a deer, if not hit, will react instantly by looking around to identify the origin of the noise. Once they have determined the source, the deer will bolt for safety. In this instance, the deer in Crockett's sights never heard that startling blast of sound, nor did it see the cloud of smoke.

Crockett's entry into Little Rock that Thursday afternoon caused quite a sensation as swarms of people thronged the streets to get a look at the living legend. As for the accuracy of their report, the *Gazette* declared that unlike the claims set forth in the tales about Crockett, their estimate of the number of people who gathered to see him was well within the confines of reality. Most in the crowd had probably never seen Crockett or a picture of Colonel Wildfire. No doubt looking much like James D. Davis described him, there was a certain naturalness as to how this scene in the streets of Little Rock unfolded. Was he not, after all, the same David Crockett who had boasted he was half-horse, half-alligator, could dive deeper and come up drier than anyone else, that anyone could look at his wrists and see they were free of political party handcuffs, and that he wore no collar around his neck designating him as the president's dog? Any doubt was put to rest for the *Gazette* confirmed this was indeed the man "better known as Davy Crockett, the *raal critter* himself." He was also the same man, who in a later day and age, would be diagnosed by America's intelligentsia as a multiple personality.

Upon learning of Crockett's arrival, a group of citizens led by Colonel Robertson Childers decided to honor their unexpected, but most welcomed guest, with a dinner. Finding the hunter at work behind a hotel butchering the deer he had shot earlier, Childers called out to Crockett, who, surprised to hear a familiar voice, responded, "Robertson Childers, as I'm alive." As one might expect, the discussion quickly turned to the subject hunters from cultures all over the world find so fascinating, the circumstances of the kill. Bragging about the shot that brought down his prey, Crockett commented, "I made him turn ends at two hundred yards." Crockett's weapon was described by one eyewitness as "a long, old fashioned, deer rifle," which the hunter affectionately called "Old Bet." Crockett initially declined the dinner invitation, stating he was in a hurry to reach Texas but soon relented.[9]

THE PRECONCEIVED IMAGE TRANSFORMED

The banquet was scheduled to be held at the Jeffries Hotel, run by Charles L. Jeffries, possibly the same man James D. Davis believed had not yet moved from Memphis. As one might well imagine, attendance would have been limited to community leaders, more or less educated men who were eager to hear the famous bear hunter speak. Scarcely qualifying as an exact science, language, and its use as both a cultivated and rational instrument of communication, was viewed by the educated as a measure of a man's intelligence and class. Some in the audience might have wondered if Crockett possessed the necessary level of proficiency to express ideas with the clarity and exactness expected of a public speaker. Was he even capable of satisfying the minimum standards of acceptability as determined by social affirmation and the common usage of speech? While it is highly unlikely that anyone in this select audience of westerners would have been anticipating a wild man covered with hair, they must surely have gone to the banquet with certain expectations. At least one invitee was expecting a clown.[10] In any event, they expected to be entertained.

During the preparation of his autobiography, an elderly Albert Pike recalled Crockett's visit to Little Rock and the banquet. He happened to have enjoyed one story in particular that Crockett told which has seen several versions in print, including one by Horace Greeley. Pike tried to recall Crockett's precise words but had to settle on an approximation. Basically, Crockett and a group of fellow members of the House of Representatives, all good friends, strolled over one day to the circus which had recently come to town. Observing the curious behavior of a caged monkey, Crockett innocently made the comment that the little guy inadvertently displayed characteristics of expression remarkably similar to those of a certain congressman. Instantly, Crockett felt a poke in the ribs, for the gentleman with whom the comparison had been made just happened to be standing nearby! Somewhat embarrassed by this indiscreet slip, Crockett tried to recover by admitting he owed an apology. Though repentant, Crockett confessed he was not sure if he should apologize to the congressman or to the monkey.[11] The subject matter of his speech which inspired debate in the local newspapers was of an altogether different nature.

Richard Penn Smith provided the readers of *Exploits* with an account of the banquet and Crockett's speech since the event actually made national news. Smith even listed the topics Crockett supposedly spoke on, some of which were interrelated. Crockett discussed the Jackson Administration, Van Buren, the transfer of the bank deposits, and how he had been swindled out of being reelected. Smith also included a lengthy discourse for young, up and coming political aspirants. Completely satirical in nature, it is the only subject of the five whose inclusion could be seriously challenged. Interestingly enough, it is the only topic Smith purports to quote from. Arkansas historian James R. Masterson suspected that this portion of the speech may have been derived from "some printed source."[12]

Both the *Gazette* and the *Advocate* confirmed that Crockett did in fact speak about the Jackson Administration, but neither mentioned any other topics. Oddly enough, Smith neglected to have Crockett say anything about Texas. One invitee who was in the audience recalled that Crockett spent a good deal of time talking about his recent political defeat in a speech, which was "devoted mainly to the subject of Texan independence."[13] Though sympathetic with their countrymen in Texas, the portion of the speech which concerned the Little Rock newspapers most was what Crockett had to say about Washington politics. And it is within the context of the Democrat/Whig conflict that the Little Rock newspaper reports on this speech should be viewed.

The first newspaper to report on Crockett's Thursday evening visit was, understandably, the *Advocate*. Though they did favor him politically, their regular day of distribution just happened to be Fridays, whereas the *Gazette* was issued on Tuesdays. In time for their November 13 issue, Pike managed to squeeze in the following little article: "We shall die contented. We have seen the Hon. David Crockett—who arrived in this place last evening, on his way to Texas, where he contemplates ending his days. A supper was given him at Jeffries' hotel, of which many citizens partook. No room for further remarks."

At the *Gazette*, Woodruff took note of just how impressed his friends at the *Advocate* were with Crockett. Four days later, Woodruff published the following article:

> A rare treat. Among the distinguished characters who have honored our City with their presence, within the last week, was no less a personage than Col. David Crockett—better known as Davy Crockett—the *raal critter* himself—who arrived on Thursday evening last, with some 6 or 8 followers, from the Western District of Tennessee, on their way to Texas, to join the patriots of that country in freeing it from the shackles of the Mexican government. The news of his arrival rapidly spread, and we believe we speak within bounds, when we say, that hundreds flocked to see the wonderful man, who, it is said, can whip his weight in wild-cats, or grin the largest panther out of the highest tree. In the evening, a supper was given him, at

Jeffries' Hotel, by several Anti-Jacksonmen, merely for the sport of hearing him abuse the Administration, in his out-landish style, and we understand they enjoyed a most delectable treat, in a speech of some length with which he amused them. Having no curiosity that way ourself, we did not attend the *show*. But our neighbor of the *Advocate* was there, and so delighted was he, that he says he can now *"die contended."* Happy man!

The Colonel and his party, all completely armed and well mounted, took their departure on Friday morning, for Texas, in which country, we understand, they intend establishing their future abode, and in the defence of which, we hope they may cover themselves with glory.

Contemptuous of Crockett's inflated image as a frontier superman, Woodruff did not take him seriously as a politician either. After all, Crockett was a former Jackson man whom Woodruff imagined would only have used this staged opportunity to ridicule the very administration he supported. Having no interest in seeing a "buffoon," Woodruff was unable to give his readers a firsthand account of the speech. He was, however, curious enough to find out what Crockett had to say about the administration.

Also notably absent from that evening's affair were the editors of the *Times*. While Smith and Reed confessed they did not hear Crockett's speech for themselves, they admitted hearing the "stamping and applause of his audience." Every bit as inquisitive as Woodruff, the *Times* explained, "we are told that 'he used up' the Administration 'head to tail.'"[14] Told, no doubt, by someone who was actually in the audience.

Though laced with sarcasm throughout, the *Gazette's* article on Crockett does not conclude that way. The line, "we hope they may cover themselves with glory," was probably a sincere statement. In the same column, just two articles above the one on Crockett, Woodruff wrote about four Little Rock residents who, having "caught the patriotic flame," departed Little Rock less than seventy-two hours after Crockett gave his speech, "to gather laurels on the plains of Texas."[15] Woodruff's ridicule was not intended so much for Crockett as it was for his competition. This prompted a response from Pike which appeared in his next edition, issued on November 20:

> We have a single word to say for Colonel Crockett. He was honored
> and hospitably received here—not because "he can whip his weight
> in wild cats, or grin a panther out of the highest tree"—(as the
> *Gazette* says)—because there are plenty of Arkansas boys who can
> do the same—but because he is an honest man, and a true friend to
> Hugh L. White. Neither was the supper given by several anti-
> Jackson men. As well men of one party as of another joined in it.
> Neither did he abuse the Administration in an outlandish style. His
> remarks were few, plain, moderate and unaffected—without
> violence or acrimony. He spoke against the Administration and
> against the heir apparent—but he did it by quietly detailing facts.
> His remarks were far from outlandish. He neither aimed at display
> or eloquence—and was simply rough, natural, and pleasant.

Pike, a staunch anti-Jackson man, obviously liked the controversial
Crockett even before the frontiersman arrived. In fact, Pike had
defended the Tennessean in print on more than one occasion, such
as when an Alabama newspaper labeled Crockett as the "King's
Fool."[16] So, however accurate Pike's appraisal of Crockett's speech
may have been, the suspicion of bias still lingers.

Were there any pro-Jackson men in attendance as Pike claimed?
And if so, were any of them offended by the speech? As a young man,
Judge William F. Pope moved to Little Rock from Kentucky in 1832.
He soon found employment as the private secretary to the Territorial
Governor of Arkansas John Pope, one of the president's most dedicated
supporters. Pope, pro-Jackson perhaps, but undeniably open-minded,
retained the following impression of the night's guest speaker:

> As a matter of course, Colonel Crockett was the principal speaker,
> and his speech was devoted mainly to the subject of Texan inde-
> pendence. He, however, dwelt at some length upon the causes that
> had brought about his recent defeat for reelection to Congress.

> I was very agreeably surprised in Colonel Crockett, both as to his
> manners and personal appearance. I had always been of the impres-
> sion that the clown was one of his leading characteristics. His manner
> was dignified and gentlemanly, and, while he showed some lack of a
> thorough education, he displayed a wide range of information upon

the leading topics of the day. While his speech abounded in flashes of wit and humor, it never descended to the clownish or vulgar.[17]

When comparing Pike's comments with those made by Pope, the similarities are clearly evident. This is all the more interesting when it is taken into consideration that Crockett was being critiqued by two men with widely differing perspectives. Unlike Pike, who not only had a political ax to grind but was concerned with defending himself against the insinuations directed at him by the *Gazette*, Pope admitted Crockett did spend some time discussing his most recent political defeat, which definitely would have required bringing up the name of Andrew Jackson. But as Pope pointed out, this was not the main thrust of the speech.

When William F. Pope moved to Arkansas as a young man, he had a perception of Crockett which corresponded remarkably well with popular opinion. Desiring to write a recollection of Arkansas' most prominent figures in his later years, Judge Pope vividly recalled his impressions of the real David Crockett. From Early Days In Arkansas *by Judge William F. Pope.*

What might be of some concern is the fact that Pope's recollections were made at the age of eighty, fifty-nine years after the fact! It should be recalled here that James D. Davis, for example, assured his readers that despite the passage of more than a quarter of a century, his reporting of Crockett's departure from Memphis was conveyed with precision from a well-tuned memory. The problem, of course, has to do precisely with the passage of time. Confidence and accuracy do not necessarily go together. Whether we wish to adopt a skeptical attitude toward Pope's assertion of confidence or not, what he has imparted to us is the recollection of his impression of Crockett. Actually seeing and hearing the real Crockett totally discredited the image projected by Woodruff. It should also be pointed out here that Pike's evaluation of Crockett was printed one week after his observations were made.

One might suggest the standards designating acceptable conversation in a frontier town like Little Rock were probably lower than those of the eastern cultural centers. During the course of his many years in the nation's capital, Benjamin Perley Poore, who served as clerk of the Senate and editor of the *Congressional Directory*, had the opportunity of meeting and getting to know a great number of intelligent and influential men from every state. Poore remembered Crockett well: "He was a true frontiersman, with a small dash of civilization and a great deal of shrewdness transplanted in political life. He was neither grammatical nor graceful, but no rudeness of language can disguise strong sense and shrewdness, and a 'demonstration,' as Bulwer says, 'will force its way through all perversions of grammar.'"[18] Crockett was far more than just the most esteemed hunter in a society of hunters.

TALL TALES IN LITTLE ROCK AND OTHER BACKWOODS PHENOMENA

For someone who may have never even visited the Ozark Mountain region, there are certainly a good number of stories about Crockett indigenous to the area. Having no known precedence in printed form, Vance Randolph published eight of these tales in 1932. Their exact age is impossible to determine.[19] In keeping with the folkloric tradition, as oral compositions they were constantly subject to amendment. These stories deal primarily with hunting, where Crockett grins the bark off of trees, coaxes animals into surrendering, or undergoes an unusually magnified alteration in his perception of the world around him.

It was precisely due to the more barbaric aspects of his public image that Crockett would be portrayed by story writers as an American version of the mythological trickster. Tales combining Crockett, nature, coonskins, and incredible performances would proliferate. One such tale, thanks to Mr. Smith of Philadelphia, quickly found its way into print.

Since there was a little time before the evening's dinner would be served, it was proposed that Crockett should go out to the local shooting range and test himself with Arkansas' best. As expected, the local challengers proved themselves to be pretty fair country shots in the very first round. When the Tennessean took his turn, he responded with a shot of almost unbelievable precision, striking the marker dead center! Possibly a little surprised but nevertheless satisfied, Crockett triumphantly blurted out, "There's no mistake in Betsey." While most of the riflemen just stood there dumbstruck, one defied the implications by remarking, "That's a chance shot, Colonel." Crockett shrugged off the comment by assuring everyone it was no big deal, he could duplicate that shot "five times out of six, any day of the week." Unfortunately, this little display of self-confidence did not generate the desired response because now they demanded that he repeat his first performance, right then and there!

Once again the Arkansas riflemen went first with each improving upon their initial score. Knowing all along there was no way he could improve upon his first shot, Crockett raised Pretty Betsey, the rifle given to him by the Whigs of Philadelphia, and "blazed away." This time, he shocked everyone, including himself, by completely missing the target. Quickly composing himself, he realized that despite the pronouncement of a complete miss not all was lost. Crockett insisted there must be some logical explanation for this aberration, so he sauntered over to inspect the target board for himself. Closer examination revealed, much to the bewilderment of the other contestants, that the second shot had followed the exact same path as the first! Concluding they had just witnessed the incredible, and that Crockett was every bit as good as his legend, it was decided everyone should retire to the tavern and have a few drinks.[20]

Of course, Crockett missed the target completely, but somehow, without anyone noticing, he managed to slip a second rifle ball into the hole occupied by the first. During his years of collecting Ozark Mountain folktales, Vance Randolph came upon a fellow by the name of Windy Bill Hatfield who recounted the story of the Little Rock shooting match, only with a slight twist. According to Windy Bill, Crockett never even loaded his rifle for the second shot. Keeping a ball in his hand, he was able to discreetly slip it into the hole while pretending to be examining the target board. Windy Bill assured Randolph of the story's veracity by stating that he heard it from an uncle who was actually there and witnessed this event.

Randolph added that amongst the hill people of Arkansas, there existed a "persistent legend" that Crockett admitted to the deception years afterward.[21]

Such a confession from a basically honest man who had first bragged about his abilities and then succumbed to the temptation to cheat in order to save his reputation would make for an ideal resolution to the story. However, in *Exploits*, in which this story first appeared, there is no direct reparation by Crockett. It is curious that Smith included this story in his book, a book in which he portrayed Crockett as thoroughly honest.

Provided there was enough time, it is possible Crockett may have participated in a shooting match at Little Rock. It is also possible Smith may have read somewhere about Crockett competing in such an event, and, lacking details or drama, substituted this familiar story line. Rourke related a brief rendition of the shooting match in her book, but she correctly noted the story line was considered to be ancient even in Crockett's day and did not accept it as an actual event.[22] It is interesting that Crockett's daughter, Matilda, thought her father had taken Pretty Betsey, the rifle allegedly used in the match, along for the journey. In reality, Pretty Betsey stayed at home.

Arkansas had a reputation for being a place inhabited by a tough bunch of characters. And they had to be, if for no other reason than for the stuff they drank. Legend says that in one Little Rock tavern, Crockett was offered, and accepted without hesitation, a drink of something labeled "Ozark corn." Crockett, who had a tough guy reputation of his own, was up to the challenge as he downed the obscene looking substance with just one tilt of the horn. But, this same legend also says Crockett later confessed, "Gentlemen, I et my victuals raw for two months afterwards. My gizzard stayed so all-fired hot, that the grub was cooked afore it got settled in my innards."[23]

There is also another tale of Crockett paying a visit, in what must have been his last, to a Little Rock tavern. Not realizing he had just entered a no-holds-barred kind of bar, Crockett asked the bartender what all those slimly looking things on the floor were. Attempting to downplay any significance to the foreign objects, the bartender politely explained that his customers just had a little fun eye gouging the night before and had not bothered cleaning up since he was expecting more shortly. Not wanting a drink all that much, Crockett vacated the premises so fast he even left Old Betsy behind![24] In reality, Crockett did not remain in Little Rock very long. But, when Crockett left, he took Old Betsy with him.

A SENSE OF URGENCY

The owners of the *Times* may have been a little bashful when it came to attending the banquet, but they eventually succumbed to their journalistic curiosities and went looking for Crockett Friday morning. Apparently, they found him in a most humbling and compromising situation. "We had some curiosity to see this celebrated man; and our eyes were gratified with a sight of him on Friday morning last—and reader where—not in the hall of legislation, not in the bar-room of a tavern, neither was it in a lady's chamber—but in a carpenter's shop grinding an axe. Oh! What a falling off was there! His Honor grinding an axe."[25] One would, after all, expect to find a gentleman in any one of the three settings mentioned by the *Times*, but not in a carpenter's shop sharpening what was probably a tomahawk. Smith and Reed knew Crockett was preparing to leave Little Rock. And like Woodruff, they knew why he was going to Texas.

The fact that Crockett's group was composed entirely of Tennesseans who were, as the *Gazette* observed, on their way to assist the Texians in "freeing themselves from the shackles of the Mexican Government," suggests they had acquired an objective for going to Texas before they crossed the Mississippi River. The *New York Sun* later quoted Crockett as having said while in Little Rock that he would "have Santa Anna's head, and wear it for a watch seal." The *Sun* went on to remark that, "Two such men as Ex-Governor Houston and David Crockett will probably handle the Mexicans rather roughly."[26] Even before the end of November, Crockett's revised intentions for going to Texas were becoming public knowledge.

Anticipating that Crockett and company would "cover themselves in glory," Woodruff's journalistic patriotism managed to unfurl itself in an article that was otherwise thoroughly infused with sarcasm. Glory— it is the stuff of war stories and even some reports from the field. Perhaps this is necessarily so. Following the destruction of the Creek

Indian Village of Tallusahatchee during the War of 1812, General Andrew Jackson announced in his official report that the butchery at Fort Mims had finally been avenged. Crockett, who participated in the carnage, would also give an account of the attack some twenty years later in his *Narrative*. Crockett's version does not necessarily contradict Jackson's, he just seems to have missed out on all the glory.

Perhaps even as Jackson was writing his report, the volunteers, out of rations and nearly starving, returned to the village searching for food. The interior of the village still littered with corpses lying about undisturbed presented a grotesque image of death for which the mind is often powerless to expel from its memory. Beneath the heap of timbers devoured by flames were found the vestiges of forty-six human forms. "They looked very awful," Crockett recalled, "for the burning had not entirely consumed them, but given them a very terrible appearance, at least what remained of them." Beneath the bodies was found a food cellar containing potatoes. As a result of the fire, human tissue had seeped down into the open cellar, giving the potates a revolting appearance. Amidst the disfigured, putrescent remains of the dead, the living found sustenance. Attempting to rationalize an incident suggestive of cannibalistic behavior to a civilized readership two decades later, Crockett could only say, "we were all hungry as wolves."[27] In war, death always seems so near.

There is no question Crockett definitely spent less than twenty-four hours in Little Rock. Even in *Exploits*, Crockett left the day after he arrived. To explain why his stay was so brief, Rourke portrayed Crockett as one who had heard a calling. She dramatized this by improvising upon a scene taken from *Exploits*. When several Little Rock residents tried to persuade the Tennessean to stay and hunt bear with them, Rourke had Crockett resisting the temptation explaining that he felt an unexplainable, irresistible urge to go to Texas.

There is good reason to believe Crockett knew more about the most recent developments in Texas than either Smith or Rourke supposed possible. Pope stated Crockett initially turned down the dinner invitation because he was in a hurry to get to Texas. Quoting Pope, "he [Crockett] and some of his neighbors were on their way to Texas to assist the people of that Province to gain their independence, and that they were anxious to reach the scene of conflict."[28] If Davis's account is interpreted correctly, an account which admittedly was not overly concerned with dates or time, Crockett probably spent almost a full twenty-four hours in Memphis. It should be pointed out here that Crockett was not just in a hurry to get to Texas, but, as Pope indicated, he had a specific destination.

The editors of both the *Advocate* and the *Gazette* followed developments in Texas with particular interest. During the summer, Pike reported that Santa Anna had soundly suppressed all resistance in the state of Zacatecas and would soon form a military government.[29] Pike also reported that Santa Anna definitely planned to march on Texas. Since Mexico, in the opinion of the editors of the *Advocate*, was no longer a republic, they candidly expressed their hope to see Texas separated from the dictator and appended to the United States. A dictatorship, wrote Pike, was undoubtedly the "best kind of government for that country," but would not be suitable for Americans living in Texas.[30]

In the days immediately preceding Crockett's arrival, the Little Rock newspapers carried several significant articles concerning the latest developments in Texas. Certain that the citizens of Little Rock would view the news from Texas with great interest, James Clark, a resident of Miller County, Arkansas, and an agent for the *Advocate*, wrote to the editors. The letter stated that several Indian tribes acting in collusion with the Mexican Army had recently been engaged by the Texians in battle. The Texians supposedly initiated the attack against the newly formed alliance, killing sixty-three.[31] This report was never substantiated but was believed to have occurred. The issue of the *Advocate*, which included Clark's letter, may have hit the streets too late for Crockett to read. Nonetheless, it is almost certain that Pike shared everything he knew about the escalating war in Texas with him.

Two days prior to Crockett's arrival, the *Gazette* devoted considerable space to the outbreak of the revolution in Texas. Under a column titled *Foreign Intelligence*, Woodruff wrote, "The war has already begun." In addition, he reported the capture of the military facility in Goliad by the Texians. A minor action as far as numbers were concerned, but seizing the military facility was important from the standpoint that the Texians confiscated an estimated ten thousand dollars in equipment and supplies. The *Gazette* also printed the October 5 letter by Sam Houston. War,

Houston wrote, was unavoidable, and he urged Americans to waste no time in coming to Texas for there was plenty of land to be occupied. Houston continued: "Let each man come with a good rifle, and one hundred rounds of ammunition, and to come soon. Our war-cry is 'Liberty or death.' Our principles are to support the constitution, and *down with the Usurper!!!*"

Also of great significance were the two Stephen F. Austin letters, dated October 4 and 5, printed in the November 3 edition of the *Gazette*. Writing prior to his election as general of the newly formed "Army of the People," Austin mentioned the skirmish at Gonzales along with some grossly exaggerated casualty figures. But the primary motive for writing these letters was to announce that a great conclusive confrontation on the Texas frontier was imminent. Austin reported that large numbers of citizen soldiers were already moving to the west, and he expected no less than eight hundred volunteers on the frontier within a week. Their military objective was to capture the city of Béxar. In one great resounding victory, the Texians were determined to drive the Mexican Army, under the command of General Martin Perfecto de Cós, south across the Nueces River. At that point in time, Austin wrote, "We will then organize a government for Texas." If, after having spent less than twenty-four hours in Memphis, Crockett crossed the Mississippi unaware of the specifics of Austin's plans, the likelihood of leaving Little Rock as equally uninformed was virtually nonexistent.

On November 13, the *Jackson Truth Teller* reported that Crockett had passed through Memphis and was on his way to Texas to join the army.[32] For what might have been the very first time, Crockett was publicly identified in writing with the revolutionary forces in Texas. That same morning, Crockett and company once again received the kind of send-off that citizens give their soldiers going off to war. Very much aware that the war in Texas was quickly escalating toward a great climax and knowing exactly where this decisive battle was to take place, Crockett and his "followers" departed Little Rock, "armed from head to foot," "amid the huzzas of men, women, girls and boys."[33]

4

The Threshold Unfolds

DOWN THE ROAD

On November 14, Crockett's friend former Representative Sam Carson, who began his journey in September, pulled into Little Rock with his family. Prior to leaving North Carolina, Carson purchased twelve hundred acres of land near the Red River where he planned to establish his new residence.[1] Also preparing to leave Little Rock about the same time as Carson was Charles E. Rice, coeditor of the *Advocate*. Apparently, Rice was sufficiently inspired by Crockett's speech on Texian independence that he decided to pull up stakes and join the revolution. Commencing the long journey with five or six others, Rice, according to Pike, was leaving with great expectations that a glorious adventure awaited him on the plains of Texas.[2]

As the mythological hero who has responded to an inner call moves from the familiar to the unfamiliar, from the known into the unknown, the forbidden zone through which they must pass is a land of paradoxes. Progressing through visually stunning landscapes of immense beauty, this enigmatic sphere also presents dangers which could imperil the adventurer's life. This is the land where the laws and customs of one's society exert no influence. The hero is often assisted in these early stages of the journey by strange beings who provide advice on how to successfully surmount the obstacles and challenges which lie ahead. In *Exploits*, Smith created a little incident which would have an impact on how the story's main character ultimately views the world and his place in the universe. This incident occurred under almost ideal Emersonian conditions, which is to say in a place where nature's dynamic qualities are readily apparent.

As he made his way through Arkansas, Smith had Crockett giving the reader a geographical description of the entire territory. This was not the sort of information Crockett could have acquired through personal observation, but rather it was the type Smith procured from printed sources. Hearing the music of a fiddle, Crockett met up with a parson, the backwoods equivalent of a holy man. The two companions discussed a variety of topics ranging from politics to bear hunting. As the parson drifted into a discourse on the nature of reality, Crockett came to realize that all the things which he had taken for granted, the trees, flowers, streams, and even inanimate rocks, resonated with the spirit of God. Crockett may have felt rejected by society, but he could never be alone even in the wilderness for that omnipresent "watchful eye" was always with him. Of course, the pantheistic words of realization were contrived by a man who had spent a great deal more time behind a desk than in the wilderness.

Before they split up, Crockett, believing the parson to be a perceptive and capable man, suggested that he consider taking up a more lucrative line of work. Seeing that the hero's consciousness

The Armstead Blevins residence was known to local residents as "The Two Pines." This photograph was taken in 1934. Courtesy of the Library of Congress.

had already lapsed back to more common concerns the parson replied, "My wealth lies not in this world."[3] The reader might well imagine Crockett now suspected his recent enlightenment was somehow incomplete. As Crockett's journey progressed in *Exploits*, a fuller meaning gradually unfolded. Having fulfilled his role as spiritual guide, the parson, whose name is never disclosed, is then dropped from the story.

Smith had enough resources available to deduce that the most logical route Crockett would have taken out of Little Rock was the southwesterly road to Texas. Once used by Indian tribes, the path that eventually became known as the Old Southwest Trail may have been originally etched in the earth by migrating herds of buffalo. After the Arkansas Territory was acquired by the United States, the federal government assimilated the path into its system of military roads. In preparation for the transfer of the Choctaw Tribe to the west, the trail was widened by sixty-one feet. With few exceptions, the Old Southwest Trail closely parallels today's Interstate 30.

Real world travelers could expect to meet a number of friendly people on their adventure and maybe even a few old friends. James Nichols was a teenager when Crockett stopped by his house in the fall of 1835. His father, a man with an ambition to live in the famed marble city of Béxar, had known Crockett when they were children back in east Tennessee. Preparing his memoirs years later, James recalled that Crockett stayed with the family "for a few days." He admired Crockett's unique attire and took a special liking to one of his rifles.[4]

Another old friend Crockett might have met along his journey was Armstead Blevins. Throughout his life, Blevins welcomed many travelers into his home which was situated alongside the Old Southwest Trail just north of Washington, Arkansas. According to family tradition, it was believed Crockett spent an entire week hunting deer with Armstead. Given his desire to reach Texas as soon as possible, a week sounds a little too long. It seems more likely that the duration of the visit gradually expanded with the passage of time.[5]

Nine miles west of the interstate on Highway 4 is the Old Washington Historic State Park. Here in Washington, roughly 125 miles southwest of Little Rock, the modern day traveler can once again pick up the Old Trail on Franklin Street, which runs right

Tradition asserts that Crockett stayed at the old Washington Tavern on Franklin Street. A private residence at the time when this photograph was taken in 1934, the old tavern was in its final days of occupancy. Courtesy of the Library of Congress.

through downtown. Situated on a hill, this state park's well-preserved structures represent different time periods in Washington's history. Yet, as old as many of the buildings are, this is not the town that existed in November 1835. Even the white court-house, constructed in 1836 on the northern end of Franklin Street post dates Crockett's visit. The old tavern, also on Franklin Street, where tradition says Crockett stayed, was still standing, dilapidated and ignored, more than one hundred years after he left town. It, too, is now gone.

Eleven months before Crockett visited Washington, George William Featherstonhaugh described the town as nothing more than a "little insignificant wooden village[6] . . . a miserable affair, built on a dry scorching sand-hill, and which has no resource or attraction whatsoever."[7] Featherstonhaugh may have thought Washington was worthless, but it was the economic center of southern Arkansas and second in the territory only to Little Rock. Men of influence from south of the Sabine River frequented Washington in those early days. According to legend, Stephen Austin, Sam Houston, and James Bowie met in the local tavern plotting revolution. All three visited the town, but not at the same time. Bowie's visits to Washington are well known. Legend says he even had a knife made there. Featherstonhaugh was there when Houston was living the life of a hermit, drinking heavily, and only coming out at night.

Since the Old Southwest Trail led directly into Washington, it is possible that Crockett passed through the town. The earliest record linking him with Washington can be traced back to none other than *Exploits*. At this point, Smith lost track of Crockett's movements. Because of the publisher's edict against an idle press, Smith could hardly afford to do much research. From the page where Crockett leaves Little Rock, virtually every detail that follows in *Exploits* is due to either Smith's reliance on erroneous sources or the result of outright invention. Only when Smith has Crockett reach the metropolitan areas of Nacogdoches and Béxar is he once again able to incorporate some fact into the story, and even then to a very limited extent.

To fill the void, Smith proposed that Crockett headed out of Washington by taking the Old Southwest Trail to Fulton, Arkansas, on the Red River. There, Crockett boarded a steamboat for a leisurely cruise down the Red River to Natchitoches. From Louisiana, Crockett set out for Nacogdoches across the border into Texas. Crockett did reach Nacogdoches but not by the route outlined by Smith.

Shackford thought Smith's route for Crockett toward Fulton was a viable possibility. From there, however, Shackford theorized that Crockett visited a settlement about ten miles to the south called Lost Prairie. He then turned northwest and rode along the northern banks of the Red River, crossing the river just above the town of Clarksville.[8] The precise point where Crockett actually crossed the Red River is still subject to debate.

There are at least four different points where Crockett is believed to have crossed the Red River. Two are on the northeastern border with Arkansas and two on the northeastern border with Oklahoma. The southernmost crossing point would have been George Dooley's Ferry at Lost Prairie.[9] Historian Skipper Steely recorded two north Texas traditions identifying the point where Crockett crossed the Red River. One tradition contends Crockett traveled west from Washington through Sevier County in Arkansas and crossed the river at Levi Davis's Ferry. Another tradition says he continued further west and crossed at the Mill Creek Landing just above Spring Hill in present-day Bowie County, Texas. In the village of DeKalb south of Spring Hill, tradition claims that not only did Crockett spend the night there, but he actually gave the community its name.[10]

The fourth version, researched by Judge Pat B. Clark, argues Crockett took the military road which extended from Washington west for approximately seventy miles to Fort Towson in the Oklahoma Territory. Intended as the southernmost fort in a line of defense running from the Canadian border down to the Red River, Fort Towson was also designed to represent the United States government amongst the relocated Choctaw and Chickasaw Tribes. The piles of rubble which now occupy the Fort Towson Military Park grounds are all that remain of the Fort's limestone structures. About fifteen miles to the south, down the Choctaw Trail, lay the Red River. It was here, according to Clark, that Crockett caught the ferry at the old Jonesboro crossing.[11]

THE LAND BETWEEN

The immediate area on the south side of the Red River once constituted a disputed zone. Although claimed by both Spain and the United States in the early 1800s, no one really knew the exact location of the borderline which separated the Louisiana Territory and the Spanish lands, including France. The Transcontinental Treaty of 1819, negotiated for the United States by then Secretary of State John Quincy Adams, established the boundary along the Sabine River. So when Crockett and company crossed the Red River into what is today the northeastern portion of Texas, they were actually still in the United States.

Created in 1820 as part of the Arkansas Territory, Old Miller County encompassed land on both sides of the Red River which included portions of what is today southwestern Arkansas, southeastern Oklahoma, and northeastern Texas. The area's first commercial center was the town of Jonesboro, which was situated on the south side of the river. Jonesboro is also remembered as one of the gateways through which many immigrants first set foot on what would eventually become Texas.

After completing his education at the University of Virginia, James Clark and his father, Benjamin, a nephew of Revolutionary War hero George Rogers Clark, headed west where they established a salt mining business in southern Arkansas. Elected to serve his community in the Arkansas Territorial Legislature, Clark was "a man of pronounced views and unrelenting determination." In 1829, Clark married Isabella Hanks, a woman recognized as possessing similar characteristics. As cofounders of Clarksville, James and Isabella were prime examples of the American pioneer class. Most notably remembered as a woman of charity and enterprise, Isabella was an active community leader throughout most of her life. In fact, she was personally responsible for financing the construction of the first courthouse in Clarksville.[12]

Historian Claude V. Hall wrote in 1931 that the northeastern section of Texas had been ignored by Texas historians as no other. Earlier that same year, the *Dallas News* printed an article wherein it was claimed that contrary to local folklore, Crockett never even came within eighty miles of what is now Paris, Texas. In response, the historical society in Paris commissioned a local historian, Carolyn S. Scott, to research the matter.[13] The contest between oral tradition and the written word proved to be no contest at all.

If Scott had little documented evidence to work with, the writer of the *Dallas News* article did not seem overly eager to reveal the source on which he based his claim. In a letter to the article's writer, Scott said that judging from the information presented in his essay, it appeared to her that he must have been reading *Exploits*. While not prepared to pronounce the entire body of Smith's work a fake, she did assert that the segment dealing with Crockett's passage through southern Arkansas contained a number of errors. Scott attempted to explain the presence of the inaccuracies by suggesting that relevant pages from his journal must have either been lost or were somehow rendered illegible. In her letter, Scott stated she had interviewed many residents whose ancestors were living in the region when Crockett passed through. Ultimately, Scott would rely on an authentic Crockett letter containing internal evidence validating the claim of local folklore that he had definitely been in the area.[14]

Scott also cited Judge Pat B. Clark, grandson of James and Isabella Clark, as one of her sources. Having spent much of his

childhood living with his grandmother, Clark was afforded the
opportunity of repeated conversations with many prominent people
from the early days of the Red River area. Much of the information
Clark obtained concerning Crockett came from his grandmother and
Henry Stout, a close friend of the family. Unfortunately, when Clark
sat down to compile the story of Crockett's visit, he had to call upon
the memory of conversations which had taken place decades earlier.
In his book *The History of Clarksville and Old Red River County,
Texas*, Clark placed Crockett in the Red River region during the
summer, an error which Scott quickly corrected. Nonetheless, Clark
offered by far the most detailed description of Crockett's route
through northeastern Texas.

Judge Clark included two versions of Crockett's travels through
the Red River area in his book. Basically, both tell the same story.
The most obvious dissimilarity between the two is that Crockett's
journey is described in greater detail in the second version.[15] Clark
designated the starting point on the Red River where his grandfather, James, crossed the Red River and tied his boat to a
cottonwood tree on the Jonesboro side, the same tree that Red River
County tradition says was also used to secure the ferryboat which

*Judge Pat B. Clark posed for this photograph next to the old cottonwood tree near the
Red River in 1931. From* The History of Clarksville and Old Red River County, Texas, *by Judge Pat Benjamin Clark.*

brought Sam Houston across in 1832. Almost one hundred years later, Clark and a few friends gathered at the site of the old tree to take photographs. Using the old tree at the Jonesboro Crossing as a starting point, Clark contended that once across the river Crockett adopted a southeasterly course for about twenty miles to the home of John Stiles near the tiny settlement of White Rock. It was his understanding that Stiles and Crockett were old friends.

Clark asserted Crockett asked Stiles for directions to the home of William Becknell, a pioneer known as the "father of the Santa Fe trade." As for the possible friendship presumed to have existed between Becknell and Crockett, Becknell's biographer Larry Beachum believed this supposed friendship had "no apparent basis in historical record, although Crockett may have been an admirer of Becknell's accomplishments and therefore desirous of meeting him."[16] Becknell had just recently moved to the area, then known as Sulphur Fork Prairie. The next morning, Crockett and Stiles rode out to the edge of the prairie. Pointing in the direction of Clarksville about ten miles to the south, Stiles instructed Crockett to pass to the north of three blackjack trees standing on high prairie ground and proceed west to a prairie encircled by timber. Stiles said he would find Becknell's house roughly five miles out of Clarksville.

Passing just north of Clarksville, Crockett stopped and spoke with a man named William Brinton. The following morning, Brinton met the thirty-one-year-old Mrs. Clark in town and mentioned his chance meeting with the famous man. Just before Crockett crossed the Red River, it was reported in Clarksville that Comanches were in the vicinity for the purpose of conducting raids. As a counter measure, James Clark led a quickly assembled force out into the countryside to drive them off. Alarmed when told of Crockett's intended course, Mrs. Clark hurriedly saddled her horse and rode out to the spot where Brinton had seen him.

Mrs. Clark picked up Crockett's trail near the property of James and Jane Latimer, which was clearly evident by the trampled grass. She was soon joined by Jane and Betty Latimer in her search. For these three ladies to have left the security of their homes to venture out into a sparsely populated region to warn a stranger meant forsaking all regards for personal safety. Though the decision they made may have been impulsive to some degree, Mrs. Clark must

A true pioneer, Isabella Clark Gordon was one of the most respected citizens in Texas. From The History of Clarksville and Old Red River County, Texas, *by Judge Pat Benjamin Clark.*

have been aware of the risks involved.

Judge Clark believed his grandmother tracked Crockett to Becknell's home.[17] The details of this story, however, as related by Mrs. Clark are a little different. She tended to downplay her own role in the story. In reading her version, one gets the impression it was just as much the Latimers' idea to go after Crockett as it was hers. In another variation, she claimed to have caught up with Crockett at the home of Edward Dean about ten miles west of Clarksville where he had spent the night. Reaching the Dean residence in the early morning hours, the three ladies were greeted by a bewildered Mrs. Dean who asked, "Mrs. Clark, what in the name of God brings you here at this time of the day?" Mrs. Clark responded by simply saying, "My horse brought me."[18]

Some sixty years after this event, the *Dallas Morning News* sent one of their reporters out to Clarksville to get a story on Mrs. Clark. By then, she was one of the most revered of all Texas pioneers. During her interview, Isabella spoke of Sam Houston, who, while in her presence, was on his best behavior. She dismissed as complete fiction the story that Houston spent his first day south of the Red River in a drunken stupor. While Isabella confessed to having less than perfect recall, her memory seemed to have served her well as she shared her impressions of Crockett.

Crockett was dressed like a gentleman, and not as a backwoodsman. He did wear a coonskin cap. It has always disgusted me to read these accounts of Crockett that characterize him as an ignorant backwoodsman. Neither in dress, conversation nor bearing could he have created the impression that he was ignorant or uncouth. He was a

man of wide practical information and was dignified and entertaining. His language was about as good as any we hear nowadays. I
was glad to see in the *News* some time ago an article correcting the
false impression about Crockett. He was a gentleman all over . . .
Crockett was a handsome fellow, tall, straight, and clean-shaven. He
rode a fine horse.[19]

Mrs. Clark knew a gentleman when she saw one, and the coonskin
cap could not disguise the obvious.

There are certain aspects of Crockett's sojourn in the Red River
area which tend to give the appearance of a man wandering from
house to house, visiting old friends. Strangely enough, Judge Clark
inadvertently contributed to the misconception that Crockett was only
there to socialize by giving two different, though not necessarily inconsistent, explanations as to why he went to Becknell's house. In his first
version of Crockett's journey, Clark stated that Crockett asked Stiles
for directions to Becknell's because he was "desirous to see another
Red River County citizen."[20] Two pages later, Clark recounted this
same story except he referred to Becknell as "another friend" of
Crockett's. The contemporaneous view, as formulated by Shackford,
that Crockett was simply there for exploration, effectively severs any
correlation between his presence in the Red River area and events to
the south.

As those who had firsthand contact with Crockett gradually died
off, their unrecorded stories became somewhat diluted with the
passage of time. However, the real reason as to why Crockett was traveling through the area was never totally lost to local residents. Within
fifty years of Crockett's sojourn, *The Independent*, a northeast Texas
newspaper unaffected by the authority of more popular accounts,
relied solely on local sources when it claimed that it was "near where
Paris now stands, Davy Crockett started with a company of men to
reach the Texan army at San Antonio by this western route."[21] Having
done his own research, Judge Clark knew very well Crockett had not
crossed the Red River to look at real estate or to make social calls.

Clark stated that "Crockett was very anxious to reach Col. Travis,
who was at that time near San Antonio."[22] Although Lieutenant
Colonel William Barret Travis would not be assigned to that post until
mid-January, he was near Béxar, later renamed San Antonio, for a

brief period during the siege of that city by the Texian forces in November though not in a position of command. Travis's name, which, by the time of Clark's writing had long been identified with the siege of the Alamo, could not have been part of the original story. Clark simply confused the two sieges. Nonetheless, it was the understanding of residents in the Red River region that Crockett was in a hurry to get to Béxar where he intended to join the multitude which had engaged the Mexican Army.

Off the Road and Into the Void

As of the first week of December the Siege of Béxar, the great engagement that Stephen Austin envisioned would expel Mexican forces from Texas, was still in progress. Having learned by the time he left Little Rock that Béxar was to be the site of this great decisive battle, Crockett must have presumed that taking the western military road out of Washington would ultimately place him in a better position to reach his destination. Taking this supposedly faster route would require him to abandon civilization once he passed Clarksville and make the rest of the journey through an unaccommodating wilderness.

Judge Clark thought his grandmother had convinced Crockett to abandon his southwesterly course and remain at Becknell's house "for a few days waiting for recruits to escort them on to join Houston's Army or Colonel Travis at San Antonio,"[23] but again, his grandmother remembered things differently. She recalled that when they all finished breakfast, Crockett and his group, after having spent only one evening at the Deans' residence, began making preparations "to resume their journey to the south."[24] The last Mrs. Clark ever saw of Crockett was when she watched him riding off.

After having traveled about twenty miles west of Deans' house, Crockett made camp on a hill beneath a canopy of oak trees. Local folklore fixed Crockett's campsite within the present day Paris city limits near what is now Clarksville Street. This spot was later named Crockett Circle. Local tradition also claimed that the tree under which the group was supposed to have camped eventually became part of someone's front yard.[25] Another local tradition claimed Crockett carved his name into one of the trees in the immediate vicinity. It was probably about this time when Henry Skidmore who, along with Ben McCulloch, had been unable to leave with the group back in November, now crossed the Red River and was following Crockett's trail in an effort to catch up to him.

Crockett and his group broke camp in the afternoon of their third day south of the Red River and passed through the future site of downtown Paris. There is a little story which says that they soon came upon eight-year-old Cecilia Peters who was playing in front of her house. Not expecting any visitors, she was startled into reality when she heard a voice ask, "Little girl, can you tell me the way to the Alamo?" Cecilia nervously replied that she had "never heard of that town" but would go and ask her father.

The fact that Crockett would once again have to ask for information concerning the terrain to the south was indicative of just how little was known about the area. But Cecilia's father warned Crockett that the region was deficient in wild game and should the group continue on their intended course with the intention of living off the land, they would soon face starvation. As an alternative, he advised them to turn around and take the safer though longer route to the east. Cecilia remembered that Crockett did not appear at all concerned. Patting his rifle, Crockett said, "As long as I have Betsy I won't starve." Ignoring the advice, Crockett and company pressed on.[26]

Citing Judge Clark as his source, historian Claude Hall wrote about an incident which must have occurred after Crockett and company departed the Peters's residence. Hall stated that when the Crockett hunting party reached the "headwaters of the Trinity River," which would have placed them near present-day Dallas, they met James Clark and his band which had gone out several days earlier to drive off the Comanches. When Crockett mentioned the woman who had risked her life to warn him, Clark responded, "That was my wife, for no other woman could do a thing like that." Clark added that his wife's advice was still very prudent counseling as the dangers posed by the Comanches had not yet dissipated.[27]

One element of this story has been questioned by northeast Texas historians Carolyn S. Scott and Skipper Steely. It appeared unlikely to Scott and Steely that James Clark and Crockett could have been in the Red River area at the same time. Both historians felt that when Crockett crossed the Red River, Clark should have already been on his way to San Felipe de Austin. Instead of speaking with Clark, they believed the man Crockett probably spoke with was Dr. George Gordon. The theory is that the confusion centers around the reference to Isabella's husband. After James Clark died in 1838, Isabella married Dr. Gordon the following year. So when Isabella subsequently told and retold the story of her husband's encounter with Crockett, she was referring to her current husband, Dr. Gordon. [28]

Another version claims that Gordon met Crockett near the Sabine River. This meeting occurred after Crockett supposedly left Natchitoches.[29] If such a meeting took place at the Sabine, it would seem that Crockett must have been on his way to Nacogdoches. This would suggest a date perhaps as late as the closing days of December or early January. The later the date one would ascribe to this meeting, the more likely it is that the man Crockett met could not have been Clark.

We can only assume with any measure of confidence that Crockett crossed the Red River sometime during the third week of November. From there, it was only a matter of days before he departed Dean's house. Now, according to Hall, Crockett was just starting out on a hunting trip when he met James Clark to the south near the Trinity River. However, Judge Clark thought the hunting party rode west from Becknell's place not south.[30] We know that James Clark had definitely reached Nacogdoches by December 23 when Judge John J. Forbes penned his letter of introduction for him to present to the authorities in San Felipe de Austin.[31] Back on December 10, the council had voted to allot the citizens of the Red River region, then known as "Pecan Point and Vicinity," a total of two delegates to the upcoming Constitutional Convention. When news of this ruling reached Clarksville, Clark was appointed by a committee to present a petition to the council requesting that the municipality be split into three separate municipalities, allotting two delegates to each.[32] Clark was still in the area as of the tenth and could not have left for several more days, allowing plenty of time for him to meet Crockett.

Possibly sometime after Clark's warning in the wilderness, Cecilia Peters was peeling potatoes on her back porch when she noticed riders approaching. She quickly recognized several men as having passed by the house with Crockett some eight to ten days earlier. It was obvious they had encountered difficulties. One of the men hastily dismounted, walked over to Cecilia, and grabbing one of the raw potatoes, said, "Sister, if you don't mind, I will eat this one now."[33]

Judge Clark was unaware that Crockett's group had continued south in an effort to reach Béxar. Nor did Clark have any idea that the three or four companions he believed had crossed the Red River with Crockett were actually part of a larger group which had broken up in the wilderness. Cecilia did not exactly say how many men returned to her house, but she apparently noticed that the number constituted "about half" of the original group. If the number of volunteers accompanying Crockett across the Red River was close to the six or eight reported by the *Arkansas Gazette*, then a drop of "about half" would have reduced the size of the group to three or four. After their first meeting, Cecilia never saw Crockett again. When her family learned of his death at the Alamo, they naturally assumed he had been successful in making it through the wilderness to Béxar.[34]

One can only speculate as to what happened out in the wilderness to precipitate the splintering of Crockett's group. To begin with, the information they had acquired in Little Rock about the impending battle would, by this time, have been about two months old. With almost three hundred miles left in their journey, there must have been increasing doubt amongst the group as to whether or not they could reach Béxar in time to participate in the battle and if they could even make it at all! While offering little in the way of sustenance, this strange and forbidding land was dominated by Comanches. The prospect of being overwhelmed while out in the open had to have been a major concern. Some members of the group must have simply accepted the futility of this drive sooner than others.

The very conditions under which this drive to the south was being carried out—the race against time, slipping unscathed through hostile territory with so few—represented for Crockett an irresistible challenge. Crockett liked to take risks, such as the time when he went to retrieve his gunpowder during a snowstorm. But considering the degree of risk involved, Crockett must have realized at some point that this mission no longer made any sense. Again, according to an old reconstruction of the story based solely on local sources, "Some of the party, seeing the danger of this route, had already returned to the settlements, and Crockett, with only a few men left, was compelled to abandon the expedition in this direction," and resort to taking the recommended eastern route.[35]

A GLIMPSE OF EDEN

While Crockett was out in the wilderness, he was making national news back in the United States. On November 28, the *New York Transcript* printed the *Jackson Truth Teller* article reporting that Crockett had "passed through Memphis a few days since on his way to Texas, where he is going to join the American forces against the Mexicans."[36] Continuing to report on the former congressman despite his recent political defeat, the *Niles' Weekly Register*, a major Whig publication operated by Hezekiah Niles out of Baltimore, began tracking the progress of Crockett's journey to Texas, printing the first report on December 5. "Col. Crockett has proceeded to Texas—to end his days there. A supper was given to him at Little Rock, Arkansas."

Convinced he had succumbed to visions of Van Buren's election, the December 6 edition of the *New York Sunday Morning News* announced, "*Davy Crockett* has actually gone to Texas, with his 'rifle, and a hundred rounds.'" Disappointed that Crockett had found the United States in a politically degenerative state, the paper not only feared he would fail to find an honest politician in Texas, but expressed concern that upon reaching this most publicized promised land, he might lose his moral virtue to the temptations offered by its low class atmosphere.[37] Five days later, the *Albany Journal* made the following observation: "Colonel Crockett who has recently gone to Texas is probably one of the best shots in the world. One hundred men like Crockett would be of immense service to the Texians at this time—if you could only make them believe that their enemies were *bears*, instead of men. Crockett has been known to send a rifle ball through the same hole nine times in successive fire."[38] Even the legendary Crockett would have found such an exhibition a little hard to believe.

Instead of attempting to retrace their trail back the way they came, Crockett and his friends might have veered off in a northeasterly direction toward Clarksville. This may have been when Crockett came upon the home of Matthias Click near present-day Mount Vernon. Originally from Tennessee, the Clicks settled in

Hempstead County, Arkansas, then moved south of present-day Paris in 1834 near a stream which would later be known for decades as Crockett's Creek. This brief yet memorable visit became part of the family's folklore, and for one of Click's sons it proved to be the event of a lifetime. This particular son told the story of Crockett's visit with such frequency and sustained enthusiasm, he was nicknamed "Davy Crockett Click."[39]

During his stay with the Clicks, Crockett made a contraption called a "spider" or "lizard." Carved out of wood, it was used for hauling water or carrying small game. Crockett gave the item to his hosts and it remained in the family for many years. There are two different stories as to what happened to the relic known locally for generations as "Davy Crockett's spider."[40] One story says it was given to the Texas State Fair, where its trail ends. The other story says the "spider" was placed on display in the Lamar County Courthouse where it was destroyed in the mid-1870s by the first of several major fires that would plague Paris.

Continuing on in a northeasterly direction after leaving the Clicks, Crockett probably made his way back to Becknell's house. This seems to have been the most plausible time during Crockett's Red River sojourn to go on the hunting trip that Judge Clark was certain had started out from Becknell's place. It is also where Henry Stout must have entered the picture. Described by Clark as "a great hunter and one of the most remarkable guides on any frontier,"[41] Stout enjoyed a heightened reputation even in his own day. With Stout as their guide, Crockett and his friends traveled more than one hundred miles west of Becknell's house where there was no shortage of wildlife.

Stout led the Crockett hunting party to a place resembling that which the mythologies of many cultures contend once existed. Nature had placed a dividing line in this region separating the dryer, open lands of the west from the moist woodlands and grasslands of the east. This line of demarcation, located in present-day Fannin and Grayson Counties, was known as Cross Timbers. A thin, yet dense forest, Cross Timbers stretched from the Red River southward for 250 miles.

Crockett did not find the time to write home until he reached the cities of east Texas in the first week of January. In his letter,

Crockett mentioned "the Bordar or Chactaw Bio of Red River."[42] The word, "Bordar" has sometimes been interpreted as a reference to the "Bordark," a stream near Washington in Hempstead County. In today's standard spelling, the word in question seems to resemble "border." But a more likely possibility, originally suggested by Carolyn S. Scott and later by Anna Grace Catron and Stanley Folmsbee, is that Crockett may have been alluding to the Bois d' Arc Creek in present-day Fannin County, Texas.[43]

As the name was applied in the 1830s, Choctaw Bayou referred to a general area the precise magnitude of which had not been determined. Lacking imaginary boundaries, Choctaw Bayou encompassed meadows and prairies to the east, south, and west. To the north, the land adjacent to the Red River was heavily timbered. Before the surveyors came, land on both sides of the Red River was called Choctaw Bayou.

Crockett said nothing in his only letter from Texas about having hunted buffalo, but he did mention a buffalo pass. This particular pass was located near the western boundary of present-day Fannin County. Approximately twenty-five miles east of the buffalo pass, the hunting party came within sight of a mass of trees standing in the wide-open prairie. They soon found themselves passing through wild prairie grass that reached up to their stirrups as they approached the wooded slope. Once inside the little grove, they made camp near a small spring nestled serenely in the woods and dined on wild honey. Depending upon which story is consulted, Crockett carved either his own name or that of "Honey Grove" into one of the trees. Although the names of the three or four men who were still with Crockett at this point were never recorded, legend has identified one of them as Andy Thomas.

According to the story, Thomas set out for Texas with Crockett from Tennessee. In their company were other settlers traveling in wagons pulled by oxen. Reaching the Red River country in the spring of 1835, they made camp in the wilderness. After trading rifles, Thomas and Crockett parted company. Thomas headed in a northeasterly direction, while Crockett rode south.[44]

Aside from the obvious flaws, there are some interesting aspects of this story which deserve consideration. In what may be an independent tradition, it was Crockett who gave the woods their name of

"Honey Grove." There was, however, one tangible artifact left behind from this brief association—the rifle Thomas received in the trade with Crockett. Its single star, said to have been engraved by Crockett himself, is supposed to represent the rise of a new republic. After remaining in the family for several generations, the rifle was donated and put on display in the Long Barracks Museum at the Alamo.

Captain Henry Stout led Crockett and what remained of his little band of volunteers on a hunting expedition into Choctaw Bayou. For years afterwards, local folks talked about the famous hunt. Courtesy of the Daughters of the Republic of Texas Library.

For the longest time, it seemed as though virtually no one knew of this place. By the end of 1836, a number of people were aware of its existence. It even had a name. One local legend says that shortly after the Crockett hunting party left the woods, a man by the name of W. B. Allen found the words "Honey Grove" carved into one of the trees. It was also said that everywhere Crockett went thereafter he spoke of this place, specifically referring to it by that name.[45]

Crockett believed his friends were the type who could make something of this land. According to local history, Crockett wrote to one friend, Samuel Erwin, telling him of this place he called "Honey Grove." Erwin, a land surveyor by profession, came looking for Honey Grove in 1842, and when he found it he stayed. As the area's first permanent settler, Erwin is considered to be one of the founders of the town of Honey Grove, which still stands there today.

When James Mallory, the Tennessee storekeeper in Dover, moved to Honey Grove, he purchased the very grounds on which the frontiersman was believed to have made camp some twenty-one years earlier.[46] According to tradition, the precise location of Crockett's camp was just north of the present-day town square. The tradition linking Crockett with the woods of Honey Grove is a very strong one, dating back to the days of Stout, Erwin, and, of course, Crockett himself.

A competing story says that it was a group of Arkansas hunters who came up with the name of Honey Grove.[47] But if the Arkansas hunters had named Honey Grove, a place known only to hunters, it is difficult to imagine that Henry Stout would not have known of the woods by this name long before Crockett arrived on the scene. Yet, while Judge Clark received his information about the hunting trip and the campsite at Honey Grove directly from Stout, he preferred to fall back on local tradition which maintained that the woods acquired their name as a result of Crockett's visit.[48]

THE LOST PRAIRIE

It was during this segment of the journey that Crockett's group may have lost one more member. Steely found evidence that Henry Skidmore just might have caught up with Crockett. Another version says Skidmore tracked Crockett as far as his Paris campsite, then gave up. Either way, Skidmore found the area so attractive, he decided to stay there for the remainder of his life.[49]

Several weeks may have elapsed between the time Crockett crossed the Red River and when he finished his hunting expedition with Stout. Exactly where Crockett went after visiting Choctaw Bayou is far from clear. Rourke attempted to reconstruct Crockett's route and came up with quite a complicated trail. She suggested the possibility that due to his interest in Indian affairs, Crockett may have visited the Choctaw Tribe, then residing on the north side of the Red River. From the Oklahoma Territory, Rourke believed he traveled east to Fulton, down to Lost Prairie, and back up to Fulton. At that point, she reverted to *Exploits* which stated that Crockett caught a steamboat down to Natchitoches.[50]

Judge Clark reported that at the conclusion of the hunt, Crockett rode eastward and stopped at the home of Collin McKinney, near Spanish Bluffs in present-day Bowie County.[51] McKinney was a man of great political influence in the Red River region. Having already been acknowledged by the Provisional Government of Texas, the Red River region was set to take its place at the upcoming Constitutional Convention. The implications of such a move were sure to cause some concern in Washington. Certainly by the time he departed McKinney's, there was no doubt in Crockett's mind that Honey Grove and Choctaw Bayou, both located within the Arkansas Territory and hence the United States, would soon fall within the boundaries of Texas.

From McKinney's, Judge Clark thought Crockett adopted a southeasterly course to Logansport on the Sabine River.[52] However, it is known that at some point during his sojourn in the region, Crockett definitely stopped in Lost Prairie. If Crockett had totally bypassed this area when he left Washington as Clark believed, it would appear that this could conceivably have been the most opportune time for him to visit the little community, which was within easy striking distance from McKinney's house near the Red River.

Located on the western banks of the Red River, approximately nine miles south of Fulton, Lost Prairie had previously been inhabited by the Caddo and Delaware Indians. In addition to being a resting place for the dead, the burial grounds they built offered sanctuary to the living when the waters of the Red River overflowed. It was during one of those periods of high water, which one early settler said covered the land from "hills to hills," that Lost Prairie got its name.[53]

When Featherstonhaugh departed Washington, he left in the company of a Mr. Pryor. Featherstonhaugh feared the same detestable living conditions awaited him in Lost Prairie that he had experienced elsewhere in the region. But instead of shacks or crude cabins, he discovered a small community of plantations. Though comfortable, the homes of the Lost Prairie plantations evinced none of the grandeur or Greco-Roman influences often associated with the antebellum estates of the South. Pleasantly surprised, Featherstonhaugh described Lost Prairie as "2000 acres of incredible beauty and fertility, . . . gracefully surrounded by picturesque woods."[54]

Featherstonhaugh's apprehension concerning the quality of the principal inhabitants of Lost Prairie also proved to be unwarranted. He noted that the Pryors owned a piano, evidence they had a sense of culture, and of course, leisure time. Yet, these same people were the administrators of a slave population, a fact which Featherstonhaugh found difficult to reconcile with their state of higher consciousness.

Nevertheless, the people of Lost Prairie afforded Featherstonhaugh an opportunity to observe how different classes of people coped with life on the frontier. "How great a contrast is shown in the results produced by settlers of the educated and uneducated classes! The individuals of this last, notwithstanding the 'sovereign' privileges with which they are dignified, seem wherever I have had an opportunity of observing them to have but one object in view, which is the immediate gratification of animal wants."[55]

Ironically, Featherstonhaugh blamed the entire situation on one of the nation's foremost promoters of public education. Having little if anything good to say about Jefferson, a man whom he considered corrupted by subversive French revolutionary philosophies, Featherstonhaugh thought the former president had irreparably damaged American society. As the acknowledged leader of the anti-Federalist forces, Jefferson, whom Featherstonhaugh was quick to point out, "did not belong to any of the old Virginia families," had proposed to replace the aristocracy of families and wealth with what he called, an "aristocracy of virtue and talent."[56] Like Tocqueville, Featherstonhaugh noted how Americans tended to celebrate their liberty, but valued their sense of equality even more. Featherstonhaugh felt that Jefferson may have ennobled the "half-horse, half-alligator race" of the Mississippi River country as much as was humanly possible, but the liberating influence of his ideas had only served to expose the amplitude of their inequalities. Of these glorified citizens, Featherstonhaugh wrote: "If an individual comes amongst them with higher views, they do not aspire to his standard, but seek to drag him down to their level, as being exactly the situation they would choose if they were in his place, for nothing seems to appear more natural to democracy than dirt."[57]

As one might suspect, Featherstonhaugh found the quality of "conversation amongst the lower classes" inhabiting the region to be "disgusting" and occasionally "unintelligible." He cited the popular colloquialism "a sin to Crockett" as an example. As a tribute to his bizarre behavior, this expression referred to any claim that was too ridiculous even for Crockett to make. Featherstonhaugh could quite easily have imagined the "well-known Tennessean,"[58] perpetrator of miraculous feats and tall tales, to be an appropriate representative of the frontier's lower classes.

Almost a year after Featherstonhaugh made his observations concerning the citizens of southwest Arkansas, Crockett arrived and mingled amongst the educated class of Lost Prairie. During his stay, Crockett spent an entire day with Dr. Isaac N. Jones, a neighbor of the Pryors. Featherstonhaugh may have been affected by the outrageous aspects of Crockett's public image, but Jones was quite impressed by the real man. In a letter written to Elizabeth describing her husband's "open frankness, his natural honesty of expression, his perfect want of concealment," Jones said he found David to be "a most agreeable companion."59

When news of the Alamo reached Lost Prairie sometime in April of 1836, Dr. Isaac Newton Jones wrote a letter to Mrs. Elizabeth Crockett expressing his sympathy for the death of her husband. Dr. Jones also wrote that he sincerely hoped she would someday be able to fulfill her husband's desire that she emigrate with the family to Texas. Accompanying the letter was the watch Dr. Jones had obtained in the trade only months earlier. Courtesy of the Southwest Arkansas Regional Archives.

According to Jones, Crockett came to Lost Prairie "in company with several other gentlemen."60 This tends to concur with Judge Clark's estimate. In addition to assisting us in tracking Crockett's movements, Jones also made an interesting observation which not only gives us a little insight into his travel habits but reveals something about the man himself. Traveling in a small group was not exactly ideal, but to separate oneself from the group was definitely ill-advised. If there is any veracity to one Texas legend, he would continue to travel in this manner and within weeks it would nearly get him killed. But for now, Crockett had another problem to contend with. Aware that he was running short on cash, Crockett offered to trade watches with Jones. Crockett received an additional thirty dollars' cash in the trade since it was agreed that his watch was of greater value.

Much had transpired in Texas since November 1. Efforts toward organizing a temporary government in Texas began the very day Crockett left home. The military engagement Crockett was so eager to take part in ended early in the second week of December with the expulsion of the Mexican Army. While media attention shifted back and forth from Texas to the Seminole War in Florida, the nation's sense of direction was clearly westward. The day after Christmas, the *Niles' Weekly Register* followed up with the latest news on Crockett's journey reporting, "Col. Crockett has left Little Rock, with his followers, for Texas. Many others had the same destination." For his opening issue of 1836, Niles wrote an article on the rapid growth of New Orleans, commenting that "Davy Crockett's saying 'go ahead' seems to pervade the entire population."

5

A Calling on Song

A TEMPORARY GOVERNMENT

The traditional telling of America's westward expansion centers around the idea of bringing civilization to the wilderness. The postmodern approach, however, does not view the west as having been an empty land, devoid of human habitation, waiting to be civilized. Instead, it prefers to see the western expansion as a conquest of cultures. Historian Samuel Eliot Morison classified the early American immigration to Texas into two divisions. First, there were those who legally immigrated to Texas and generally attempted to be good Mexican citizens. *Empersarios*, like Austin, were required by law to screen applicants according to moral standards. As for the Americans who arrived in the 1830s, Morison characterized them as adventurers. He cited "Davy Crockett, a publicity-mad professional backwoodsman, . . . " as one of "many who had left their country for their country's good."[1] Morison was correct about the overall quality of those who entered Texas during this time.

On the first Sunday in December 1835, Z. N. Morrell, a Baptist preacher living in Mississippi, returned home to find five friends had just arrived from Tennessee.[2] All five enjoyed close ties with President Jackson. Having acquired inside information convincing them Texas would soon become part of the United States, Morrell's friends were on their way to survey land suitable for the eventual establishment of a colony. At their urging, Morrell agreed to accompany them. Unconcerned about the fact that Texas had a reputation for attracting vagabonds, social rejects, and fugitives from the law, they seemed confident in their ability to help shape the future.

Morrell and his group reached the Sabine River on December 21. Just as they were preparing to cross, an unexpected commotion distracted them. Right in full view of the group, a fugitive made a dramatic escape to the promised land, eluding U.S. law enforcement by simply crossing the river. Emerging on the Texas side, the escapee pronounced himself saved by the waters of the Sabine and berated his pursuers, who remained on the U.S. side. As if having just witnessed complete confirmation that Texas was indeed everything they had heard it was, the group stood on the river bank speechless. The ferryboat operator then welcomed them to Texas by asking, "And, gentlemen, what have you done that you have come to Texas?"[3]

When the *Philadelphia Public Ledger* learned Crockett had reached Texas, the paper proclaimed the frontiersman was now one of "several distinguished men" who had relocated to an environment suitable to their personalities. "ROBERT POTTER, whose domestic exploits will live on the historic pages: HOUSTON, ditto, and CROCKETT, ditto. The course of this last 'stupendous man,' is somewhat more eccentric than that of his crusading compeers."[4] As a Jacksonian democrat from the Twenty-first Congress, Robert Potter also had the distinction of having been expelled from the North Carolina state legislature after he was caught cheating in a card game. But Potter's behavior was not simply eccentric, it was volatile. Not one to be crossed, the retribution he was capable of personally administering was rather extreme. In fact, Potter had justifiably earned a solid reputation for cruelty never associated with the other two.

Rumors persisted in the United States that Houston had removed himself across the Mississippi, not because of personal problems but to realize his expansionist ambitions. Some, like Thomas Hart Benton of Missouri, encouraged him to pursue his aspirations down in Texas. Certain individuals alleged there was a conspiracy afloat involving President Jackson to forcibly appropriate Texas from Mexico. Though nothing was ever proven, former President John Quincy Adams, among others, steadfastly maintained that Houston was acting as Jackson's personal agent. The president was still attempting in late 1835 to arrange for the purchase of Texas through diplomatic means. Houston's vision of the future did not involve a financial settlement.

The story that Houston went to Texas at the request of President Jackson for the specific purpose of starting a revolution, the ultimate objective of which was annexation by the United States, was perpetuated by late nineteenth century historians. A fanciful notion, clearly intended to better illustrate the process of "Manifest Destiny," it seemed almost made for Hollywood. There is a brief scene in the 1956 film *The First Texan*, starring Joel McCrea as Houston, where the former governor, an easy-going private citizen pursuing a low intensity law practice, meets his old friend, Crockett, played by James Griffith, in Nacogdoches. Handing Houston a letter, Crockett tells his compatriot, in a tone suggesting something big is in the works, that the president wants to see him. It is high-level stuff which will ultimately terminate Houston's quiet life. Houston then returns to Washington where he receives his instructions directly from Jackson.

When Houston first reached Texas, he observed and analyzed the state's leadership. Overall, he found them to be less than first rate and felt confident of his eventual ascension in the ranks. Shortly after General Cós arrived with reinforcements in September 1835, Houston was elected commander-in-chief of the militia in the municipality of Nacogdoches. Houston actually viewed this as the beginning of the movement toward independence, though he was not saying so publicly. Soon after, Houston was elected to represent Nacogdoches at the Consultation in San Felipe de Austin.

Texians were predisposed to the concept of local autonomy, which they believed was guaranteed them under the Constitution of 1824. Having been without an elected state government since April, Texian leadership wanted to create some sense of stability during this period of uncertainty, until a clearer assessment of their situation could be determined. Fully aware that on October 3, military officers had nullified the Constitution of 1824, the Consultation accused President Santa Anna in a public statement of destroying the federal system. On that date, the constitutional government, its limitations effectively removed, assumed the appearance of a despotic government. Therefore, the Consultation concluded that the pact between Texas and the other states had been broken.[5] However, while making it clear they preferred the reinstatement of the Constitution of 1824 and separate statehood within the Republic of Mexico, the Consultation insisted in Resolution Five upon their right to pursue the political course "best calculated to protect their rights and liberties."[6] The cautious majority, desiring that the language of this resolution not provoke the Central Government or disrupt the statement's overall conciliatory mood, reiterated that Texians would remain "faithful to the Mexican Government so long as that nation is governed by the Constitution and Laws that were formed for the government of the Political Association."[7]

It must have seemed to some Texians that ever since its creation as a nation, Mexico had taken Jefferson's admonition about the sobering effects of revolution to the extreme. Clearly, the inability of the Federalists to establish a stable, functional government was frustrating. With the scraping of the Constitution of 1824, a small number of Texians envisioned the creation of a new political state, one which would not be associated with Mexico City. Their primary problem was convincing the majority of Texians that the time for independence had come.

The two main groups represented at the Consultation were informally designated the "war and peace parties." Though imprecise, the terms at least emphasized a contrast. While both favored armed resistance to military occupation, they differed regarding the political solution to be applied. The war party vigorously promoted the dissolution of all ties with Mexico, whereas the peace party urged restraint. Viewing the independence movement as a conspiracy of land speculators and slave owners, many at the Consultation were openly suspicious of the minority war party. The Consultation's disposition against independence was not based solely on their partiality toward the Mexican Constitution, but more than anything else it was pragmatic. Both parties anticipated war with the Centralists and were well aware that the funds needed to conduct a war were nonexistent.

The Provisional Government of Texas formed by the Consultation consisted of a governor, council, and lieutenant governor, who also acted as president of the council. With this creation and the election of its officers, the Consultation concluded their meetings, agreeing to reconvene on March 1 of the following year. The Provisional Government began operations on November 14, the day after the

Consultation adjourned. Though the officers chosen to lead the Provisional Government were to varying degrees able men, the amalgamation of personalities proved to be disastrous. To begin with, the explosive Henry Smith was selected as governor. Smith is usually depicted in history to have been the main problem. Anticipating war, the Consultation also prepared plans for the creation of an organized military force. The day Crockett rode into Little Rock, Houston was elected major general of the Armies of Texas.

THE ARMIES OF TEXAS

The military committee created by the Consultation determined that the regular army should consist of 1,120 men. This was to be evenly divided into regiments of infantry and artillery. Regulars, enrolling for a term of two years, were to be governed by the same regulations used by the United States Army. In an attempt to encourage men to enlist in the regular army rather than the militia, a bonus of 640 acres was offered, receivable upon separation from service with an honorable discharge. An unspecified number of the regulars were to be designated "permanent volunteers." Expected to serve throughout the duration of the war, these volunteers would be subject to the same regulations as the regulars and were to receive the same pay and bounty of land.[8]

The militia, the standard first line of defense, had not even been organized leaving Texians totally unprepared for war. Aware of this fact, the Consultation decreed that all able-bodied men between the ages of sixteen and fifty were to report to a designated location within their municipality on December 3 for the purpose of electing officers. This program never even had a chance to get off the ground.

In his opening address, a somewhat overbearing Governor Smith set about explaining his understanding of the "separation of powers." Apparently, the job descriptions delineating the functions of the various offices were lacking in clarity. In what turned out to be an unfortunate choice of words, Smith referred to himself as "the Supreme Executive." The council quickly moved to head off this apparent assertion of power by passing a counter measure limiting the governor's veto power. The governor then gave the council a demonstration of his veto power.

No sooner had the governor and the council established that they disagreed on the scope of each other's duties, but they extended their quarreling into the realm of military matters. Governor Smith believed the first order in the building of the armed forces should be to organize the militia. Fearing a long drawn out conflict, perhaps spanning years, Houston advocated focusing on the regular army. In fact, Houston was now telling anyone who would listen that Texas must be prepared to field an army no later than mid-March. Apprehensive about the very idea of creating a regular army, the council turned their attention to a more immediate problem.

It should be noted here that the first military campaign of the war had started before the Consultation assembled. Since a volunteer army, formed and led by Stephen Austin, was already in the field, the Consultation decided that Austin's army should not be subject to the orders of the Provisional Government. The day after Houston was elected major general, he recommended that Austin's force cease all military operations and disband. Two days later, the council voted unanimously to support the volunteers. Even though the council gave Austin's volunteers top priority, they did not completely ignore the other branches of service, despite what Houston claimed. As Houston ignited a barrage of complaints, the council finally began appointing field officers for the regular army, some of whom, like James C. Neill, Frank W. Johnson, and Edward Burleson, were members of General Austin's independent volunteer army.

In Austin's army, officers had to be careful how they spoke to subordinates. Unable to enforce any kind of behavior expected of military personnel, orders were sometimes given in the form of requests. Occasionally, it was necessary for officers to supplement orders with apologetic explanations assuring the volunteer there was no intention of violating his rights. As volunteers freely came and went, Austin could never be sure just how many men he would have in camp from one day to the next.

Constantly having to deal with the formidable combination of the soldier's individualistic spirit and the spirits brought forth through the consumption of alcoholic beverages left the ever patient Austin thoroughly frustrated. The worst moment came when Austin, under pressure to order an all-out assault on Béxar, finally did so, only to have the rank and file overrule him! Austin then turned over his command and left to pursue the less strenuous duty of ambassador to the United States. Two officers, also frustrated by the lack of discipline and organization, wrote letters to the governor and the council in early December. The first letter was written by James W. Fannin and the second came from William Travis. One letter was influential, the other almost prophetic.

Having attended West Point certainly qualified Fannin as one of the more knowledgeable men in Texas where military procedures were concerned. Fannin began by saying that the 1,120 proposed for the regular army would not be sufficient to successfully confront the Mexican Army. Besides the fact that Texas could not hope to raise an army comparable in size to Mexico's, its men, while brave and determined, were, as soldiers, completely lacking in discipline. He estimated it would take at least six months of intense training to produce a soldier of acceptable quality. Officers were another matter all together. Fannin added that Mexico would no doubt send its best officers, men educated and experienced in the business of making war. Some of the men the council had in mind for filling officer's positions were as untrained and undisciplined as the men they were expected to lead! To rectify what was clearly an alarming disadvantage, Fannin proposed that the council undertake a program of attracting professional officers from the United States Army.[9]

Fannin's letter is credited with having had an impact on the council's way of thinking. On December 4, the Military Committee presented an ordinance designed to create an auxiliary volunteer corps to be attached to the regular army. The Auxiliary Volunteers were designed to work in conjunction with the regular army, receiving the same pay while being subject to the same regulations. The main difference between the Permanent and Auxiliary Volunteers was that the latter would be permitted to choose their own officers. On December 6, the council authorized the enlistment of "at least 5,000 auxiliary volunteers," greatly eclipsing the number recommended by Fannin.

At the request of a council member, Travis jotted down his thoughts concerning the building of the army and addressed them to both the governor and the council. Already familiar with the contents of the Fannin letter, which he wholeheartedly endorsed, Travis wished to limit his discussion to a subject which had thus far been completely ignored—the cavalry. Acknowledging that "considerable time must necessarily elapse before the regular Army, can be raised, and brought into the field duly equipped for service," Travis admitted that the cavalry must, out of necessity, be composed of volunteers. Furthermore, Travis insisted that volunteers "should be subject to regular discipline and the 'rules and articles' of War." Expressing a low opinion of the volunteer's overall dependability, Travis wrote, "A mob can do wonders in a sudden burst of patriotism or of passion, but cannot be depended on, as soldiers for a campaign."[10]

While the council discussed organizing the regulars and Auxiliary Volunteers, word came that the "mob" was in the streets of Béxar battling the Mexican Army and desperately in need of reinforcements and ammunition. Struck by the sudden realization that the only Texian army in existence might be in serious trouble, the council designated forty thousand dollars in nonexistent funds to finance the regulars. Unaware the Mexican Army had already surrendered, Houston issued his *Proclamation to the Citizens of Texas* on December 12.

In this document, Houston elaborated on the grievances against President Santa Anna and warned Texians they must be prepared for a full scale war by no later than March 1. Houston deliberately wrote his *Proclamation* in such a way that it would appeal to both supporters of the annulled Constitution of 1824 and those favoring independence. Houston cited the example of Austin's volunteers as one worthy of emulation. Attempting to rouse a response from those Texians still at home, Houston told them, "your rights must be defended." Houston finished with the invocation, "Let the brave rally to our standard."[11]

The Matamoros Expedition

Certain the war was not over, Texian leaders considered it imperative that in order to insure continued military success volunteers from the United States had to continue to enter Texas. If rumors spread into the United States that the war was over, they feared a valuable and indispensable source of recruits would be lost.

Secondly, while having no discipline and little interest in acquiring any, these volunteers needed to be given something to do. Not wanting to see them dissolve from boredom and just drift off into oblivion, authorities hit upon a solution that included a new campaign.

Just below the mouth of the Río Grande on the Gulf of Mexico was the prosperous seaport of Matamoros. If captured, the city could conceivably provide the Texians with much needed revenue to defray the costs of war. By late 1835, the Texians learned that most of the troops stationed there had been called away, leaving the city lightly garrisoned. For Texians wishing to move the war against the Centralist Government southward, these factors made Matamoros an especially attractive target.

The idea of transferring the war to the south was a widely shared view amongst the Texian leadership, and the inspiration for actually attempting to make the campaign a reality may have come from one man, Dr. James Grant. Born in Scotland, Grant had lived in Coahuila y Tejas, as Texas was then known, for more than ten years. A staunch Federalist, Grant was a member of the state legislature in Monclova until it was shut down by Cós in April 1835.

That Grant was really pushing for an expedition to move south of the Río Grande is evident from his mid-November letter to Austin. Grant's presentation of the political climate below the river sounded very favorable and tended to confirm most everything those who endorsed reinstating the Constitution of 1824 wanted to believe. Grant assured Austin that every state was either openly in protest of Santa Anna or waiting for the right moment to rise up in revolt. He even went so far as to say this of Zacatecas, a state crushed and sacked by Santa Anna only months earlier. The key to Grant's position was that the revolution had to center around restoration of the constitution.

Preparations for the Matamoros Expedition began under suspicious circumstances. For once, it appeared Governor Smith, the council, and General Houston had actually found something they could all agree upon. In mid-December, the council requested the governor to instruct Houston to begin organizing the campaign. While the governor instructed the major general to comply, neither man was overly excited about the project. To begin with, the governor had difficulty disguising the fact he thoroughly distrusted Mexicans, and Houston had serious reservations about the expedition's feasibility. As ordered, Houston instructed Colonel James Bowie, a volunteer, to begin making plans for the expedition but only if he deemed it practical. Since Bowie was en route to his home in Béxar when Houston penned those orders, the receipt of his new assignment was delayed. This was just about the extent of the roles played by the governor and Houston in preparing for the expedition. This was not, however, the end of preparations.

Following General Burleson's departure from Béxar in mid-December, the volunteers elected Frank W. Johnson as successor. Johnson's election seemed appropriate because he, along with Ben Milam, had led the volunteers in the storming of Béxar. Unlike most of those who elected him, General Johnson was a resident of Texas and considered himself a Mexican citizen. Favoring the restoration of the Constitution of 1824, Johnson found himself in the same political camp as Grant.

By the close of the third week in December, Houston moved to place Béxar under the control of the regular army by assigning Colonel Neill to take command of the garrison. It was well known amongst the garrison that Smith and Houston wanted to replace them with regulars, a fact which made both men suspects in the eyes of the volunteers. Unbeknownst to Houston, Wyatt Hanks and Joseph D. Clements of the council, had entered into a silent partnership with the only Texian army in existence. Soon after his election, Johnson received a communication from the council addressed to Burleson suggesting that preparations for an assault upon Matamoros should begin immediately. On December 24, Johnson wrote back to sympathetic members of the Council's Committee for Military Affairs informing them he had succeeded Burleson and would gladly comply with their expectations.[12]

On Christmas Day, six captains representing their respective companies submitted a letter of protest to Johnson regarding the possible threat of interference from the regular army into their operations. Neither willing to be dissolved nor absorbed by the regulars, the Federal Volunteers demanded their right to remain independent and completely autonomous of all regular army regulations and authority. The captains stated that in no way could "we induce our men under any circumstances to subject themselves to the Organic laws of the Regular Army, or to serve under any other terms than those under which they have at present volunteer'd." Furthermore, the officers insisted they were not "subject to the Comdr. in Chief of the Regular Army," that is, of course, unless they were to *invite* him to assume command.[13]

Johnson, the newly designated commander-in-chief of the Federal Volunteer Army of Texas, had, in fact, already made the same complaint in his letter written the day before. Johnson firmly asserted that the decree creating the Auxiliary Volunteers simply did not apply to them.[14] By insisting upon these conditions, the officers of the Federal Volunteers had egregiously expanded upon the same intractable, unsophisticated spirit of independence exhibited by their forefathers which had so encumbered military operations in both wars with Great Britain.

It would appear, however, that as the spirit of the Matamoros Expedition swept through the Alamo garrison in late December, doubts must have been raised in the minds of some concerning the volunteer system's effectiveness and viability. Those who planned to remain in Béxar quickly realized just how vulnerable they would be as soon as the Johnson and Grant volunteers left on December 30. On the last day of 1835, the remaining volunteers held a meeting.

The public statement which resulted from this meeting contained seven resolutions.[15] One through five are of primary concern to us. Most important, as evidenced by the fact that it was listed first, the volunteers wanted their rights as citizen soldiers publicly recognized. The second, fourth, and fifth resolutions were all directly related to the question of who would command. Finding Houston's selection acceptable, the volunteers decided to allow Neill to assume a position of leadership amongst the garrison.[16]

That the garrison even managed to stay together brings us to the third, and possibly most significant resolution—the decision that the post would be maintained even under the conditions which existed as of December 31. As noted in the postscript by Captain William Blazeby, chairman of the meeting, the question of whether or not to sustain the post arose out of the situation created by the departure of the majority of the volunteers for Matamoros. Johnson believed that 150 volunteers would be sufficient to effectively man the fort.[17] Very democratic-like, the issue was put to a vote. This decision to remain and defend the fort did not come from the governor, the council, or Major General Houston, let alone from any regular army officer. That decision was made by the citizen soldiers, many of whom would eventually die at the Alamo.

POINT OF CONVERGENCE

Even as plans were being made for the Matamoros Expedition, volunteers from the United States were making their way to Texas. In Newport, Kentucky, Captain Sidney Sherman organized and equipped a group of fifty-plus volunteers for Texas. Having taken divergent paths, three small groups of volunteers reached Natchitoches in December.

One of those aspiring volunteers was forty-one-year-old Micajah Autry. An attorney by profession, Autry wrote poetry, painted, played the violin, and possessed a pleasant singing voice. His exuberance for life was contagious. Hearing about the promise of a future in Texas while on a business trip to New York, Autry contemplated making a new start. Then came the news of war.

Autry was only one of approximately twenty volunteers who boarded a steamboat in Memphis on December 7. Within a week, Autry reached Natchitoches where a group of volunteers from Jackson had passed through three weeks earlier. Unable to procure any horses in Natchitoches, a determined Autry set out to complete the journey to Nacogdoches on foot.

In mid-October, Daniel Cloud, Peter James Bailey, B. Archer, M. Thomas, William Keener Fauntleroy, and Joseph G. Washington departed Kentucky in search of a place to establish their law practices. Fauntleroy separated from the group early in their journey. Instead of crossing the Mississippi, he boarded a steamboat headed down river. Despite having found numerous places offering opportunities to establish their careers, Cloud's group turned south at Springfield after hearing that the war in Texas had started. Crossing the Ozark Mountains, the group made their way south through Arkansas to a place on the Red River, which from Cloud's description sounds as if it could have been Lost Prairie.[18] This is only speculation, but Washington may have remained behind there. Ten weeks after leaving Kentucky, Cloud, Bailey, and Thomas reached Louisiana.

While descending the Mississippi River, Fauntleroy met up with Herbert Simms Kimble and William Irving Lewis. Kimble, an attorney from Clarksville, Tennessee, was leading a group of six or seven also bound for Texas. By Christmas Day, the Cloud and Kimble groups were in Natchitoches. Although running out of writing paper, Cloud, unable to contain his excitement about crossing the border and joining the revolution, wrote home to a friend, "now we stand on the shores of the United States, but next week, heaven willing, we shall breathe the air of Texas."[19] Being that Fauntleroy knew the men in both groups, he may very well have played an important part in bringing them together.

After they crossed the border, Kimble met up with Autry in San Augustine, Texas. It seems Autry may have already been acquainted with Kimble. Free to travel and form associations with whomever they wished, Autry was quite pleased to learn that Kimble's "small company of select men" included four attorneys. Autry was also pleased to report to his wife Martha that he found them all to be "perfect gentlemen."[20] Kimble's group rode on ahead toward Nacogdoches.

Thirty-year-old James Madison Rose was a nephew of the former president of the United States. Rose left home in either late December or earlier January with the intent of joining the Texas Revolution. According to family members, he headed west toward Nacogdoches.[21]

One of the oldest cities in Texas, Nacogdoches was officially established by the Spanish government in 1779. Political chief Antonio Ybarbo constructed a two-story brick building on the north side of the public square near the Old San Antonio Road. Initially intended to be a trading post, it would be used as a military head-quarters, mayor's office, courtroom, polling place, and reception center for immigrants. From within its walls the province of Texas was prematurely declared to be free and independent no less than three times. According to local tradition, it was also within the walls of this building, which would later become known as the Old Stone Fort, that the Oath of Allegiance was administered.

There are two excellent descriptions of Nacogdoches as it existed in the mid-1830s. When Amos Andrew Parker ventured through Nacogdoches in the fall of 1834, he found the city located in a rather attractive setting between two rivers. The city itself was quite another matter. "I could not but smile," wrote Parker, "at the odd and grotesque appearance of Nacogdoches, as I entered the principal street of the town."[22] The old church, built of logs and mud, stood in a pathetic state of disrepair and was a conspicuous eyesore. Nacogdoches had not improved very much when Colonel William Fairfax Gray, scouting the Texas real estate market on behalf of two friends, arrived from Virginia on January 31, 1836.

Whereas Parker looked upon the scene with some degree of humor, Gray took a dimmer view. Three days after his arrival, Gray went on a tour of Nacogdoches. Finding it destitute of anything aesthetically rewarding, he described the city's appearance as "old, . . . miserable," and "shabby in the extreme." Worse yet, Gray concluded there was "not a decent tavern in the place."[23]

In spite of the city's decadent features, there were fewer places in Texas capable of offering such a wide variety of the advantages associated with metropolitan life. As a trading center located on the region's major highway, Nacogdoches saw a great many transients, many of whom were regular customers who crossed the border from Louisiana merely to drink and gamble. As for Morrell and his friends, the first couple of days in Texas tended to be a little stressful. Unlike the fugitive from justice who had acquired his freedom by simply crossing the Sabine, Morrell's little group began to feel an aggravated sense of concern for their personal safety when they reached San Augustine. In Nacogdoches, Morrell observed a number of enthusiastic young men who imagined themselves becoming heroic leaders of the anonymous multitude of men aimlessly milling about town. Morrell categorized these specimens of humanity, the somnolent patriots whom these young men were intent on leading, as the "dregs and renegades"[24] of Texas. However, as their journey progressed, Morrell gradually encountered enough people possessing an "intellect of a higher type, and morality of a better cast" than most of what he had thus far seen for him to conclude that "a good society might be formed."[25]

By previous arrangement, Morrell's companions had agreed to meet their old friend and hunting partner, David Crockett, at a place called the Falls of the Brazos, near present-day Marlin. From the falls, they planned to embark upon a bear hunt. Apparently unaware there had been a change in Crockett's plans, they took the Old San Antonio Road to the southwest and pushed hard to reach the falls by Christmas Day, the date of their appointment.[26] Arriving two days late, Morrell found an encampment of about forty Tennesseans. They asked if anyone had seen Crockett. The response was always the same.[27]

Soon after Morrell and his group left Nacogdoches, an observant young man from Bangor, Maine, named Edward Warren, arrived by Christmas Day. During his travels, Warren routinely wrote to an uncle back in Maine. It is believed he composed at least thirteen letters, two of which have survived. The letters, numbered twelve and thirteen at the top presumably by Warren's uncle, cover almost the entire five to six weeks Warren spent in Texas. Letter number twelve was written on New Year's Day from a little Texas town known as Washington.

The highlight of Warren's visit to Washington was having the opportunity to meet General Houston with whom he spent several days. Instantly impressed with the young man, the general offered Warren the position of aide-de-camp, which was declined. Instead of remaining with Houston, Warren decided to visit Béxar. The only delay was in finding a group of sufficient size to warrant making the trip a safe one. In his New Year's Day letter, Warren described to his uncle just how well he had adapted to the climate of barbarism then existing in Texas by stating, "I never go out doors, or move within, without my pistols close about me—they are, day and night, my constant companions. Next to these is a knife about the length of our largest carving knives & weighing about two pounds. This I tote at my left side in my pistol belt. When [torn] it may serve to amuse the pacific & harmless people of the north to show them the present and remarkable state of society in Texas."[28]

Warren then briefly discussed the suspected fate of another traveler: "You may have heard that David Crockett set out for this country with a company of men to join the army. He has forgotten or waved his original intention & stopped some 80 or 100 miles to the north of this place to hunt Buffalo for the winter! For a long time, it was feared that he & his party had been destroyed by the tribes of wild Indians through which he intended to pass. But, at last, it is ascertained that he is at his favorite amusement."[29]

Warren probably first learned that Crockett was attempting to break through Comanche country while he was in Nacogdoches. The rumor that Crockett did not make it soon followed. The final development in the story was the report that Crockett was vacationing near the falls. Of course, Crockett was no where near the falls. It is possible the seeds for speculation about Crockett's death could have been unintentionally provided by James Clark and the information refuting his demise supplied by Morrell's group, all of whom were present in Nacogdoches in the days preceding Warren's departure on December 26.

Warren did, however, know exactly why the famous frontiersman was traveling through Comanche country. Though this particular rumor of Crockett's death had a happy ending, one can sense in Warren's correspondence the subtle expression of disappointment. For a man, and a national celebrity at that, to risk his life traveling a great distance to join these people struggling for their ideals was certainly indicative of noble intentions. But to fear the worst fate had befallen this man, only then to discover he had been out playing around in the wilderness, suggested something other than responsible behavior to Warren; it suggested that the real-life Crockett was indeed an unreliable eccentric whose sense of duty could easily be distracted by his recreational interests.

By New Year's Day, Crockett was probably riding south toward Nacogdoches on a road called Trammel's Trace. Named after Nicholas Trammel, the trace was not really much of a road as far as roads went, but until the mid-1840s it served as the main link between the Red River country and Texas. Sometime during the first week of the new year, Crockett crossed the Sabine River and the border into Mexico. Postmodernists, who view the Texas Revolution as a morally questionable undertaking, tend to look at Crockett's entry into Texas with varying degrees of suspicion. Jeff Long divided the illegal immigration of Americans to Texas during the revolutionary phase into two waves of mercenaries. According to Long, not only was Crockett a mercenary who just happened to wander across the Mexican border, he was a "'wetback' congressman."[30] Historian Garry Wills also classified the latest wave of American immigrants into one of two categories, either as "squatters," or "'filibusters' who came to take advantage of the unrest." However, Wills saw Crockett as one "of the last-minute military 'filibusters,'" an individual singularly focused on reviving his spent political career through martial conquest.[31]

While hardly expecting Crockett to show up, local leaders in Nacogdoches were greatly anticipating the arrival of Don Agustín Viesca, the deposed governor of Coahuila y Tejas. A refugee in his own state, Viesca admonished all who would listen to rise up in revolt against the central government. He assured Texians and Tejanos alike that unless they responded to the impending crisis like "true republicans," the tyranny of Santa Anna would soon engulf them.[32]

Crockett rode into Nacogdoches while the dinner honoring Viesca was in progress. A welcoming party was immediately dispatched to escort him to the banquet hall where the best citizens of Nacogdoches were gathered. Entering the hall, Crockett was saluted with three robust cheers. Naturally, a little speech followed. Several months later, this eyewitness account appeared in papers throughout the United States:

> A gentleman from Nacogdoches, in Texas, informs us, that, whilst there, he dined in public with col. Crockett, who had just arrived from Tennessee. The old bear-hunter, on being toasted, made a speech to the Texians, replete with his usual dry humor. He began nearly in this style: "I am told, gentlemen, that, when a stranger, like myself, arrives among you, the first inquiry is—what brought you here? To satisfy your curiosity at once as to myself, I will tell you all about it. I was, for some years, a member of Congress. In my last canvass, I told the people of my district, that, if they saw fit to reelect me, I would serve them faithfully as I had done; but, if not, they might go to h___, and I would go to Texas. I was beaten, gentlemen, and here I am." The roar of applause was like a thunder-burst.[33]

Here, Crockett modified the story of his campaign promise for a Texas audience, an audience well aware of their solid reputation in some circles as a repository for low class undesirables. Having set his own terms, Crockett was the only man in Texas who could brag that he had been expelled by an entire congressional district. True to his word, the man whose motto was to always make sure he was right before going "ahead," had acted; he had come to Texas.

6

Return to Civilization

SOMETHING TO WRITE HOME ABOUT

Crockett's arrival in Nacogdoches, the northernmost population center in the Mexican state of Coahuila y Tejas, marks the completion of a major segment of his journey. One of the influential people he would meet in Nacogdoches was businessman Nicholas Adolphus Sterne. Over the course of his life, Sterne would serve Nacogdoches in just about every public office possible. When Sam Houston came to Nacogdoches in 1832 to begin a new life again, he took up residence with Mr. and Mrs. Sterne who helped him get started in his law practice. Recalling those early years, one of the Sterne's daughters observed that her mother "probably entertained more distinguished guests in her home than other women in Texas." Among her mother's "distinguished guests" she listed the name of David Crockett.[1]

Crockett probably managed to pick up bits and pieces of information since leaving Little Rock, some of which was no doubt conflicting. However, a most significant development took place while Crockett was out in the wilderness. Instead of permitting delegates of the Consultation to reconvene on the first of March, they decided that a body of newly elected delegates should meet for the purpose of creating a new state government and constitution.[2] The ordinance, passed by the council on December 10, would, at just about the precise moment of its nadir, unintentionally provide Texas with an opportunity to declare itself independent.

For many years, Nicholas Adolphus Sterne was one of the most influential citizens of Nacogdoches. Courtesy of the East Texas Research Center, Stephen F. Austin University.

As election day for the Constitutional Convention neared, concerns about a new state government evolved into a question of whether to declare for independence or continue to support the Constitution of 1824. Writing to Lt. Governor James Robinson, ferryboat operator Judge James Gaines noted, "From St. Phillip to Nacogdoches one Entire Kind of Indeppendence pervades all Classs of Men."[3] Gaines may not have noticed, but there existed in Nacogdoches a political faction organized by John Durst comprised almost exclusively of non-Anglo Mexicans, which not only favored restoring the Mexican Constitution but refused to acknowledge the

The Sterne-Hoya House is now a Texas Historic Landmark. Descendants of the Sternes maintained that Crockett stayed here during his two-week stopover in Nacogdoches. Courtesy of the East Texas Research Center, Stephen F. Austin University.

legitimacy of the Provisional Government. Energized by the arrival of the exiled Governor Viesca, supporters for the constitution began mounting public demonstrations. On January 7, both Houston and Austin publicly came out in favor of independence.

Crockett may have learned, possibly through Judge John J. Forbes, that Houston, whom he had not seen since April 1834, was expected to arrive in Nacogdoches any day. In the interim, Crockett decided to ride east to San Augustine, where there were more old friends, the political currents were not so turbulent, and a most pleasant surprise awaited him. He probably left for San Augustine sometime on the eighth.

It was during his stay in the Nacogdoches-San Augustine area that Crockett found the time to write to his family. Dated January 9, his letter to his daughter, Margaret, both confirms his presence in San Augustine on that date and the fact that he had already been to Nacogdoches. Shackford's objection to the story contrived by Richard Penn Smith and perpetuated by Rourke, among others, that Crockett entered San Augustine from the east, continued on to Nacogdoches, doubled back to San Augustine, only then to backtrack to Nacogdoches, must be sustained.

Located thirty miles east of Nacogdoches on the Old San Antonio Road, San Augustine was named after an early Spanish mission. Not quite two years old, the city, consisting of only about a dozen buildings, was set in the Redlands amongst the pine trees of the beautiful east Texas hill country. Despite the fact Mexican legislation required the building of communities to follow traditional format as stipulated in the Spanish Royal Ordinance of 1563, San Augustine was quite possibly the first city constructed in Texas with a total disregard for this law. In place of a town square, a business district quickly established itself as most of the early townsfolk randomly settled on either the northern or southern side of the Old San Antonio Road.[4] This segment of the thoroughfare soon became known as Main Street. The San Augustine that existed in January of 1836 has long since disappeared.

Discounting the organization of the local government, the Spanish-sounding name was about the extent of Mexican influence on San Augustine. Colonel Almonte noted in his 1834 tour of Texas that Spanish was not a language of major consequence in this region of the Mexican state. Although an overwhelming percentage of its inhabitants spoke only English, San Augustine did not rush to embrace revolution. The complacency exhibited by the citizens of San Augustine peaked in the summer of 1835. By December, many in San Augustine and elsewhere began to view the council's proposal for a Constitutional Convention as an opportunity to forever alter the course of events. At a public meeting held on December 22, Jonas Harrison, a conservative in the peace party, proposed that the Municipality of San Augustine publicly recognize the upcoming Constitutional Convention as an opportunity, not to write a new state constitution, but to make a formal declaration of independence for Texas and compose a constitution creating a new republic.[5] The resolution passed without opposition, making San Augustine the second municipality in Texas to do so.

Crockett's grand entry into San Augustine was acted out in fine style as the city fired its cannon to announce his arrival. A dinner in his honor naturally followed. Crockett's reception, possibly the most enthusiastic thus far in his journey, may have been due to the existence of an enclave residing just outside the city known as the "Tennessee Colony."[6] The most prominent member of this community was an east Tennessean named Elisha Roberts. Venerated as a man of wisdom amongst his peers, Roberts was an active community member who served for a number of years as judge. Roberts's home, located about six miles east of the city at a place called the Old Brick Spring, was open to all. His guests included Sam Houston, who actually lived there for an extended period, James Bowie, William Barret Travis, and, in the second week of 1836, David Crockett.[7] Mrs. Elizabeth White, daughter of Judge Shelby Corzine, always remembered the day when Crockett was a guest in their home.[8] It may have been at either the Roberts or Corzine residence that a long forgotten proposal was presented to Crockett by a small group of leading citizens.

The news that "Colonel" Crockett had turned up in east Texas gradually made its way across the United States and up the east coast. The *Morning Courier and New York Enquirer* made the following report: "He was warmly received at San Augustine, Texas, and urged to become a candidate for the Convention; but the Colonel told the Texians that he came to fight for them and not seek office; but as he took care at the same time to tell them that he had rather be a member of the Convention than the Senate of the United States, we dare say he will be elected."[9] Crockett's apparent popularity seems to have impressed James Gaines enough for him to write the Lt. Governor, "David Crockett deliverd one of his Corner Speeches yesterday at San Augustine and is To Represent them in the Convention on the first of March."[10]

By the time Crockett sat down to write Margaret, there could not possibly have been any question in his mind as to where he belonged. A true sense of exhilaration permeates this entire letter. He wrote, "I have but little doubt of being elected a member to form a Constitution for this province I am rejoiced at my fate I had rather be in my present situation than to be elected to a seat in Congress for life I am in hopes of making a fortune yet for myself and family bad as my prospect has been. . . ."[11] Starting over had always been tough, but starting over had never been this good.

The earliest known reference to Texas attributed to Crockett comes from a congressional session in 1830 during a debate on the proposed Buffalo to New Orleans Road Bill. Crockett suggested the road should end in Memphis, not because the city just happened to be in his district but because it stood in a direct line to Texas! Referring to Texas, Crockett was then quoted as saying, "which I hope will one day belong to the United States, and that at no great distance of time."[12] In the years following that statement, President Santa Anna had managed to do to the Mexican Constitution what Crockett claimed Jackson wished he could do to the one in the United States. While there are grounds for debate as to whether or not Crockett would have acquiesced to the idea of Texas being annexed by a country that would even consider Martin Van Buren as a presidential candidate, there can be no question that he favored complete separation from Mexico. Crockett and San Augustine seemed to have an analogous perspective on what the future of Texas should be.

CHECKS WITHOUT BALANCES: A GOVERNMENT MOST TEMPORARY

By January 3, General Johnson was in San Felipe de Austin where he formally requested permission from the council to lead the

Matamoros Expedition. Permission was granted. Three days later, Bowie arrived with his orders from Houston. Upon presentation to the council, the orders were filed.

Once Governor Smith discovered what the council was up to, he did not hesitate to make his disapproval known. Johnson was so stunned by the governor's aggressive protest, he wrote to the council on January 6 informing them of his decision to withdraw from the campaign. The council, intent as they were upon having a new campaign, deliberated and on the following day gave the assignment to Fannin. Despite having already been appointed to the rank of colonel in the regular army by the council, Fannin was now assigned, by this same governing body, to lead this new military campaign as a special agent.

The speed with which the council moved to replace him surprised even Johnson. But on January 7, the day of Fannin's appointment, Johnson wrote again to the council informing them he had reconsidered and wanted to lead the campaign after all. Faced with a situation in which they now had two men who considered themselves to be the leaders of the campaign, the council proceeded to do nothing.

While Crockett was entertaining the citizens of San Augustine, Fannin issued a formal call for volunteers. Signing this invitation as "J. W. Fannin Jr.," the colonel made no pretense of acting in the capacity of an officer in the regular army. Two days later, Johnson came out with an invitation of his own. Instead of being short and to the point like Fannin, Johnson wrote at length and demonstrated an awareness that he was competing for volunteers. To add credibility to his leadership claim, he stated that the march to Matamoros, already begun by the Federal Volunteers under his command, had the approval of the council. With all the bases covered regarding his authority, Johnson then discussed the purpose behind this new campaign. Fannin had touched on this briefly, citing the advantage of taking the war to the south. But whereas Fannin made no connection between driving the Mexican Army out of Texas and this new campaign, Johnson presented these two operations as separate phases of the same war. First drive the Centralists from Texas, then out of Mexico City, and, finally, restore the Constitution of 1824.

Johnson trusted Dr. James Grant. Johnson had even recommended Grant receive a commission for the rank of colonel. The decision to place Grant, the man who had perhaps the most lucid vision of the expedition, in charge of overseeing the army's departure from the Alamo may have been Johnson's biggest blunder. Within days, Houston began receiving letters from Béxar accusing Grant of having sacked the Alamo!

At this time, it is necessary to refer to a letter written by Houston to Smith. The occasion for the general's writing was the receipt of a very disturbing letter from Colonel Neill in Béxar. Houston felt Neill's letter was important enough for him to attach it to his so both the governor and the council could read it for themselves. Unfortunately, Neill's letter has since been lost.

With Johnson and Fannin openly competing for troops, where did this leave Houston, the duly appointed major general of the Armies of Texas? The expedition, as coordinated by the council, suddenly looked as though it was being undertaken without regard for the fact that, as of November 12, a major general had been chosen specifically for the purpose of organizing and conducting military operations. Houston called the officers of this campaign, "self-created" and concluded that submission to the "despotism of a single man" was preferable to the current "state of deplorable anarchy."[13]

In what was an entirely inexcusable act, these "marauders upon human rights," as Houston called them,[14] confiscated supplies and medicine needed by the sick and wounded at the Alamo. And this operation was carried out under the auspices of James Grant, a medical doctor! Johnson would later deny this ever took place; however, only days after leaving the Alamo, Grant struck again and seized all the horses belonging to the volunteers stationed in Goliad.

Houston, in what was a departure from his usual practice of requesting permission from the governor, informed him that he would leave headquarters in Washington on January 8 to meet with the volunteers in the hope of persuading them to withdraw from the campaign against Matamoros. As of January 6, the last instructions Houston had received from the governor was that he should proceed to Nacogdoches where he was to join with Judge Forbes in negotiating a treaty with various Indian tribes. But due to the present emergency, that meeting would have to wait.

Clearly, the council's communication addressed to Burleson suggesting that a new campaign should begin immediately was made without the knowledge of either the governor or the major general of the army. From the council's point of view, this was a campaign involving the volunteers from Austin's command, who, in fact, had never disbanded. But once the governor became aware of the council's involvement with Johnson's group, he instantly made the connection between the Matamoros Expedition and Mexican statehood.

The governor received Houston's letter along with Neill's message on Saturday, January 9. Already irritated by the council's deceptive maneuvering and expropriation of military authority, Smith now learned of the condition of the Alamo garrison. Smith wrote to the council that same day. His intention was to motivate them into taking what he considered to be the appropriate step to rectify the mess. His message was not received that way.

After reading Neill's letter, the council was then treated to the governor's. Denouncing the council's meddling in the Matamoros campaign as "predatory," the governor proceeded to accuse certain members of being "Mexican like." Among other reprimands, he censured their appointment of Fannin as a special agent entrusted with unlimited powers.[15] From that day forward, Smith has been cast as an ill-tempered man who lost all self-control. However, before these two letters were presented to the council, the governor sent a letter to Lt. Governor Robinson explaining the reasons behind the harsh message to be directed at the legislative body. In that letter, Smith assured Robinson that nothing in his letter to the council was directed at him.[16]

Twice in his letter to the council, Smith stated that the lieutenant governor was not the target of his attacks. He even extended this exemption to the council's "honest" members. It was instead only for the "Judases in the camp" that he had aimed his remarks. Leaving it up to the more responsible members of the council to purge the "wolves" in their midst, Smith gave them until noon of the following day to publicly acknowledge their errors and take the appropriate corrective measures, or else he would suspend the council from further operation! As governor, he would carry on alone.[17]

By threatening to dismiss the council, a group which viewed itself as the representatives of the people, and vowing to execute the responsibilities of government all by himself, the governor, according to the council, had revealed his tyrannical temperament. The council therefore decreed that Governor Smith was now the ex-governor and would subsequently be answerable to charges according to the provisions in the Constitution of 1824, a document which he had sworn to uphold. The next day, Lt. Governor Robinson was sworn in as acting governor.

Writing a somewhat apologetic letter to the council the following day, Smith made a proposal—if they would simply admit their wrong-doing and rescind the authority granted to Fannin, all would be forgiven. Hardly in a conciliatory mood, the council informed Smith he had three days to respond to charges of malfeasance and misconduct in office. But when the council demanded that Smith relinquish all governmental documents in his possession, he refused! As far as Smith was concerned, he was still the governor.

Possibly because of all the excitement, the Military Committee did not get around to taking up the matter of Johnson's reconsideration of his withdrawal from the Matamoros Expedition until January 14. In what turned out to be an ambiguous statement, Johnson received the council's endorsement to lead his forces and unite with Fannin.[18] As the second week of January came to a close, the council still had two commanders for their expedition and the Provisional Government of Texas had two governors. The schism in the government would effectively divide the volunteers in Texas into two political camps, those supporting the acting governor and the council versus those supporting the governor and the major general.

THE OATHS OF ALLEGIANCE

Attracted by the promise of revolution, thirty-eight-year-old John J. Forbes left Cincinnati in the fall of 1835. Settling in Nacogdoches, Forbes quickly impressed local leaders with his apparent abilities. On November 13, he was appointed first municipal judge of Nacogdoches. By mid-January, Forbes had composed a document he titled the "Oath of Allegiance."

As of January 12, Forbes was still anxiously awaiting the arrival of General Houston. News of the schism in the government had not yet reached Nacogdoches by the time Forbes finished his letter addressed to the "Lieutenant Governor" in mid-January. Hearing only that Houston had moved to gain control of the volunteers, Forbes wrote, "I was truly gratifyed to learn of Genl. Houstons departure for the Army it will have an excellent effect. . . ."[19]

Forbes prepared at least four versions of the oath. Except for two significant variations, the versions are substantially the same. For example, the pledge signed by the Autry, Kimble, and Cloud group is preceded by an introduction. The volunteers who took this oath acknowledged they were enlisting in the Auxiliary Volunteers for a specific term of six months. The second variation occurs in the closing sentence, wherein it states that the volunteer will follow the orders of the government's officers "according to the rules and articles for the Government *OF THE ARMIES* of Texas."[20] Certainly, an army not under the authority of the government is a most unsettling prospect for a republic. What Forbes may have intended to clarify was that unlike the volunteers already in the field, the Auxiliary Volunteers, as a creation of the Provisional Government, were expected to submit themselves to its authority. The question is, does the presence of the introduction suggest that Forbes may have thought about how to improve upon an earlier version of the oath?

According to Rourke, Crockett took the Oath of Allegiance immediately following the banquet.[21] Challenging this assertion, Shackford presented a copy of the document as prepared by Forbes, signed by Crockett, and dated January 14, 1836.[22] Though not entirely convinced of this date's accuracy himself, Shackford went on to state that "Miss Rourke referred to this document as being dated January 5, on what authority I cannot say . . . ."[23] But that is not exactly what Rourke said. She simply said Crockett signed the document on January 5. The original oath Crockett signed was destroyed by fire in 1855. The document that survived was Forbes's "true copy."

In addressing the dating problem, Shackford came up with four possible explanations. First, he believed it was conceivable that Crockett could have taken the oath on two different occasions from Forbes, once verbally and then a second time wherein he actually signed the document. Secondly, either Crockett's letter of January 9, wherein he mentions having already taken the pledge, or the oath could have been incorrectly dated. A third possibility is that the list of names appearing on the document may have been accumulated over a number of days, with January 14 being the day the sixty-eighth and final signature was added. And finally, in preparing a copy of the original, Forbes may have applied the date the duplicate was prepared. Shackford was unable to reach a conclusion as to which possibility was the most plausible.[24]

In his letter of the twelfth to Robinson, Forbes discussed the progress of dispensing the oath to new volunteers. He mentioned having given the oath to Crockett. However, about halfway through the letter, he entered a new date of "Jany 15."[25] In the January 12 segment, Forbes was waiting for the arrival of either John Henrie or Sam Houston. When he resumed his letter three days later, he noted that Henrie had arrived. Finding the excerpt about Crockett under the January 15 portion instead of January 12 would still allow one to argue that he could have taken the oath as late as the fourteenth. But in the second half of the letter, Forbes confused matters by writing, "I would recommend to your particular attention Captn. Kimble, Major Autry, and Major Gilmore I hear that [these] are on the [road] for this place."[26] Assuming the supplemented words appearing in the brackets are correct, and they make perfect sense, this sentence only requires that more questions be raised.

All four oaths prepared by Forbes were dated January 14.[27] The lists contain the names of the three officers mentioned above. The fact that Autry was definitely in Nacogdoches on the thirteenth suggests that Forbes was probably mistaken with regards to certain details. There could be any number of explanations why Crockett's name does not appear on the same list with Autry, Cloud, and Kimble.

Forbes's third attestation to this event was recounted in greater detail in the *Telegraph & Texas Register*,[28] a newspaper published by Gail Borden, later of powdered milk fame. Evidently, Forbes did not provide a date for the event. The article merely stated that Crockett and his companions took the oath "Soon after their arrival." If the newspaper understood Forbes correctly, Crockett was accompanied to the judge's office by "several volunteers." The article also presents a copy of what it purports to be the first draft of the document. Because it states Forbes did not prepare the paper until

Crockett entered his office, the reader is left with the impression that the frontiersman might have been the very first to sign the document. The fact that his name is nineteenth on a list, which has no apparent order, would seem to indicate that though he may not have been the first, he at least signed it early on. Finally, and perhaps most important, Forbes alluded to a single event, not two.

Forbes's observation as to when Crockett and his friends took the oath seems to be a little more in line with the information found in Crockett's letter of January 9. But is his letter dated correctly? A quick glance at the letter written by Judge Gaines, also dated the ninth, places Crockett in San Augustine on the eighth. The dates of these letters compliment each other well enough so as to preclude the probability that both could be off by no more than a day or so.

As for how she came about a date of January 5, Rourke did not designate her sources with precision. She did, however, list her sources by section in the back of her book. Among those listed as a reference for the section on Crockett's travels through Texas is Henderson Yoakum's *History of Texas*, published in 1855. The story of Crockett's arrival in Nacogdoches, his attendance at the banquet, and taking of the oath on January 5 can be found on pages seventy and seventy-one in volume two of Yoakum's work. Yoakum footnoted two sources, a newspaper and a history book.

Yoakum's source for the arrival date and the banquet story was the January 16 issue of a Nacogdoches newspaper called the *Emigrants Guide*. Officially titled the *Texian and Emigrants Guide*, the paper began weekly publication in about mid-November of 1835. The paper was only able to continue running for approximately four months before shutting down. Unfortunately, of the three issues known to exist, the latest is dated January 2, 1836.[29] With the designation of Crockett's arrival date, Yoakum ceased to treat time with any further significance whatsoever in his story, so much so that the reader could easily assume that Crockett arrived in Nacogdoches, went to the banquet, took the oath, and left town all in the same day!

Writing about the Oath of Allegiance, Yoakum seems not to have relied on the aforementioned newspaper but instead turned to William Kennedy's book, *Texas: The Rise, Progress, And Prospects of the Republic of Texas*, published in 1841 out of London.[30] Kennedy appears to have relied almost entirely on the information provided by Forbes in the 1838 newspaper article. Because the article neglects to give the reader a date, or any real perspective on the passage of time, Kennedy chose to omit any reference to that matter. Considering Yoakum's sources, it is understandable why he too, with the exception of mentioning the arrival date, tended to be so vague where time was concerned.

Supporting January 5 as an approximate date the dinner honoring Viesca was held is the letter from Arthur Henrie, a local political activist who wrote to Henry Smith on January 3, stating that the event was scheduled for the following day.[31] It is therefore very likely that Crockett arrived in Nacogdoches on either the fourth or fifth. But does this necessarily imply Crockett signed the oath the same day? Could Forbes's statement that Crockett took the oath shortly after his "arrival" actually have been an allusion to his return to Nacogdoches from San Augustine? There is even the possibility that the version signed by Crockett was the last of the

The Old Stone Fort once served Nacogdoches as the Government House, but soon after the revolution, it would be used for pursuits that were not exactly above reproach. By the time this photograph was made in 1885, its reputation was such that ladies were embarrassed to be seen near the building. Today, however, the image of the Old Stone Fort is symbolic of the city of Nacogdoches. Courtesy of the East Texas Research Center, Stephen F. Austin University.

four, hastily prepared by Forbes on the fourteenth with the sixty-eighth signature being appended several days later.

William C. Davis has proposed an interesting solution to the dating problem. Davis theorizes Crockett started his letter to Margaret on January 9 in San Augustine but did not finish it there. In the first half of the letter, Crockett discussed Choctaw Bayou and mentioned having been to Nacogdoches. But then Crockett announced he had taken the oath, joined the army, and would depart for the Río Grande in a few days. Davis contends that this segment of the letter was written after he returned to Nacogdoches.[32] In support of Davis's theory, one can look at the oath in which sixty-eight men subscribed their signatures and see the names of those belonging to Captain Sidney Sherman's Kentucky Volunteers, listed both before and after Crockett's name appears. The Kentucky Volunteers did not begin arriving in Nacogdoches until sometime in the second week of January. But even if January 14 is not the correct date, we are nonetheless left with a profoundly important event, one which Shackford concluded was authentic beyond doubt.[33]

THE OATH OF GOVERNMENT

Although Forbes thought of Crockett's signing the Oath of Allegiance as a meaningful event, postmodern historians have generally tended to be less impressed. Shackford argued that Crockett's reasons for signing the oath were linked to farsighted personal goals, which entailed an eventual resumption of his political career. It was also Shackford's contention that much of the impetus behind Crockett's behavior in Texas, including an incident which occurred during the signing of the oath, was attributable to his maniacal hate of anything even remotely associated with Andrew Jackson.

In 1958, Stanley J. Folmsbee and Anna Grace Catron took a look at Shackford's theory. Folmsbee and Catron rejected the more complicated tenet of Shackford's theory which maintained that Crockett envisioned Texas as a new battleground between the pro and anti-Jackson forces and instead emphasized personal objectives. Referring to the January 9 letter to Margaret, they asserted that Crockett did not decide to volunteer for military service until after he arrived in Texas, and that this decision "was not without its political overtones. . . ."[34] With the premise of personal objectives established as valid, other historians would work out the details.

In sharp contrast to historian Lon Tinkle's depiction of Crockett's taking of the oath as described in his 1958 book *Thirteen Days to Glory*, Walter Lord adopted a cynical, Bohemian approach toward the event. Lord pointed out that back in November, his ego mauled by political defeat, Crockett had no interest in revolution. But now, with public adoration hurled upon him at every turn, the exploitable David Crockett, suddenly became a revolutionary.[35] Mark Derr, who wrote a biography of Crockett in 1993, noted that he joined the Texas Revolution "to fight for an ideal—freedom," a tantalizing statement which he did not let slip by without qualification, for the "key to liberty and opportunity was land." Derr then concluded by firmly linking Crockett with "Manifest Destiny,"[36] a land appropriation venture viewed by many postmodern thinkers with suspicion, if not outright condemnation.

Crockett may have signed the oath in Nacogdoches, but the real turning point from the current perspective came in San Augustine where Crockett suddenly discovered he had a constituency. "He had come to Texas to fight, not to seek office, he told them disingenuously, for getting involved in the rebellion formed no part of his original intention," wrote William C. Davis.[37] Thus, with "his very equivocal denial of the town's offer," he committed himself publicly for the first time to joining the revolution. Besides, this was, Davis contends, "his last chance to be a boy again." [38]

Davis's interpretation of the letter to Margaret definitely complicates matters. Clearly, the sequence of events which took place in east Texas suggests that Crockett may not have acquired an interest in the revolution, or the oath, until after he visited San Augustine. Maybe Crockett ignored the opportunity to take the oath during his first stay in Nacogdoches. But how do we even know if Forbes had prepared the oath prior to Crockett's return from San Augustine? As we have already seen, Crockett's commitment to Texas and revolution did not develop as suddenly as some maintain.

By the 1990s, when it was still widely accepted that Crockett had traveled most of the way to Little Rock via America's waterways, much as Smith described in *Exploits*, the Shackford, Folmsbee, and Catron theory had gained the approbation of professional historians. The recent surfacing of pertinent documents supporting west Tennessee folklore that Crockett's route took him overland also reveals he joined volunteers bound for Texas long before he crossed the Mississippi River and more than a month before the council transformed the next scheduled assembly into that of a Constitutional Convention. However, the recent appearance of this information does not explain why historians reached the conclusion that Crockett displayed so little in the way of patriotic devotion until being tempted by the opportunity for personal advancement. Though possibly unknown to Shackford, Folmsbee, and Catron, the November 17 edition of the *Arkansas Gazette*, which not only mentioned Crockett's plans to reside in Texas but clearly reported his intentions to take an active part in the revolution a full six weeks before he crossed the Sabine River, has long been available and widely known to historians. However, these recently found documents have apparently had little, if any, impact on the generally accepted view.[39]

There is some evidence demonstrating that once Crockett reached Nacogdoches, he still had every intention of participating in the war yet to be won. In second Lt. Peter Harper's discharge papers, prepared by General Houston during the spring of 1836, it states, "8th Jany commenced at Nacogdoches under Col. D. Crockett. . . ."[40] Harper had joined Crockett before he visited San Augustine and before he took the oath. Perfectly consistent with the accounts which came out of Jackson, Bolivar, Little Rock, and the Red River country, this would suggest Crockett began reforming his company of volunteers in Nacogdoches. As one who saw himself as a future resident with a vested interest in the well-being of Texas, Crockett responded to the call for assistance in precisely the manner expected of citizens aeons ago in ancient Greece. In fact, the little encounter Forbes found so memorable provides us with some insight into Crockett's perspective and how this view relates to the ancient tradition.

Forbes left behind two versions of the oath as it related to Crockett. When Forbes's "true copy," which he prepared for the secretary of war, is compared with the one he supplied to the newspaper, the differences are few and insignificant. On the following page is a copy of the oath as Forbes presented it to Crockett:

I do solemnly swear that I will bear true allegiance to the provisional government of Texas, or any future government that may be hereafter declared, and that I will serve her honestly and faithfully against all her enemies and oppressors whatsoever, and observe and obey the orders of the governor of Texas, the orders and decrees of the present and future authorities, and the orders of the officers appointed over me according to the rules and articles for the government of Texas so help me God.[41]

As volunteers from the United States began entering Nacogdoches in January of 1836, Judge John J. Forbes created the Oath of Allegiance. Although Forbes was an active supporter of independence, the question of what course Texas should take politically was not addressed in the oath. Forbes understood that such a question should be left until a more appropriate time. Courtesy of the Texas State Library and Archives Commission.

Inside his office at the Old Stone Fort, Forbes tendered the oath to Crockett for signature. Naturally, he wanted to read the document before signing. When Crockett came to the part about supporting "any future government," he stopped. There was a problem. Not interested in supporting just any kind of government, Crockett explained to Forbes that he was only willing to support a "republican government." Forbes then inserted the word "republican" in between the words "future" and "government." Satisfied that it now conformed to standards, Crockett signed his name without reservation. Forbes sent the original containing the words "any future *republican* government" and Crockett's signature to the secretary of war.[42]

Constance Rourke told this story in an unassuming, straightforward manner.[43] Even during the Great Depression, readers in America could understand its implications. In the second half of the twentieth century, it became possible for us to see this story in a different light. Crockett could be seen as the famous frontier bumpkin who, unable to resist being the center of attention, imprudently interrupts the proceed-ings,[44] while Forbes, in a supporting role as the star-struck judge, cheerfully complies with the demanding luminary standing before him.[45] Obviously, Forbes did not mean to imply that just any kind of government was acceptable. Working from the premise that the Texians were also admirers of the American Founders, the attorneys in the Autry/Kimble/Cloud group saw nothing alarming about pledging to sustain "any future government."[46] So, was it really necessary for Crockett to create a scene over one word? And why would Crockett, a man so closely identified with the common people, even in his own time, claim that he would only support a "republican" government? If he was truly worthy of our admiration, shouldn't Crockett have proclaimed that he would only support a "democratic" government?

Contrary to popular perception, the distinction between democ-racies and republics has nothing to do with either direct participation or representation. James Madison, in what historian William R. Everdell described as "an error of the first conse-quence,"[47] unintentionally misled many of his contemporaries into thinking of representation as the distinguishing characteristic between democracies and republics. Madison was actually attempting to work out a mechanism that would provide the new nation with the capability of averting the seemingly inevitable tyranny of the masses which had afflicted republics throughout history. Ironically, several years after the Democratic-Republican Party discovered the second half of their name to be irrelevant, President Jackson was able to convincingly project himself as the direct "representative of the people."

Like many other words, "democracy" has come to signify some-thing quite different from what it originally meant. As the word "republic" gradually fell into disuse during the twentieth century, "democracy" practically became synonymous with liberty and equality. There is currently a concerted effort to further modify the meaning of democracy by dissociating it entirely with the idea of majority rule.[48] Whatever values may be assigned, democracy remains first and fore-most the "making of law and policy by a majority of all."[49]

Everdell has studied the history of republics and republicans in great detail. Noting that Israel and Greece had established republican societies long before the Romans invented the word and long before the

Athenians came up with democracy, Everdell concluded that republics are in fact an ancient and flexible institution. The Latin *res publica* refers to the almost indeterminate well-being of the general public. Everdell believes John Adams has provided us with the best definition. In a letter to Roger Sherman, Adams defined a republic as "A government whose sovereignty is vested in more than one person."[50]

Since the very concept of being ruled by one man or one woman is inherently repugnant to the republican, the classic fear shared by republicans down through the ages has been the possible emergence of a despot or tyrant. Republicans learned in ancient times how tempting it was to lend one's devotion to a popular individual rather than remaining loyal to abstract ideals. As distinguished from other forms of government, a republic is seen as a government of laws. For this reason, republicans have tended to view the world as a battleground between the forces favoring governments without limitations versus those advocating governments with limitations.

From Crockett's standpoint, the oath, as it was originally worded, definitely allowed for the ascension of a popular individual, potentially a tyrant. When Crockett took sides against the president of the United States, a very popular political figure who, it was argued, had exceeded his constitutionally assigned authority, he was acting in the republican tradition. Now, Crockett was on foreign soil, opposing the *de facto* government of another president-general, a despot who, according to some Texians, was in the final stages of destroying the last vestiges of the Republic of Mexico. In January 1836, Crockett formally joined "the people" of Texas, citizens recently dispossessed of their constitutional rights, who were determined to reestablish their political liberties. More specifically, Crockett joined a modest number of revolutionaries who firmly believed they were capable of building a better republic than the Centralists. In his letter to Margaret, Crockett appropriately referred to the document in which he pledged his allegiance as the "oath of government," for it accurately characterized the nature of the crisis in Texas.[51]

THE OTHER SIDE OF FREEDOM

Leaders in Texas had once hoped the Federal Government in Mexico City would grant their petition to split Coahuila y Tejas into two states. The events which led up to the termination of all realistic hopes of statehood within the Republic of Mexico included the overthrow and forced exile of the acting president and duly elected vice president, Valentin Gómez Farias, the imprisonment of Stephen Austin, the shutting down of the national legislature and state governments, the brutal subjugation of dissident states, and finally, the revocation of the Constitution of 1824. Many observers in Texas concluded that the newly formed Centralist Government in Mexico City, under the domineering leadership of President Santa Anna, once a self-proclaimed Federalist, was despotic. In accordance with the traditional American view, Crockett believed that corrupt men were incapable of governing justly, and people who were ruled by a tyrant, even a benevolent one, were no more free than subjects, or slaves. And although the annulled Constitution was to be replaced by another, one created by Centralists, many leaders in Texas were of the opinion that living without having any input into the laws by which they were to govern, and be governed, was simply unacceptable. That was not the way a free, self-governing people should be treated.

For republics, constitutions not only represent the political philosophy of the citizen-constituents, but they are the fundamental laws which confer rightful authority upon the offices of government and bestow the political liberty which comes with full-fledged citizenship. In the modern era, constitutions are not usually created by magnanimous individuals like Lycurgus of Sparta and Solon of Athens. Following the newly formed tradition set by nations like the United States, Spain, and Mexico, the upcoming Constitutional Convention to be staged in the primitive little settlement of Washington would feature an assembly of elected representatives who were leading citizens from various communities. With the example set before them, what had taken the thirteen individual states more than ten years to accomplish, the Texians would do in less than three weeks.

Having studied more than one hundred constitutions from throughout all of Greece, Aristotle knew and understood that the implementation and maintenance of constitutional governments requires the participation of capable, self-governing citizens who possess certain qualities. Traditionally, republicans have acknowledged a number of values identifying the standard of conduct appropriate for citizens. Among the values deemed absolutely crucial for maintaining political equilibrium are honesty, frugality, civility, self-assertion, tempered by self-discipline and justice. These values are thought to manifest themselves through certain visible characteristics. For example, it is anticipated that citizens possessing such qualities will be property owners with an established residence. Residence signifies a certain degree of stability, whereas the ownership of property implies responsibility. It is also presumed they are independent in their thinking, independent in the means by which they provide for their families, and free from the burdening debt or personal obligations which have the potential of compromising their public service. Unlike democracy, republicanism does not make a clear distinction between public and private behavior.

Republicans have a long history of recognizing that the values encouraged by society and the aspirations we have as individuals are not always in harmony. In fact, they seldom parallel each other. As Aristotle noted, to consistently choose values over personal desires requires nothing less than moral virtue. Nonetheless, republics have generally sought ways to entice society's best citizens to channel their talents and energies into politics. Though frequently thought of as a dangerous combination, republicanism contends that ambition and politics are compatible; however, one must not lose proper perspective. Naturally, the best citizens are not expected to act like everybody else.

It is not necessary here to elaborate on the fact that unlike subjects or slaves, citizens possess rights which are publicly recognized. Yet natural and constitutional rights, however essential, do not form the primary or critical feature of citizenship. Prior to the revitalization of republics, the principle of bloodlines determined the leaders of society. Expected by people of all classes to exercise paternal care over their communities, "noblesse oblige" referred to the standard of behavior persons of high rank and birth had set for themselves. Born into a life of responsibility, children of the aristocracy, as future rulers and leaders, underwent intellectual and moral instruction in preparation for their assigned roles. The responsibilities once shouldered by the aristocracy are now assumed by citizens. Consequently, it is the citizenry which makes up the ruling class in a republic.

As the *Morning Courier and New York Enquirer* article implied, Crockett was an ambitious man. Folmsbee might have believed Crockett's political aspirations were suddenly rekindled in east Texas, but a few historians have since speculated that he probably possessed a little more ambition than previously thought. If Crockett could think of himself as president of the United States, then he surely could have imagined himself becoming president of the Republic of Texas.

Crockett was experienced enough in politics to know that no matter how alluring the San Augustine overture was, proper republican etiquette required him to politely decline and display a certain degree of disinterest in the offer. Had he not come to Texas to fight in the revolution? Absolutely. Did he not want to leap at this once-in-a-lifetime opportunity to participate in a constitutional convention and take part in the creation of a new nation? And if the citizens of San Augustine offered him that opportunity, would he not accept? Of course he would, but only if they insisted. Citizen-constituents approaching the prospective candidate was precisely how the very ideal of republicanism was supposed to work. Had Jefferson or Madison witnessed this event, they would have given the participants a standing ovation.

The governing principle which remains constant throughout every facet of republicanism, whether in times of peace or war, is that the interests of the republic are always paramount. In Crockett's particular case, it was the republic yet to be announced. It was known in Jackson, Bolivar, Memphis, Little Rock, Clarksville, and rumored in Nacogdoches prior to his arrival, that Crockett intended to join the Texas Army. There was nothing in writing, just a sincere commitment. This commitment became a matter of public record when he signed the Oath of Allegiance. With this public commitment, Crockett formally ceased being an independent individual.

Although Disney portrayed Crockett as a man who definitely went to Texas with personal ambitions, [52] he maintained a proper balance between his private interests and those of society. Neoprogressive cultural attitudes, however, insist on an entirely different perspective. Although new explanations have been offered to rationalize Crockett's conduct in Texas, the basic premise is undeviating in its assessment. To explain precisely what motivated and guided Crockett's behavior in Texas, one need look no further than his personal ambitions. Upon determining there existed substantial opportunity for personal gain, Crockett calculated how to best attain his objectives by exploiting the prevailing conditions in the existing unstable political climate. If this viewpoint is correct, Crockett's conduct upon leaving Nacogdoches should then be consistent with what we might expect of a man preoccupied with acting in his own self-interest.

7

Down the King's Road

A GATHERING OF FRIENDS

While it is impossible to determine for certain the names of those who crossed the Mississippi with Crockett, it is possible to make a reasonable guess as to whom might have accompanied him into Nacogdoches. Since Forbes described the "several" men who entered his office along with Crockett as "volunteers," it naturally follows that we would expect to find their names on the Oath of Allegiance. However, a search of the list on which Crockett's name appears yields only one familiar name—William Patton.[1] The names of Burgin and Tinkle are nowhere to be found on any of the surviving lists of volunteers who signed the oath. It would appear that Burgin, Tinkle, and Patton must have continued on with him after departing Jackson. However, at some point prior to taking the oath in Nacogdoches, Burgin and Tinkle must have turned back to Tennessee.

The name immediately following Crockett's on the oath is that of Henry W. Hardeman. Members of the Hardeman family of west Tennessee had moved to Texas in 1835, but it is pure speculation that Henry, assuming he was in fact of this family, might have ridden into Nacogdoches with Crockett. With his signature, Henry W. Hardeman disappears from our story as quickly as he entered.

The twenty-first name and second below Crockett's belongs to Joseph G. Washington. This is the second volunteer who separated from the Cloud group. It is possible that the group Crockett rode into

Nacogdoches with consisted of Hardeman, Washington, and Patton. This may hinge upon whether or not the signature below Washington's belonged to the same William Patton who left Tennessee with Crockett. Shackford believed he was and proposed that Patton's name should be added to the list of Alamo casualties. This proposal has not gained much acceptance. It is known there was at least one other William Patton in Texas at that time. A captain in the regular army, this second Patton is believed to have reached Béxar circa January 18. It would be one of those rare coincidences if the William Patton who signed the oath was not Crockett's nephew.

Herbert Simms Kimble thought his little group might have reached Nacogdoches as early as January 4 but definitely no later than the eighth.[2] Having traversed the entire 115 miles from Natchitoches through poor terrain and foul weather on foot, Autry probably arrived in Nacogdoches shortly thereafter. By this time, Joseph G. Washington would have reunited with his friends Cloud, Bailey, Thomas, and Fauntleroy. It was during the second week of January that Autry and the Kimble and Cloud groups came together and formed a new squad.

At least three other volunteers not associated with any of these groups also reached Nacogdoches sometime in early January. William McDowell arrived with Dr. John P. Reynolds, a graduate of Jefferson College in Philadelphia, ready to join the army. Even though the name of Ben McCulloch does not appear on any version of the oaths, William C. Davis found evidence indicating that he just might have caught up with Crockett in Nacogdoches.[3]

In his mid-January letter, Forbes also stated he was expecting the arrival of a Major Gilmore. Historian Amelia Williams found the name of Gilmore, minus a first name and initials, on every single list of Alamo casualties. Further research by Williams into the records yielded two men with the name of William Gilmore, both of whom were honorably discharged from separate units in September 1836. Williams eliminated both of these men because neither appeared to her to have been well educated. While the name of William Gilmore does not appear on any version of the Oath of Allegiance, she did find the name of William Gilmer.[4] Since Williams's work, the name of Gilmore has been permanently removed from the list of Alamo casualties.

At the request of the commissioner of claims in Texas, the circuit court judge of Giles County, Tennessee, took a deposition from William Ray Gilmer on April 12, 1859, regarding the fate of Dr. John W. Thompson. Under oath, Gilmer stated that he and Thompson left Columbia, Tennessee, for Nashville. There, they boarded a steamboat bound for New Orleans. Gilmer said that at Natchitoches, Crockett, with whom they had been traveling, moved on ahead while they walked the remaining distance to Texas. In Nacogdoches, the two volunteers signed the same oath and joined the same company. Thompson enlisted as a private and Gilmer as a captain. This company, as Gilmer remembered, was formed on about January 1, 1836.[5]

Even though the first reaction might be to dismiss Gilmer as a credible witness, we should bear in mind that this information was being related twenty-three years after the fact. The records verify both Gilmer and Thompson were definitely in Nacogdoches at about the same time as Crockett. Williams also obtained a statement from a relative of Thompson's, claiming he was a member of "Crockett's company."[6] Although Gilmer insisted on a connection with Crockett, it appears that Thompson formed no association with the newly formed Autry, Cloud, and Kimble group. On January 13, Autry composed his third and final letter to Martha from Nacogdoches. In the last of three postscripts, he wrote, "P.S. Col. Crockett has joined our company."[7]

Despite repeated attempts by scholars to reach a conclusive figure, the question still remains; exactly how many volunteers were in Crockett's group? Dr. Nicholas Labadie recalled having heard that Crockett passed through Nacogdoches "with some fifteen others" on his way "to join the army."[8] In 1841, the *Austin City Gazette* published a letter addressed to the paper's editor which tends to confirm Labadie's figure. The letter's author, who would only identify himself as a "Volunteer of 1836," claimed to have departed Nacogdoches in February with a company of "about sixteen men under the command of Col. Crockett."[9] In the process of verifying the Alamo casualties, Amelia Williams came up with a list of sixteen men who joined Crockett, most of whom were made up of the Autry, Cloud, and Kimble group, and signed the Oath of Allegiance together.[10] With a few exceptions, the following list is similar to the one compiled by Williams.

Micajah Autry
Peter James Bailey
Joseph Bayliss
Robert Bowen
Daniel William Cloud
William Keener Fauntleroy
Herbert Simms Kimble
William Irvine Lewis
J. E. Massie
Ben McCulloch
William McDowell
William Patton
Dr. John Purdy Reynolds
Richard L. Stockton
B. Archer M. Thomas
Joseph G. Washington

An Assemblage of Talent

No story, not even Richard Penn Smith's, portrays Crockett as traveling through Texas alone. Since Smith had limited access to news from the west, he resorted to his imagination and came up with four characters Crockett just happened to encounter along the way. Intended to be symbolic, their names were never revealed to the reader.

The first to join Crockett in *Exploits* was an aspiring aristocrat called Thimblerig. Their meeting occurred on board a Red River steamboat where Thimblerig tried to manipulate Crockett into taking a chance on his pea and thimble game. After he was caught cheating, a composed Thimblerig inadvertently exposed the philosophy behind his deceitful lifestyle. A gambler by profession, Thimblerig earnestly sought a life of freedom, totally devoid of either work or responsibility, one which would forever set him apart from mainstream society. He boasted of having been raised to be a gentleman, only to have recently fallen upon hard times. Failing to marry into wealth, Thimblerig took to the stage. Cast in an anonymous role as the rear end of an elephant, he abruptly deserted the theater after only one performance. Thimblerig then found employment in a gambling establishment but was fired when he was caught cheating more than the customers.

Of course, prior to meeting Crockett, Thimblerig had never given any thought to the Texas Revolution. But before he could join Crockett on a journey which would become his own, Thimblerig had to first undergo a change in his view of the world. As the relationship between Thimblerig and Crockett developed, the hero of *Exploits* assumed a role similar to that previously played by the parson. Thimblerig's manner of living, essentially a life aimed at avoiding risk and responsibility, could not spare him from the ultimate reality.

Although counseled to rise above his self-degradation, Thimblerig confessed that he was beyond help. Crockett then invited, or rather challenged, Thimblerig to undergo a spiritual transformation. "Accompany me to Texas. Cut aloof from your degrading habits and associates here, and in fighting for their freedom, regain your own."[11] Thimblerig's immediate reaction was to pick up his thimbles and walk away. But after having taken only a few steps, he suddenly turned and vowed to accompany Crockett to Texas. The Bee Hunter congratulated Thimblerig, for Texas was a land where no one would care about his past.

Patterned after a character from a James Fenimore Cooper novel, the Bee Hunter wore a finely decorated hunting shirt. His boots, as the reader of *Exploits* might well imagine, were of the finest quality and always polished. The first impression of the Bee Hunter is one of an actor, who was ever mindful that with his next move he may encounter the very dirt which will soil his attire and his image. Whereas Smith and his associates would have the prospective buyer to judge their book by its cover, the Crockett of their imagination was not so easily deceived by outward appearances. Unlike Thimblerig, who sought to rise above the rest of society, the Bee Hunter preferred to physically separate himself from civilization. Hearing that Crockett was in Natchitoches and on his way to Texas, the Bee Hunter offered his services as a guide.

Smith introduced Crockett's last two companions in *Exploits* after he leaves Nacogdoches. One was an Indian and the other a pirate who used to sail with Jean Lafitte. Although born outside of the white man's community the Indian, who belonged to a Galveston Bay settler, spoke fluent English and sought assimilation into the culture of his adoption as an equal. Conversely the pirate, ostracized by the culture of his birth after having deliberately lived outside its laws, was reticent and sought atonement. Traveling together on foot, both men were already on their way to join the fight for freedom when they met up with Crockett.

In effect, Smith created four characters intended to represent individuals who would not have been considered typical of mainstream American society, the very society the author's readers belonged to. Truly romantic figures in every respect, Smith's make-believe characters had little in common with the majority of volunteers who were actually entering Texas in late December 1835 and January 1836. Familiar with the work Amelia Williams did on Alamo casualties for her doctoral thesis, Rourke acknowledged that Crockett actually traveled in the company of sixteen or seventeen men, yet she deliberately chose to ignore the historical aspect of the story and incorporated Smith's characters.[12] Smith obviously portrayed his characters in a very sympathetic light and though it might be nice to think, as Rourke did, that Crockett mingled with all kinds of people as a matter of routine, he actually seems to have been rather selective. In her own book, Rourke titled the chapter in which Smith's characters were introduced, "The Story of Five Strange Companions." Whereas Rourke acknowledged the characters in Smith's fictitious cast were nowhere near as dignified as those with whom Crockett actually traveled,[13] one historian reached the conclusion that Crockett's real life companions were the ones who were kind of peculiar.

In his critique of the letters written by Autry and Cloud, Jeff Long offered the quintessential postmodern interpretation of their reasons for going to Texas. A decade before the creation of the now infamous expression "Manifest Destiny," Cloud viewed the westward immigration of Americans as inevitable and good. Cloud imagined himself, his friends, and even future generations of Americans as the "apostles of liberty and republicanism."[14] When viewed from the highly tolerant postmodern perspective, it becomes obvious how Cloud's fervent and amplified proclamations about fighting for freedom contrasted with his materialistic designs. Having already denigrated Crockett earlier in his book as a mercenary of sorts, a man whose behavior was dominated by a drive for personal gain, Long then alleged that other Americans had gone to Texas for precisely the same reason.[15] Unlike Cloud, who was ready to enter the revolution, the older Autry supposedly intended to avoid the actual fighting.[16] Ultimately, Long found Crockett and his fellow volunteers to be a "strange set of mercenaries."[17]

Even though they came to Texas from another country, the term "mercenary" as applied to Crockett and the volunteers who formed the Autry, Cloud, and Kimble group seems inappropriate. Mercenaries normally have no intention of establishing permanent residences in the lands where they work. In addition, mercenaries typically receive compensation without any thought or consideration as to the moral implications of their actions. True, these volunteers, like their predecessors in the United States, understood they would be compensated for their services. But receiving compensation in exchange for military service does not necessarily make one a mercenary.

The contention that these letters proved they wanted to conceal their true intentions from the world[18] is simply a misunderstanding. From the republican point of view, there was nothing hypocritical about confidentially communicating personal aspirations through letters. For them to have shared their personal aspirations in a public forum would have risked violating proper republican etiquette. Accordingly, one should never even give the slightest impression that personal aspirations supersede or equal the interests of the community. While Autry and Cloud did in fact seek personal advancement, they clearly disclosed their intention to contribute to the establishment and building of a new society. Perhaps even more cognizant of the inherent risks to be undertaken than Cloud, Autry wrote, "I expect to help them gain their independence and also to form their civil government, for it is worth risking many lives for."[19]

Crockett's friends came from the same neck of the woods as he did. That is certainly the impression one gets when viewing Hollywood screen productions such as *The Last Command* and *The Alamo*. Obviously less sophisticated than their leader, they were not exactly the type to devote much time to writing letters. In *The Alamo*, they were not even aware of the real reason Crockett had brought them to Texas!

The men who made up the Autry, Cloud, and Kimble group would hardly have fulfilled our perception of the stereotypical backwoodsman, nor did they have much in common with the sordid individuals who actually frequented Nacogdoches on a regular basis. Unlike regular soldiers, who are assigned to units by an unbiased authority, these men were free to form associations and travel with whomever they felt so inclined. Therefore, it is almost certain that the men who comprised this newly formed squad were of complementary backgrounds, shared similar interests, and had comparable educations. Rather than escaping creditors, having been exiled for political reasons, inappropriate behavior, or unlawful conduct, most of these men and their families were respected members of their communities. Some even came from distinguished families. Describing the quality of new recruits entering Nacogdoches in early January, Judge Forbes wrote in a letter to the lieutenant governor, "almost all are Gentlemen of the best respectability and mostly hailing from Tennessee They have come to fight the battles of Texas and maintain its rights, . . . I have had the honor of administering the oath of allegiance to them the Celebrated David Crockett is of the number."[20] As a whole, the group of men with whom Crockett became associated tended to represent the quality of those volunteers.

Not the kind to be content with remaining mere followers for long, many of these volunteers almost certainly expected to take on leadership roles with varying levels of responsibility at the first opportunity. Based on his own observations, Autry confessed to Martha that considering the general overall quality of these men, the competition for those roles would be stiff.[21] But one day the war was going to end. Although these men were willing to meet the challenges and sacrifices they would surely encounter in the campaign ahead, their primary focus was on the long term. Capable of assuming responsible roles in the building of new communities, they were precisely the kind of men any republic would want to attract. And from Forbes's point of view, the most notable citizen-constituent in this group of distinguished individuals for whom he had the honor of administering the oath was David Crockett.

NEW SENSE OF DIRECTION

It is not surprising that of all the people Crockett came into contact with he would align himself with highly capable men. And this is something Amelia Williams picked up on.[22] The question is, why would a group of intelligent, educated individuals have allowed themselves to become affiliated with a man whose scholastic achievements were virtually nonexistent? Within the confines of a homogeneous group, a leader can afford to flaunt a sophisticated resumé, that is to say a reputation which has narrow appeal but rich in detail. For example, in a society of hunters, the premier hunter could very well emerge as a leader of the community. However, if the hunter's role as a leader is to expand beyond the indigenous circle, the list of qualifications must be simplified and the image transformed into one appealing to a broader audience.

Having the right to elect their own officers, citizen soldiers tended to choose the men whom they respected as community leaders. Being the oldest in the group, Crockett was more experienced in every facet of life, except attending school. But was Crockett really elected to serve in such a capacity by his fellow volunteers? Judging from the postscript in Autry's letter, it would appear that as of January 13, Crockett had merely joined the group, not assumed a position of leadership. However, the reader should recall here that the anonymous "Volunteer of 1836" claimed to have departed Nacogdoches with a group led by Crockett.

Williams believed that Private Achilles L. Harrison, a man who did not make anyone's list of Alamo casualties, left Nacogdoches with the Crockett group but contracted an illness on the road and was unable to continue on to Béxar. Captain Sidney Sherman stated that Harrison's horse and gun had been appraised at eighty-five and thirty-five dollars respectively by Captain William B. Harrison, Colonel Crockett, and Lieutenant Robert Campbell.[23] Williams therefore concluded that Private Harrison and the "Volunteer of 1836" were one in the same.[24]

Since Dr. William P. Smith confirmed his patient was also a member of Captain William B. Harrison's Company, this definitely presented Williams with a problem. Having accepted that Private Harrison, Captain Harrison, Robert Campbell, and Crockett were all members of the same outfit, Williams needed to explain how two men could be in command of the same small group. To reconcile this dilemma, she settled upon the explanation that Captain Harrison must have been the official leader of the "so-called Crockett men," a loosely knit group over which Crockett himself exercised "at least a nominal command."[25]

Crockett had definitely returned to Nacogdoches by January 13. However, there is a very good possibility that Captain Harrison's Company may have already departed Nacogdoches. Dr. Smith specifically stated they left Washington for Béxar on "about the 15th of last January."[26] This would place Harrison's group at least 125 miles to the southwest, while Crockett, Autry, Kimble, and the rest were still in Nacogdoches.

On January 15, Crockett's horse, one rifle, and equipment were valued at $240 and placed into the service of Texas.[27] The fifteenth also yielded another fact about Crockett's situation. As previously noted, the character of Crockett's journey changed dramatically within days, if not hours, of his departure from home. In agreement with Matilda's observation, James Davis recalled that Crockett had only one rifle in his possession while preparing to cross the Mississippi River. Approximately seventy-two hours later, both the *Gazette* and the *Advocate* noted Crockett and company were leaving Little Rock "heavily armed." At some point, possibly in Little Rock, Crockett must have purchased a number of rifles, thereby incurring an expense he had not initially anticipated. In Lost Prairie, he attempted to replenish his supply of cash by trading watches with Dr. Jones. The need for cash soon resurfaced. On January 15, Crockett sold "two rifle guns" to Thomas J. Rusk of Nacogdoches for sixty dollars.[28] Crockett actually received only two dollars and fifty cents in cash from the sale. A promissory note was issued for the remainder.

In preparation for their impending departure, Crockett appears to have had a prominent role in preparing the group for their journey. For example, there is the receipt prepared by the Nacogdoches Committee of Vigilance and Safety. This was issued in the amount of ten dollars for materials purchased on credit. "To A. McLaughlin for a tent cloth furnished Davy Crockett and ordered to be paid by said committee."[29]

During the course of writing *Exploits*, Smith tried to incorporate reports from Texas whenever possible. Several months before Smith's project was completed, the *New York Sun* printed an article titled "Davy Crockett's Last" in which the paper purported to quote from a speech given in Nacogdoches. Totally relying on the article's

distorted perception, Smith erro-
neously placed Crockett in
Nacogdoches during the Siege of
Béxar. Obviously aware he was a
celebrity, Crockett reportedly told a
Nacogdoches crowd which had
gathered to see him off that he
would die with his rifle, Pretty
Betsey, in his arms. But perhaps
sensing this sounded a little melodramatic and a little out of
character, Crockett immediately
compensated by saying, "No, I will
not die, I'll grin down the walls of
the Alamo, and the Americans will
lick up the Mexicans like fine
salt."[30]

Thomas Jefferson Rusk purchased two rifles from Crockett in mid-January. Rusk would serve Texas as the secretary of war. Courtesy of the East Texas Research Center, Stephen F. Austin University.

We know from Crockett's letter
to Margaret that a dinner was also
given in his honor by the ladies of
Nacogdoches.[31] Perhaps it was at
such a dinner that twenty-six-year-old Bennett Blake, another recent
arrival who would serve Nacogdoches as a county judge for many
years, heard Crockett make one of his speeches about Texian independence. Blake would later recall "Old Davy" wrapped up his
speech in fine form by declaring, "We'll go to the city of Mexico and
shake Santa Anna as a coon dog would a possum."[32] Of course, no
army in Texas was capable of accomplishing such a feat, but
Crockett probably got a healthy response from the audience anyway.
Soon after these words were spoken, there would be a change in
plans.

Since the council was not advertising that their version of the
expedition was being conducted independently of Houston and the
regular army, anyone hearing of troop movements in the early days of
January could easily have assumed this was all part of a concerted
effort. Forbes, who maintained a regular correspondence with
Lieutenant Governor Robinson and was loyal to Houston, knew little
about what had recently transpired concerning the expedition. As one

Judge Bennett Blake may have attended the dinner hosted by the ladies of Nacogdoches honoring David Crockett. Courtesy of the East Texas Research Center, Stephen F. Austin University.

might imagine, there was the typical assortment of unconfirmed rumors circulating amongst the volunteers in mid-January. One of the more prevalent stories, which Autry tended to discount as improbable, was that Santa Anna had become so frightened by the impending expedition he had already made preparations to flee to Europe. An altogether conflicting rumor claimed Santa Anna was personally preparing to lead a large invasion force northward into Texas.[33]

Instead of going to Matamoros, Autry, Cloud, Kimble, and the others decided on a different destination. When Crockett joined his new friends he may not have been aware that his immediate destination had also changed. "We are waiting for a company daily expected from Columbia, Ten. under Col. Hill with whom we expect to march to head quarters (Washington) 125 miles from here, where we shall join Houston the commander in chief and receive our destination," Autry wrote.[34] As Auxiliary Volunteers they would do exactly what was expected of them, which was to submit to Houston's authority. Their ultimate destination was something for Houston or an officer under his command to decide. By the fifteenth, Forbes had learned that Houston's journey to Nacogdoches had been delayed. They may have decided that by the time they reached Washington, Houston would have concluded his business with the volunteers down south.

There can be little doubt that Crockett very much wanted to attend the convention. However, the postmodern perspective suggests that Crockett did not just want to attend the convention, he was determined to ensure his attendance. Crockett was savvy enough to have known that the election results in San Augustine could not be guaranteed. Therefore, in order to ensure his seat at the convention just in case the voters in San Augustine did not come through, Crockett implemented a backup plan. Having no real plans for going to the front, he would impersonate the self-sacrificing citizen by playing army for the time being. From behind this facade of legitimacy, Crockett would discreetly hunt for a second constituency, one more predictably sympathetic to his situation. This constituency would be composed of men who, like himself, had earned the right to vote by joining the volunteers.[35] One of the two constituencies was bound to deliver. Ultimately, we are left with the image of a slick opportunist.

AT THE SPRING BY THE ROAD

Period maps may have labeled Texas as Mexican, but most everyone living there knew who actually ruled. Having driven the Apaches further south, the triumphant Comanches thought of this land as theirs. Even though a party atmosphere prevailed within Béxar, life itself remained one of constant fear for those who had to venture outside the city limits. Despite the fact that the Mexicans did not trust the Comanches, they still permitted them to enter their city. And why wouldn't the Comanches go into Béxar? As far as they were concerned, it belonged to them too! On January 8, a lone Comanche ambassador entered the city to inform local authorities that Béxar and the Comanche Nation were in a state of war.[36]

Anxious to see Béxar for himself, Edward Warren embarked on his journey from Washington to the great city despite having only one companion. As their journey progressed, others joined. Warren later remembered thinking while camped on the banks of the San Antonio River this was the clearest and most beautiful river he had yet seen. Deceptive though his immediate surroundings may have been, Warren did not totally forget where he was. "Our party," he wrote, "had now increased to five (including myself) well armed, each carrying from two to four pistols and rifle or double barrelled gun."[37] Warren and his group never made it to their destination.

During their encampment, the group was joined by a refugee from Béxar. The stranger related how two or three hundred Comanches had entered the confines of the city, while an unknown number waited outside on the prairies. He was convinced it was their intention to kill all of the inhabitants and pillage the city. His recommendation that the group turn back was taken quite seriously by everyone in the camp except Warren. But as the only dissenter, Warren had no intention of making the journey alone. Late in the afternoon of January 14, Warren decided to take the main road back toward the United States.

Also known as *El Camino Real* or the King's Road, the Old San Antonio Road was the principal thoroughfare in Texas. Mapped out by the Spaniards in 1691, it stretched all the way from Natchitoches to the Río Grande and beyond. The Old Road eventually became part of the state's new highway system in 1929 and was renamed Highway 21.

With the exception of some divergence, Highway 21 parallels the Old Road much of the way from Nacogdoches to San Antonio.

In the mid-1830s, the Old San Antonio Road made its way through unpopulated lands as settlements along the route were few. Interspersed along the Old Road from Nacogdoches to Washington were nineteen hospitality establishments called "stands." Though mostly windowless farmhouses, the traveler could obtain meals and lodging for both himself and his horse. Warren adjusted his schedule so as to ensure that he reached a stand by nightfall. But at the cost of one dollar a night, he found the hospitality industry in this part of the world backward and grossly overpriced. Served only cornbread and meat whether he ordered it or not, Warren learned that complaining about the menus accomplished nothing.

After waiting a few days without any sign of Colonel Hill, Crockett finally started down the road from Nacogdoches he had long been advised to take. For the first eighty miles or so out of Nacogdoches, Highway 21 closely follows the Old Road over the rolling hills and diverges no more than two miles at the most and coming as close as a half-mile at certain points. Amos Parker had also taken the Old Road to the southwest when he left Nacogdoches in November 1834. A little disappointed about encountering the same old pine trees he had been looking at since he left Mississippi, Parker found the scenery quite "monotonous." For the first twenty miles out of Nacogdoches, it was nothing but pine trees.[38]

The progress of one's journey often depended to a great extent upon the weather. This tended to be especially true during the rainy season, as rivers were prone to overflowing. Unfortunately, bridges were quite scarce in the Texas of 1836. Between Nacogdoches and Béxar, the traveler would have to contend with numerous rivers in addition to many smaller streams, each posing unique hazards. Parker acknowledged the fording of rivers and streams proved to be formidable obstacles.

Having crossed the Angelina and Neches Rivers, Crockett continued in a southwesterly direction, past the ancient Indian mounds, until he entered an area known as Hurricane Bayou. Finding a pleasant setting adjacent to a spring about sixty-five miles out of Nacogdoches, Crockett decided to make camp just off the Road. Overlooking the spring, at the top of a slope, lived twenty-three-year-old

Andrew Edwards Gossett and his family. His father, Elijah, happened to be his nearest neighbor, residing three miles to the northwest. A native of east Tennessee, Elijah Gossett had lived in Spring Creek near Bolivar for about a decade, prior to moving the entire family to Texas in 1833.[39]

Obtaining information from his father, Frank Mulder Gossett wrote a brief narrative in 1969 about his grandfather, Andrew Edwards Gossett. Elijah and David had definitely been childhood friends, and continued to see each other periodically throughout adulthood. According to family tradition, their paths crossed again, one last time in Texas, as Crockett happened to come upon men working on a public building, when he recognized Elijah and stopped to greet him. That evening, Elijah, Andrew, and a few neighbors, visited with Crockett at their camp by the spring. Sufficiently impressed, Andrew, who was already preparing plans to lay out a new town on the site, suggested to his father that they should name the town in honor of "Colonel Davey." From this brief meeting, the Gossetts, Elijah, Andrew Edwards, and their descendants, liked to think of themselves as "the only family that knew David Crockett in both Tennessee and Texas."[40]

There is another variation of this less than eventful meeting, wherein it was Elijah who happened upon the encampment at the spring and recognized Crockett. In this version, which qualifies as local legend, Crockett had no idea when he made camp, just how glad he would be to see an old friend. The rendition below of what might have happened, is pieced together from assorted fragments of information,[41] and takes place in a crime-ridden Texas. As a general rule, Texians preferred to deal with suspected criminals swiftly, administering their brand of justice with as little formality as possible. No one in Texas was dealt with more severely than the suspected horse thief. Punishment by hanging quickly followed apprehension. Periodically, bodies of the accused were left hanging in the trees as a reminder of what thieves could expect if caught.

We know that Crockett's group in Nacogdoches probably consisted of as many as fifteen or sixteen men. Yet, this local legend says Crockett made camp at the spring with only two companions. Their journey almost ended right there. Apparently, horse thieves had been working in the immediate vicinity. A posse discovered these three strangers camped in a place where they did not belong. We can imagine all of the accused protested, assuring their captors that they were innocent of any wrongdoing. They must have explained they were merely passing through, volunteers on their way to join General Houston. To add credibility to their story, one of the accused might have even claimed he was a former congressman and nationally known celebrity back in the United States. If he did make such a claim, we may presume from local legend that he was not believed.

It is not known if Elijah just happened upon the scene, or if he was summoned to witness the hanging, but in either case, he made it just in time. Recognizing Crockett

Like his father, Elijah, Andrew Edwards Gossett would serve his community in a number of capacities, including judge. Courtesy of Dorothy Gossett Jones.

as an old friend from back home, the elder Gossett put an immediate halt to the proceedings. Afterwards, "the two joked about Crockett's almost getting mistaken for a 'hoss thief.'"[42] It is conceivable that by separating himself from the main group, Crockett may have contributed to the circumstances which led to the realization of this incident. Imagine, Davy Crockett, hung as a horse thief! But with Gossett's intervention, Crockett's fate, and that of his two friends, was reserved for a more spectacular conclusion. His last reunion with the Gossetts was no doubt reassuring. The following morning, Crockett and his friends resumed their journey.

As Crockett and his friends were making their way south, the schism in San Felipe de Austin was reaching melodramatic proportions. Following Governor Smith's failed attempt at reconciliation, both sides launched campaigns to discredit the other. Accusations soon erupted over the contents of a letter written by Smith to Major William Ward, who was a recent arrival from Georgia. Writing to Acting Governor Robinson, Fannin quoted the governor as saying, "A mob, nick-named an Army, has just been disbanded amongst us—and I am threatened with assassination, by an internal enemy at home (the mob volunteer army) and an external enemy from abroad."[43] This quote would be incorporated into the first of three formal charges against the governor.

As promised, Smith sent what was left of the land's only representative body "to the devil" and carried on alone. Most of the council, while not taking the governor's directive literally, gradually quit and went home, fed up with the state of Texas politics. No longer able to achieve a quorum as of January 17, the remnants of the council adopted a new moniker, calling themselves the Advisory Committee to the General Executive.

Momentarily ignoring General Houston, Acting Governor Robinson issued a public appeal on January 19 and called upon the citizen soldiers of Texas to duplicate their patriotic performance of the previous fall by descending upon Béxar.[44] Two days later, Robinson attempted to assume full, undisputed control when he ordered Smith to relinquish all governmental documents in his possession. Should the governor refuse to comply, the marshall of Texas had orders to procure the military personnel necessary to seize the documents. Naturally, Smith refused. But when the marshall ordered twelve men to take the documents by force, three-fourths of the squad refused to obey. Among the nine refusing was Colonel Travis.

THE ENIGMATIC DECISION

Passing through Mustang Prairie, the largest he had encountered thus far, Crockett reached the deep and muddy Trinity again this time to the southwest. Though as much as one hundred yards wide in some places, the Trinity was only half that where it intersected with the Old San Antonio Road. An enterprising man named Nathaniel Robbins operated a ferry there and charged twenty-five cents per crossing.

Once across the Trinity, travelers could easily see how the landscape was changing. Although the timbered lands were gradually receding, the trees did not altogether disappear. Following the road southwest, wayfarers continually passed large clusters of trees called "islands." With those wearisome pine trees behind him, Amos

Parker had described the next ten miles as consisting of the "most beautiful rolling prairies."[45] Crockett kept no journal with which to record his impressions, but less than a month after he passed through, William F. Gray would be quite impressed by what he saw after crossing the Trinity. In his journal, Gray wrote, "we passed through a most beautiful prairie of several miles extent, presenting all the appearance of cultivation."[46]

Approaching the Navasota River, the Old San Antonio Road made a sharp detour to the south for several miles. Backtracking, the highway then resumed its southwesterly course following the current day Leon-Madison County line to the Navasota. At some point, Crockett and his group abandoned the highway and headed due south. It was probably at about this time that Herbert Simms Kimble broke from the main group to take a sightseeing tour of the Falls of the Brazos. Kimble and the group agreed to rendezvous in Washington.[47] Just above their destination, the Navasota merged with the Brazos River.

Just north of Washington, Crockett and company entered a swamp. The four-mile path they were now on was frequently blanketed by muddy water, sometimes as much as two feet deep in places. Emerging from the swamp, they reached the banks of the Brazos River. Longest of all Texas rivers, the Brazos was originally named El Río de Brazos de Dios or the River of the Arms of God.

The town of Washington was laid out on a steep slope overlooking Hall's ferry crossing. When the Brazos was at normal levels, John Hall charged the standard twenty-five cents per man and horse. Due to its proximity to the La Bahía Road and because the site could also be reached by boat from the coast, Washington was thought to have tremendous commercial potential. This prime real estate location was also considered to be exceptionally beautiful. Towering over the river bed, shading its brownish waters from the noonday sun, the area was dominated by varieties of red cedar, oak, and hickory trees.

Crockett crossed the Brazos and ascended the earthen ramp known as Ferry Street. Hastily built in the midst of the woods, nature had not yet given way to the work of man. The downtown area, complete with tree stumps still clinging to the earth that was Main Street, consisted of two hotels, a few shops, and other small buildings.

Offering what were perhaps the finest accommodations in all of Texas, Lott's hotel was the first building one encountered. By this time, Washington's population was already in the neighborhood of one hundred residents.

There are two documents in the Audited Military Claims Collection relating to Crockett's stay in Washington. Both are promissory notes written to reimburse hotel owner John Lott. Some questions have recently been raised as to whether the note reputedly written and signed by Crockett is the genuine article. It is the opinion of at least one historian that the handwriting does not compare favorably with samples known to be his.

Concluding that the style of composition was definitely Crockett's, Shackford was convinced that the note itself was authentic. The actual handwriting aside, there is some internal evidence to support the belief that the document was written in Crockett's style. For example, Crockett frequently divided words like "myself" into two distinct words. Another typical feature of his style, also evident in this document as shown, is the absence of punctuation.[48] Could a forger have intended to infer that the other four volunteers were Crockett's companions from *Exploits*? Maybe, but if so, the forger did not read Smith's book very carefully. Smith had no idea Crockett went through a Texas town called Washington.

Now, regarding the curious dating of this document. There is a document ascribed to Captain William B. Harrison, also written in Washington and dated January 23. This is especially interesting since according to Dr. Smith, Harrison's company should have left Washington eight days earlier. Regardless of how this date was ascribed to the Crockett note, there is still good reason to believe he was not only in Washington circa the twenty-third but that he was traveling with a group separate from Harrison's. If the document in question were totally without any basis in fact, it would be amazing that a forger could have assigned it a date of January 23.

The second promissory note relating to Crockett and Washington came from B. Archer M. Thomas who signed as "one of D. Crocketts Com."[49] This second note, also to John Lott, was dated January 24, 1836. This almost certainly assures Crockett's presence in Washington on or about January 23. We also have here a clear indication that Thomas understood Crockett's company to be an actual unit. More

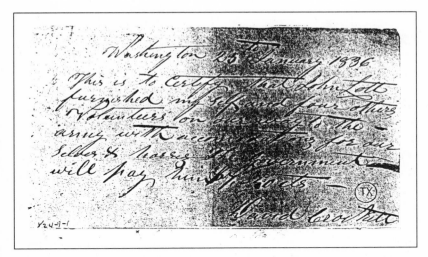

Promissory note from Crockett to Washington tavern owner John Lott. The note reads:

Washington 23 January 1836

This is to Certify that John Lott
furnished my self and four others
Volunteers on our way to the -
army with accomodations for our
Selves & horses The Government
will pay him $7.-50 cts -

David Crockett

Courtesy of the Texas State Library and Archives Commission.

important, it would appear that Thomas, like the "Volunteer of 1836," recognized Crockett as the group's leader.

As previously noted, Washington was not just another town for Crockett and company to pass through. They had come to present themselves to Houston and receive their assignment. As for Houston, he was still down south debating the volunteers led by Johnson and Fannin. By now, the general had already been gone for more than two weeks. Crockett could have opted to wait around but apparently did not.

Crockett certainly spoke with civil authorities such as John Lott. For the first time, he would have acquired information suggesting that Texas was in a tailspin toward anarchy. Assuming they were present, one would expect Crockett to have spoken at length with members of the general's staff concerning the current state of affairs in Texas. Whatever doubts Crockett and his friends may have had concerning an impending invasion by the Mexican Army would have been quickly dispelled. As far as the general and his staff were concerned, the invasion was imminent. By Texian standards of the day, all indications were that the invasion would be made on a massive scale. They even knew the primary target. If Houston's forecast of an invasion sometime in March was even somewhat accurate, it would have been apparent to even the nonprofessional that Texas could not possibly field a combat-ready army in time.

The governor, acting governor and his advisory committee, major general, and the officers at the Alamo all believed maintaining the post was crucial to the security of Texas. Having received no assistance whatsoever, Neill wrote an urgent appeal on January 14 to Houston stating that he expected to be attacked within eight days![50] This letter probably bypassed Washington entirely. Receiving Neill's letter on the seventeenth, Houston immediately wrote Smith informing him that he was sending James Bowie to Béxar with thirty men. Captain Patton, previously dispatched by Houston to Béxar, was believed to have already arrived there with his company. Captain Philip Dimitt of Goliad was instructed to stand by with another one hundred men ready to deploy to Béxar on order. After reading Houston's letter, Smith ordered Travis to recruit one hundred men and proceed directly to Béxar.

Crockett once expressed his faith before his fellow congressmen that the settlers of the frontiers were always first in responding to the call to defend their homeland. He himself had been part of such a response twenty years earlier. In the final week of January, it just might have appeared from Washington that Texians were once again making preparations to converge upon Béxar. Whether Crockett was ordered, asked, or decided to go there on his own, the decision to proceed to Béxar was made during the twenty-four to thirty-six hour period he spent in Washington.

The traditional version of Crockett's Texas adventure left previous generations of Americans with the unmistakable impression that he joined this revolution and went to the Alamo on his own initiative. Until recently, this perception captured the essence of what the "volunteer" was all about and as such stood as one of the most impressive examples of patriotism in American history. Proponents of the postmodern viewpoint seem to concur with the basics, albeit for entirely different reasons. As Richard Boyd Hauck wrote, "I believe David Crockett went to the Alamo because he intended to live up to his legend." In what would have been a deliberate, calculated decision, Crockett saw the road to the Alamo as the "right path to fame and political fortune in Texas."[51] Either way, there can be little doubt Crockett left Washington knowing the Mexican Army had definitely targeted Béxar.

8

In No Particular Hurry

THE VISIT

Nathaniel Mitchell was just a youngster when Crockett and company came by his parents' farm in the municipality of Washington. At the age of seventy-five, Mitchell claimed he could still picture Crockett whom he recalled was not wearing a buckskin outfit. One member of the group proposed to trade his "stove pipe hat" for Mitchell's fur cap. The deal was closed when the volunteer offered to throw in a ten-dollar gold piece. Initially, Mitchell felt like he had made a real bargain until the winter winds picked up. Stuck with the fancy new hat, Mitchell jokingly called it his "Davy Crockett." He would wear it into battle at San Jacinto.[1]

Mitchell said that Crockett stopped by his ranch with twelve other men.[2] If the Texas legend about Crockett almost getting himself hanged as a horse thief has any factual basis, then we could only conclude that he had not learned anything from his near-fatal episode at Hurricane Bayou. In no apparent hurry to reach Béxar, Crockett and B. Archer M. Thomas traveling apart from everyone else stopped at the home of James Gibson Swisher, a native of Tennessee, who also lived in the municipality of Washington.

The recording of Crockett's visit would be left up to Swisher's son John Milton. Seventeen years old at the time of Crockett's visit, John was a bright young man who had already opened and taught school three years earlier at Fort Tenoxtitlan. In 1841, John was hired to

145

work in the treasury department where he eventually rose to the position of state auditor of public accounts.

In late January of 1836, John returned home from hunting with a few friends to find his father had a special guest. Crockett came out of the house and assisted the teenager with a deer he had killed. Naturally, Crockett enquired about the circumstances of the kill. The master frontiersman complimented John on a fine kill and called him "his young hunter." John said his "pride swelled" and that he could not even imagine changing places with the president of the United States.[3] And in this instance, all things were as they should have been for the president would not have changed places with the young man either.

Crockett challenged the younger Swisher to a shooting match and there were actually several between the two, all in fun. According to Swisher, even though Crockett always shot at a disadvantage, the matches pretty much ended in a draw. He recalled that Crockett's rifle, "Bessie," was decorated with a silver plate over the stock where the name "David Crockett" was engraved.[4] While certain aspects of Crockett's physical description, as presented below, may not be entirely accurate, Swisher's appraisal of the man's character was insightful.

> At the time I saw Colonel Crockett, I judged him to be about forty years old. He was stout and muscular, about six feet in height, and weighing 180 to 200 pounds. He was of a florid complexion, with intelligent gray eyes. He had small side whiskers inclining to sandy. His countenance, although firm and determined, wore a pleasant and genial expression. Although his early education had been neglected, he had acquired such a polish from his contact with good society, that few men could eclipse him in conversation. He was fond of talking and had an ease and grace about him which, added to his strong natural sense and the fund of anecdotes that he had gathered, rendered him irresistible.[5]

The Swisher family was not accustomed to staying up late at night, but they never went to bed before midnight during the time Crockett spent with them. John did not specify how long their special guest stayed, but one gets the impression from reading his memoirs that it must have been several days. Only weeks earlier, the elder Swisher had led his company into the streets of Béxar when the city was captured from Cós. As one of four officers who accepted Cós's formal surrender, he must have had a great deal to tell Crockett.

John recalled that Crockett "conversed about himself in the most unaffected manner without the slightest attempt to display any genius or even smartness. He told us a great many anecdotes, many of which were common place and amounted to nothing within themselves, but his inimitable way of telling them would convulse one with laughter."[6] Swisher related four stories Crockett told.

John Milton Swisher was only a teenager when Crockett stopped by his father's farm on the way to the Alamo. Courtesy of the Texas State Library and Archives Commission.

One story, which concerned Andrew Jackson and Martin Van Buren, tends to confirm Crockett was blaming the president less and less for the nation's ills, while condemning the vice president more and more. Swisher recalled Crockett had such an aversion to Van Buren that he had no interest in even speaking to the man. Scheming to meet the famous congressman, Van Buren enlisted the help of a mutual friend who offered to arrange an introduction. One evening at a Washington theater, Van Buren and the mutual friend sat in the seats directly behind Crockett. Tapping him on the shoulder, the mutual friend politely asked, "allow me to take the liberty of introducing to you the future president of the United States." At this point, Van Buren must have been confident Crockett would have to acknowledge the overture, which he did. Turning around with a smile on his face, but careful so as not to look directly at Van Buren, Crockett said, "Really, my friend, anything in reason, but by heaven I cannot permit anyone to take such a liberty with me."[7]

The last story Swisher recounted had to do with Crockett's last campaign. Swisher basically related the same story Crockett had been telling everyone else—how he told the voters back home that in the event of his defeat, they could go to hell, and he would go to Texas. Swisher stated that in Crockett's version of the story, he made his pronouncement to the people a couple of days before the election.[8]

Looking ahead, Crockett told the Swishers that his future was with Texas. The youngster admired Crockett, as he was a man who knew how to get along in the world. He vividly recalled the sight of B. Archer M. Thomas and Crockett riding off to join the army. The young man had no reason to suspect he would never see him again.

Possibly about the time Crockett was visiting the Swisher residence, news from San Felipe de Austin reached Béxar. On January 26, the garrison's officers held another meeting, this time for the purpose of drafting a statement expressing their disapproval of the recent political developments. Again, seven resolutions were drafted. First and foremost they wanted to communicate their unequivocal support for Governor Smith. Whereas the governor and Houston had clearly demonstrated their support for the Alamo by attempting to provide reinforcements, the council, while claiming to favor sustenance of the post, not only ordered the extraction of much needed personnel but had also, in an action the garrison believed to be "in the highest degree criminal and unjust," diverted a five-hundred-dollar loan originally intended for the Alamo.[9]

The second, third, and fourth resolutions were directed toward Smith's political adversaries. In the second, they emphatically stated their refusal to submit to the "anarchial assumptions of power" exhibited by Acting Governor Robinson and the council. Thirdly, they issued an open invitation to every soldier in the army to publicly express their agreement with the first two resolutions. And in the fourth resolution, in support of General Houston, they refused to recognize the appointments of Johnson and Fannin to lead the Matamoros Expedition.[10] These resolutions, adopted by the same fiercely independent volunteers who just one month earlier had demanded that the regular army mind its own business, represented a dramatic transformation of political allegiances at the Alamo. Regardless of the council's inconsiderate attitude, they concluded, "we cannot be driven from the post of Honor and the sacred cause of freedom."[11]

THE SONS OF DARKNESS

Fannin heard the rumor of Houston's instructions to blow up the Alamo but could not confirm that such an order had actually been issued. Houston, who knew that a regular army could not become a reality anytime soon, had in fact made such a suggestion to Governor Smith in writing. And though this was followed up by a reminder, Houston never received a response. Travis, who was dispatched by the governor to the Alamo, correctly understood his orders were to assist in defending the post in the event of an attack. The Advisory Committee could have cleared up the question by simply asking the governor, but then again, they were not talking to each other.

Houston had ridden south determined to learn exactly who was responsible for the unauthorized campaign against Matamoros, the appointment of its leaders, and the mess at the Alamo. Houston trusted Robinson, but the general had no idea that as he was writing to the lieutenant governor back on the eleventh the Provisional Government was fracturing. On his own before the volunteers of Johnson and Fannin, Houston was in prime form. Houston told them they were wrong if they expected the other Mexican states to join them against the Centralists. Ultimately, he was able to win over a number of converts by convincing them that this campaign had no official government sanction.

Johnson's letter of January 30 yields some idea as to the extent of Houston's success. He wrote to the council, by then the Advisory Committee, that Houston's visit with the volunteers had left the new Volunteer Army of the Frontiers in a "most mortifying" condition. With his army disintegrating around him, including some companies disbanding entirely, Johnson suggested that Acting Governor Robinson should send a deliberate message in writing to the volunteers authorizing the campaign without making any reference whatsoever to Houston![12]

Returning to Washington with plenty to write about, Houston resumed his correspondence with Governor Smith on January 30. In a rather lengthy discourse on the condition of the largest military organization in Texas, Houston attacked the legitimacy of the Matamoros

Sam Houston arrived in Texas with a vision of the future, but as Stephen F. Austin had to learn the hard way, attempting to lead Texians was a tempestuous test of a man's leadership capabilities. This is one of the earliest photographs of Houston taken during the days of the Republic of Texas. Courtesy of the Daughters of the Republic of Texas Library.

Expedition. First, he evaluated the authorizations granted to Johnson, Fannin, and Grant. Then, he pressed his attack against the council.

During his meeting with Johnson on the evening of January 20, Houston was presented with a copy of the council's resolution relevant to Johnson's assigned role in the expedition. Rather than acknowledge in Johnson any legitimate military standing, General Houston referred to him in his letter as either "F. W. Johnson, Esq.," "F. W. Johnson," or simply "Mr. Johnson." Houston stopped short of actually assigning any blame to Johnson, but instead depicted him as a manipulated man. He was not so lenient in his treatment of either Grant or Fannin.

Dr. James Grant was truly one of those officers Houston had labeled as "self-created." By having proclaimed himself the "acting commander-in-chief," Grant had adopted a ranking which Houston insisted was "unknown to the world."[13] He went on to point out that there was no provision in the military chain of command for Grant to actually take charge of anything. Houston further asserted that Grant, hardly a disinterested patriot, was using the Matamoros Expedition as a means of recovering the property taken from him by the Centralist Government.

Unlike Johnson and Grant, Fannin was another case entirely. Obtaining a copy of Fannin's January 21 letter to the council, Houston quoted the colonel as saying that if the major general of the Armies of Texas would only submit to the council, then he (Fannin) would do all he could to promote harmony. Houston noted that this was not the expressed conviction of an officer in the regular army but of "J. W. Fannin, jr." agent of the Provisional Government![14] From

Houston's perspective, it appeared that Fannin had more than a few priorities confused.

Even more disturbing to Houston was the fact that Fannin, with whom he was unable to meet, had in an impudent maneuver promised the troops whatever spoils they could take. Fannin's version of the war's objectives had, in Houston's words, stripped "the campaign of any character save that of piratical or predatory war."[15] Houston could not help but to wonder if Fannin really believed that a city of twelve thousand people was going to quietly stand by and allow itself to be overrun by a handful of soldiers pillaging in the name of liberty? Above all else, Houston insisted that this must remain a war based on principles.[16]

No longer in doubt that the council was well aware of his orders to Bowie, Houston now knew exactly who was responsible for the army being in total disarray. Houston had learned that Wyatt Hanks and Joseph D. Clements of the council were actively engaged in writing to Johnson and were promoting their own program, in secret, even after having learned the governor had already assigned him to lead the campaign. Houston's condemnation of the council was emphatic:

While the Council was passing resolutions affecting the army of Texas, and transferring to J. W. Fannin, jr. and F. W. Johnson the whole control of the army and resources of Texas, they could order them to be furnished with copies of the several resolutions passed by that body, but did not think proper even to notify the major general of the army of their adoption; nor have they yet caused him to be furnished with the acts of the council relative to the army. True it is, that they passed a resolution to that effect, but it never was complied with. Their object must have been to conceal, and not to promulgate their acts. "They have loved darkness rather than light, because their deeds are evil."

I do not consider the council as a constitutional body, nor their acts lawful. They have no quorum agreeably to the organic law, and therefore I am compelled to regard all their acts as void.[17]

On January 31, the Advisory Committee which included Don Carlos Barrett and Joseph D. Clements delivered four resolutions to

Acting Governor Robinson. Resolutions three and four are of particular interest. Convinced Houston had issued orders for the evacuation and destruction of the Alamo, the Advisory Committee recommended that Robinson immediately order Neill to maintain the fortress "and in no case abandon or surrender the place unless in the last extremity."[18] While they felt the Alamo must be defended, their sources had led them to believe that the garrison was already sufficient in size to sustain the post if attacked. This conclusion may have been influenced by Johnson's letter of January 3 wherein he stated that in addition to the one hundred men he had left behind to garrison the Alamo, another fifty men would be adequate for the fort's defense. Taking into consideration the Advisory Committee had just received a letter from Neill that a Mexican force of only "a few hundred cavalry"[19] was being sent toward Béxar, their conclusion is understandable. Having determined that the garrison was now sufficiently manned, they recommended instructions be sent to the government's agent in Washington, John Lott, to redirect all volunteers headed for Béxar to Goliad and Copano.[20]

When Johnson wrote to the council in late January, he was still unaware that they had downgraded themselves to a committee. With his army crumbling around him in the wake of Houston's visit, Johnson tenaciously clung to news that was all too good to be true. Based on the sources available to him as of January 30, Johnson was certain the opportunity for victory never seemed greater.[21]

Having just missed Crockett when he returned to Washington in late January, Houston's next assignment was to negotiate a peace treaty with various Indian tribes. The last time Texians assembled for war, they unwittingly left their homes and families vulnerable to Indian attack. Governor Smith, being of the opinion such meetings were crucial, approved Houston's leave of absence. This was, however, a critical time for the general to take a furlough from an army that did not yet exist. Almost immediately after Houston departed for Nacogdoches, rumor spread amongst the volunteers that he had been relieved of command.

Election Day: A Celebration of Rights

Some degree of confusion concerning the election had existed almost since the very idea of the convention was conceived. The biggest problem centered around the question of who was eligible to vote. The council's ordinance conferred upon "all free white males and Mexicans" the right to vote provided they were "opposed to a Centralist Government." Proxy votes would not be accepted unless cast by "Citizen Volunteers" serving in the military.[22] This ordinance, passed on December 10, was composed at a time when Austin's Federal Volunteers were still in Béxar. By February 1, the ratio between those meeting the criteria of a "Citizen Volunteer" and recent arrivals volunteering for service was clearly changing. In fact, the question as to just who qualified as a "Citizen Volunteer" was raised in several municipalities.

As if relations between the Spanish and English-speaking residents of Nacogdoches had not already been strained enough, the rambunctious Kentucky Volunteers aggravated matters further. On election day, they assembled at the Old Stone Fort, ready to perform their civic duties. When told they would not be permitted to vote, the first lieutenant lined up the volunteers in front of the building and threatened to open fire! Attempting to appeal to their sense of republican values, election officials asked the crowd to determine by a show of hands whether or not the Kentuckians should be allowed to vote. The Kentuckians lost and clearly became quite agitated when the crowd began to openly demonstrate their approval of the outcome. Fearing they might begin shooting civilians, Judge Augustus Hotchkiss and William F. Gray intervened and spoke to the soldiers.

Also occupying center stage in the fracas was candidate Robert Potter. In what was his second speech of the day, Potter urged the volunteers to demand their right to vote. Gray had the opportunity of observing Potter in action and made the following assessment of his political role in Nacogdoches, a divided city both ethnically and politically: "It is manifest that much ill blood exists in this little community. Potter is regarded as a disorganizer, and his coming among them is greatly deprecated by the intelligent and well disposed. He is courting popular favor with all his art, and is succeeding to a wonderful degree. He can only float in troubled water."[23]

After listening to several more speakers, the volunteers finally settled down and resigned themselves not to press the issue further. In a surprising move, the judges relented and decided to permit the volunteers to vote. Gray described what then followed as "a shameful spectacle."[24] Celebrating their rights, the volunteers marched up and down the streets of Nacogdoches in total disarray, playing what few musical instruments they had and brandishing their weapons for all to see. In the final count, Potter finished fourth in a municipality which had been allotted four delegates.

Convinced that the council's ordinance of December 10 had granted them the rights of full suffrage, volunteers in Refugio and Béxar also showed up at the polls on February 1 only to be turned away. Election officials in both cities rejected the soldier's arguments on the grounds that they were not residents of the municipality. The officials' contended that the election results must reflect the preferences of the citizens living in the municipality. In both instances, responsible officers were present and the volunteers peacefully withdrew.

Alamo head surgeon Dr. Amos Pollard, who trusted Mexicans almost as much as Governor Smith, was certain that the rejection by local election officials was designed to ensure the entire delegation representing the municipality of Béxar would vote against independence. In spite of the fact that he must have known these delegates were not obligated to express the sentiments of the garrison, Pollard insisted that should they deviate from his instructions it would be in their best interest to think twice about returning to Béxar.[25] Pollard was clearly out of line. It should be noted here that republican principles would not have required any delegate to vote in favor of independence.

Like Nacogdoches, Béxar was allocated a total of four delegates. Béxar voters selected Miguel Arciniega, Juan Nepomuceno Seguín, José Francisco Ruiz, and State Senator José Antonio Navarro who were all respected men of experience. While Johnson and Grant, both staunch republicans, were endeavoring to restore the Constitution of 1824, Seguín, Ruiz, and Navarro shared a bolder, far more ambitious vision of the future. Neither Navarro nor Ruiz, the only two who would actually attend the convention, were in any need of lessons on republicanism from Pollard or anybody else. Like Ruiz whose reputation was well established,

Navarro would earn the unequivocal respect of virtually everyone in Texas. Men as republican as Ruiz and Navarro were a rare breed indeed.

While most all of the delegates chosen by the municipalities were local residents, there were a few scattered exceptions. For example, Dr. Junius William Mottley came to Texas in 1835, and in January he was assigned by Houston to the garrison in Goliad. Mottley received more votes in the municipality of Goliad than any other candidate, despite the fact that he did not have an established residence.[26]

Stranger still was the case of candidate Major General Sam Houston. He received the most votes in the municipality of Refugio, the same town where election officials had denied the right to vote to volunteers. No one really knew how his name wound up on the ballot in Refugio since he did not claim to live there, but it is understandable why he was a candidate in the municipality of Nacogdoches. However, the general did not do very well in his home municipality, finishing next to last in a field of seventeen. In the precinct of Nacogdoches where he lived, Houston did even worse and received only a microscopic percentage of the votes.[27]

The question of residency never surfaced in the Red River Municipality where judges went ahead with their election despite not having obtained a response to their petition to have the region broken up into three separate municipalities. On January 27, Red River officials announced the election of five delegates. While all five delegates claimed to be citizens of Arkansas, four lived in Old Miller County. The most unique situation was that of Crockett's friend Sam Carson. Though Carson had only been living in southern Arkansas a little more than two months, he at least had an established residence and plenty of legislative experience. At no time did Carson ever reside on, or even own, land that would eventually become part of Texas.

The municipality of San Augustine, where Crockett seemed certain of being elected, was assigned a total of three delegates. When all of the votes were tallied, Edwin LeGrand, Martin Parmer, and Stephen Blount, had been selected as representatives. The document prepared by San Augustine judges certifying election returns listed the candidates by name and the number of votes received by each. In the final tally, Crockett did not receive one single vote![28] Crockett had been wrong before in predicting the outcome of elections but not even one vote? Since Judge Gaines concurred with Crockett's evaluation of his chances, we may conclude the former congressman's assessment of his chances was not the product of an overactive ego.

Considering his apparent popularity, the fact he did not receive any votes suggests that someone or some group must have challenged Crockett's qualifications to represent San Augustine. While the council's ordinance calling for an election was completely silent as to the qualifications for candidates, it is plausible, judging from the irregularities which had arisen in a number of other municipalities, that any challenge to Crockett's eligibility would almost certainly have been based on the old republican requirement of residency. If this was the case, it would stand to reason that all of the candidates receiving votes would have been resident property owners in the San Augustine Municipality.

Due to a lack of detailed records covering this particular year, it is impossible to say with absolute certainty whether or not all of the candidates were residents of the municipality as of February 1. However, many of the eleven candidates like Robert Kuykendall, David Cunningham, and Jacob Garrett were among San Augustine's earliest settlers. There is indirect evidence indicating that all three men elected to serve as delegates had established residences within the municipality of San Augustine prior to the close of 1835. Therefore, it is highly probable that sometime between his writing to Margaret and election day, Crockett's name must have been removed from the list of eligible candidates.

Property qualifications for candidates had always been far more stringent than for voters in virtually every state of the United States, though these requirements had become more relaxed in recent years. Familiar with the tradition of property requirements for candidates, Crockett would have known from the very beginning that his eligibility as a candidate to represent either a municipality or a garrison of propertyless volunteers was susceptible to dispute. Assuming Crockett had learned of his disqualification prior to leaving east Texas, he would not have been surprised. Ironically, as he was preparing to leave Washington a week before the election, Crockett must have at least suspected that he probably would not even be voting.

A MATTER OF PRIORITIES

It has been alleged that on February 1, Crockett was still "rocking in his saddle" out on the open prairie, one hundred miles east of Béxar. At this point in his journey, Crockett supposedly came to the realization that "his last minute bid for office had crumbled" and was now cornered into remaining with the army. If he wanted a political future in Texas, he had no choice but to continue the journey to Béxar.[29] Long's depiction of Crockett as an egocentric individual confused as to his own identity is an expansion upon the theory promoted by Hauck and Hutton which contends that Crockett willingly pursued his public image and personal ambitions to Béxar and once there "was trapped by his own legend" into remaining with the Alamo garrison.[30] Even if one were to explain Crockett's leisurely excursion through the countryside from Nacogdoches to Béxar by claiming he must have been under the impression that everything was all set in San Augustine, the conclusion would still be the same with regards to the magnitude of his personal interests.

At this time, it is appropriate to assess the validity of the supposition discussed in an earlier chapter which proposes that with his departure from Nacogdoches in mid-January, Crockett implemented his backup plan by embarking upon a quiet campaign in which he searched for a garrison of volunteers to join in order to qualify for candidacy. If Crockett headed south masquerading as a volunteer for the specific purpose of securing a seat for himself at the convention, then he definitely needed to reach a garrison no later than February 1. The best estimation is that Crockett probably left Nacogdoches on either January 15 or 16.[31] But even if he had departed as late as the twentieth, reaching Béxar, Refugio, or Goliad within twelve days would not have posed much of a challenge.

We can be fairly certain that Crockett reached Washington by January 23. Assuming Crockett had left Nacogdoches on either the fifteenth or sixteenth, it would appear that he managed to cover the 125 miles to Washington in approximately seven or eight days.

Moving at a rate of less than twenty miles a day would seem to suggest Crockett felt he had plenty of time to reach his destination. With approximately 160 miles remaining in his journey and eight days before the election, Crockett needed to accelerate the pace a little if he intended to reach Béxar by the first. All indications are that he did not.

Crockett probably left Washington on the twenty-fourth. The next major town was Bastrop, only seventy miles to the southwest. Though the exact date of Crockett's entry into Béxar remains unclear, there is no question he definitely arrived at least several days after the garrison had elected their representatives. Based on his probable time of arrival in Béxar, it is within reason to suppose he may not have even left Bastrop by election day. Over all, it definitely took Crockett more than sixteen days to cover roughly 285 miles on horseback. Not exactly the pace indicative of someone determined to reach their destination by February 1. In conclusion, there was simply nothing about Crockett's behavior during this period that would warrant taking the idea of a hidden agenda beyond the stage of mere speculation.

Certainly, the perception of individual rights has always occupied a prominent place in the American mind. It has been said that Americans of the Jacksonian Era took their rights with them wherever they went. It has also been said that Americans went to Texas to fight for their rights. As confirmation, we have already seen that Captain Sherman's Kentucky Volunteers were not hesitant about fighting for what they perceived to be their rights. And judging from his letter to Margaret, Crockett also seemed confident that by becoming an Auxiliary Volunteer, he too had been accorded the same political rights as the citizen-residents of Texas.

Had the volunteers been permitted to vote by the election officials in Béxar and Refugio, they would have been voting as constituents of a political community. The fact that these same officials prevented the volunteers from voting alongside the citizenry of the municipalities, however, did not necessarily mean they were denying them the right to vote. It just meant they were not going to have a voice in expressing the preferences of the municipality. Once again, the problem came down to a question of residence. In fact, the officers in Béxar admitted that the overwhelming majority of volunteers in the army did not "yet possess any local habitation whatsoever."[32] To compound matters, the council's ordinance recognized the municipalities as the only truly legitimate political communities. This raised more perplexing questions. Assuming they even had the right to vote, did the volunteers, as members of a military unit without a municipality to call home, also have the right to be represented? And if so, who was qualified to represent them?

After having staged elections of their own, officers at both stations wrote letters to convention authorities requesting that their representatives be accepted on equal footing with those of the municipalities. In their letter, the officers in Refugio specifically stated they attached no special significance to the fact that they were in the army. They based their argument on the premise that having been granted the rights of full suffrage by the council's ordinance, all volunteers serving on active duty were instantly elevated to a status commensurate to the citizens of the municipalities, and as such were deserving of "an equal right to Representation."[33] However, in Béxar the officers did base their argument on the fact that they were in military service, contending it was their "duty, . . . to represent the Anglo American and Army interest" at the convention.[34] One of the two delegates elected to represent the Alamo garrison was Jesse B. Badgett, who along with his brother had departed Little Rock for Texas just a few days before Crockett gave his banquet speech.

Delayed in his journey because of illness, Captain Sidney Sherman finally reached Nacogdoches in late January where he rejoined his company of volunteers. Sherman, however, did not immediately resume command of his outfit. Sherman temporarily abdicated his role as leader, thereby allowing a subordinate officer to assume the corresponding responsibilities. In the absence of mature and responsible leadership, Colonel Gray and Judge Hotchkiss stepped in to do what Sherman should have done! In his journal, Gray described what he said to the soldiers:

> I addressed them publicly, and attempted to convince them that by the law of the country and the ordinance under which the Convention was held, they had not the right to vote—or that it was at least a questionable right; that it was unbecoming in them,

coming into the country as soldiers, to be stickling at the threshold for political rights; that it was derogatory to their character to be mingling in the political and personal squabbles of the country, contrary to all the principles of republicanism, and destructive of the freedom of elections for soldiers with arms in their hands to interfere in elections; exhorted them to abstain from violence, reserve their weapons for the enemies of the country, etc.[35]

Gray argued that under the provisions of the council's ordinance authorizing the election, it was far from obvious that they were, as of yet, deserving of any political rights in Texas. But as Gray told the volunteers even if they were entirely correct in their presumptions, their conduct was not only inappropriate it was unethical. In the excitement of the moment and under the influence of self-interested manipulators, the Kentucky Volunteers lost focus. In effect, what the Kentuckians had unintentionally managed to accomplish was to establish the supremacy of rights over duties. But just how far would Crockett, the most famous "Kentuckian" of his day and the politician who once said he would vote to have a road built through a rich man's property if it promoted the general welfare, have pushed the volunteers' rights issue? As a recent arrival and prospective citizen of the future Republic of Texas, would Crockett have viewed the demanding of individual rights as warranted and proper? Would he have considered it the duty of prospective citizens to openly challenge the existing order upon their arrival and conduct themselves in such a manner so as to become an imposition upon the established political community? But, of course, the preservation of individual rights requires constant vigil. This was no less true for the volunteers who made up the garrison in Béxar.

THE LOST PINES

The route Crockett followed from Nacogdoches to Béxar was very similar to the one taken in October by another group of volunteers, the New Orleans Greys. Volunteer Herman Ehrenberg described the open prairies west of Washington as a land of "beauty which no word could depict."[36] Three days out of Washington, Ehrenberg noted that a "rolling country dotted with pines gradually replaced the level land through which we had been traveling since leaving Washington. The pine forests among which we were now riding were tall and dark."[37] The land they had entered was a seventy square mile forest known as the Lost Pines. Separated from the nearest forest of southern pines by one hundred miles of prairies, it is theorized by scientists that this dichotomy in the landscape may have occurred as a result of the Ice Age. Their proximity to the Colorado River might have allowed the pines to survive in a terrain not normally considered hospitable to this type of tree.

The Greys planned to reach Austin's army then besieging Béxar by reconnecting with the Old San Antonio Road. With the sun sinking on the horizon, the trail beneath them seemed to gradually disappear. Pushing on well into the night, Ehrenberg noted the fatigue of both the horses and their riders. Straining their eyes, the riders peered diligently into the darkness for any sign of low hanging branches. After trudging on this way for several hours, they approached the Colorado River. A flicker of lights through the trees revealed the town of Bastrop.

Named by Stephen Austin after Philip Henrick Nering Bogel the Baron of Bastrop, who had assisted Austin in procuring a land grant from the Mexican Government, Bastrop was founded in 1829. The site chosen for the town was actually a favorite fishing spot of several Indian tribes. They also came here to gather pecans from the trees that grew along the river banks and nearby creeks.

This first version of Bastrop consisted of wooden buildings and Spanish-style narrow streets. It is believed that the Old San Antonio Road ran right through Bastrop. It is also believed, though with less certainty, the precise location was on or near what is today Loop 150 and Chestnut Street. Crockett and B. Archer M. Thomas probably intended to pick up the Old Road in Bastrop and follow it into Béxar. But somewhere along the way, probably after leaving the Swisher residence, a more urgent reason for going to Bastrop developed when Crockett damaged one of his rifles.

Mrs. Hannah Berry was living in Bastrop when Crockett passed through either in late January or early February. Hannah came to Texas in 1828 from Louisiana with her parents when her last name was still Devoe. In 1831, she married John Berry who was a gunsmith from Kentucky. Three years later, the couple moved to

Bastrop where he set up shop. When Crockett came to town looking for a gunsmith, he was taken directly to Berry. She even recalled the name of the man who brought Crockett to her husband's shop.

Decades later, historian Andrew Jackson Sowell found Mrs. Berry living in Bandera County, just west of San Antonio. Though she apparently did not give Sowell a detailed description of how Crockett looked, Hannah said she could still picture him in her mind. She did not recall seeing him wearing a coonskin cap.

Hannah recalled the rifle Crockett brought into her husband's shop "had been broken off at the breech." Over the break, Mr. Berry fastened a silver band. Once the band had been polished, Hannah thought this made the rifle most attractive. Impressed with the quality of workmanship, Crockett was said to have commented that the rifle was now in better condition than when it was new. Because of that silver band, Hannah was confident she could recognize that rifle anywhere.[38]

Noah Smithwick was also in Bastrop that winter. He had left his Kentucky home in 1827 for Texas at the age of twenty and never went back. At the age of eighty-nine, Smithwick and his daughter, Nanna, began working on his memoirs. In his book, published in 1900, Smithwick recounted that after having participated in the taking of Béxar, he left the army and rode to Bastrop. It appears from Smithwick's perspective, Crockett was just passing through Bastrop on his way to join the army in Béxar. Smithwick stated, "I was taken down with fever while in Bastrop, but was convalescent when Crockett came on, and wanted to return with him to San Antonio, but, seeing that I was not in condition to do so, he persuaded me to wait for another party to arrive a few days later. But the expected party did not come that route, and there were too many risks for a lone man to start out."[39]

Smithwick's illness was not life threatening, but his youthful enthusiasm was. Some sixty years after the event, Smithwick was able to reflect back on his impetuous urge to fight alongside the famous Davy Crockett and how such an opportunity would have dramatically altered the course of events as he knew them. It was an older, much wiser Noah Smithwick who recalled with some amusement his puerile reaction to hearing the news about the Alamo's fall. "I cursed my ill-luck," he said, for having missed out on all the "fun."[40]

The last leg of Crockett's journey was through the almost one hundred miles of open terrain between Bastrop and Béxar. When future President Rutherford B. Hayes journeyed over this "fine rolling country" in February 1849, he did so at his own leisure. It was in this region that Hayes came across what he called "two of the most beautiful streams I ever saw, the Guadaloupe and the Comal." Of the latter, Hayes described the waters as "so transparent" that the fish appeared to be suspended in midair. Though Hayes would pass through the newly founded town of New Braunfels, the region was still largely unsettled. One day out of San Antonio, Hayes stopped to pick flowers. Like much of his journey through this region, the last thirty-five miles into San Antonio were traversed without any undue concern for his safety.[41]

Anyone contemplating journeying down the Old San Antonio Road through this idyllic pastoral setting toward the great city in early 1836 would not have permitted themselves to be deluded into such a false sense of security. This was Comanche territory. Unable to find a group going to Béxar, Smithwick wisely decided against making the trip alone. While it is certainly possible for Crockett to have picked up a few extra volunteers by the time he was ready to leave Bastrop, it could not have been a considerable number. He clearly had no intention of waiting in Bastrop for the larger group to join him. The New Orleans Greys, a fairly good sized group, managed to make the trip without any problems but not without a great deal of apprehension. Upon leaving Bastrop, the Greys employed extreme caution. Ehrenberg said, "stricter order and keener vigilance prevailed in our ranks; our guns were loaded; and the slightest alarm found us ready against aggression."[42]

9

Fandango in San Antone

ARRIVAL IN THE MARBLE CITY

As late as the mid-1830s, the city of Béxar was still known as San Fernando de Béxar. For much of its first one hundred years, the city that would become San Antonio in 1837 was actually composed of four separate communities. Following European tradition, the San Fernando Church was the centerpiece of the city. Constructed in the shape of a cross, the old church served worshippers for almost 130 years. When the cathedral was erected on this same site in 1868, the builders retained a small segment of history by incorporating the apse of the old church into the new structure. This polygonal section housing the altar of the San Fernando Church is all that remains of the edifice Crockett saw. By the 1830s, what had grown up around the San Fernando Church was a city with a population in excess of two thousand residents. And unlike almost any other community in Texas, San Fernando de Béxar was thoroughly Mexican. Here, Spanish was the only language of consequence.

If eyewitness accounts are to be believed, the descriptions of Béxar, comfortably situated between the San Antonio River and the San Pedro Creek, sound as if they could have been extracted from a storybook. From a distance, the metropolis, which appeared to one observer as a "city of white marble,"[1] projected a romantic image to the weary traveler ready to perceive it as such. The Moresque dome of the San Fernando Church marked a focal point in this majestic panorama as the city's sunbaked structures of white stone formed a clear contrast to their natural surroundings.

At a reasonable pace, the ride from Bastrop to Béxar would have taken at least three or four days. The subject of Crockett's date of arrival in Béxar was briefly touched upon by historian William C. Binkley. Included in the *Official Correspondence of the Texan Revolution, 1835–1836*, a compilation of documents edited by Binkley, is a copy of the resolution from the Alamo petitioning convention authorities to recognize the garrison's request for representation. Unfortunately, the resolution itself was not dated. Since the material in his book was to be arranged chronologically, Binkley's problem was determining just exactly where this document should be placed. It was Binkley's contention that had Crockett been present in Béxar when the request was drafted, we should expect to see his signature at the bottom of the resolution.

Scanning the list of signatures at the end of the article, Binkley found the name of Travis, who reached his assignment on February 3. Neill, the garrison's commander and the first to sign, left the Alamo on February 11. In a footnote, Binkley stated that Crockett "seems to have arrived on February 7th or 8th."[2] Binkley gave no explanation as to how he came up with these dates.

In his letter to the governor dated February 11, Major Green B. Jameson, the Alamo's engineer, wrote, "We are now one hundred and fifty strong Col Crockett and Col Travis both here. . . ."[3] In accordance with Jameson's observation, Dr. John Sutherland later recalled that Crockett arrived "in a few days—less than a week" after Travis.[4] While we still end up dealing with approximates, Crockett could have reached Béxar as early as the fifth but certainly no later than the tenth.

Clearly, something big was going to happen in Béxar. Somewhere along the way, Crockett came up with the idea for a dramatic entry that meant being escorted into the city by its most famous resident. Camped on the west side of the San Pedro Creek near the old cemetery, Crockett sent one of his companions, possibly B. Archer M. Thomas, into Béxar to present his request to James Bowie.[5]

As an eleven-year-old boy, Enrique Esparza spent a lot of his time playing in the Main Plaza. As an elderly man, Esparza would visit San Antonio schools telling children his story of the Alamo. He recalled thinking of the Texians as men who "could do anything," even beat Santa Anna. He also remembered when the man whose legendary image could do just about anything came to Béxar. Esparza explained, "There was great cheering when Señor Crockett came with his friends. He wore a buckskin suit and a coonskin cap. He made everybody laugh and forget their worries. He had a gun he called 'Betsey.' They told me that he had killed many bears. I knew he would kill many of Santa Anna's soldiers."[6]

Albert Pike obviously believed a dictatorship was the appropriate form of government for the Mexican people, but this was not an opinion shared by everyone. Many of the leading families in Béxar, known as *republicanos,* were not only intolerant of Santa Anna but also of the centralist form of republican government as well. In fact, these leading families went beyond merely cooperating with the Anglos; they played a very conspicuous role in securing Texas independence. Family elder Judge Juan Erasmo Seguín who owned a ranch, *Casa Blanca,* about thirty miles southeast of the city, literally fed Austin's army during the Siege of Béxar. His thirty-year-old son, Captain Juan Nepomuceno Seguín, would soon become one of the heroes of the revolution. After being escorted into Béxar by Bowie and his friend Antonio Menchaca, Crockett was conducted to the Seguín residence on Military Plaza. Crockett, Bowie, and the Seguíns were joined by Neill and Travis to discuss the defense of the city.

IN THE ABSENCE OF A PLAN

In October 1835, as Austin's army of amateurs marched across the open prairies toward Béxar confident they could beat the enemy anytime or anyplace, some of the volunteers began to wonder aloud what would happen if the Mexican Cavalry were to suddenly appear on the horizon? And once they had fired their weapons, would they have time to reload? Coping with their newly discovered sense of vulnerability, a feeling which no military instructor could adequately impart to a student, talk of meeting the enemy anytime or anyplace began to quietly subside. Confronting the Mexican Cavalry in the open was a concern that never really went away.

Anticipating a resumption of hostilities, the council placed a purchase order for firearms in late 1835. If the fact they ordered smoothbore muskets by a ratio of two to one over the more advanced rifle is any indication of their thinking, it could be assumed they were preparing for a conventional field confrontation where the emphasis would be on linear formations, mass, and volley. And this is exactly what Santa Anna was hoping for. As General Joaquín Ramírez y Sesma was preparing in December to go to the aid of General Cós, Santa Anna reminded him not to hesitate to form lines if the Texians dared show themselves on an open field. Operating as a cohesive unit under battlefield conditions required strict discipline. Part of the problem was Texians did not like to salute.

Since the open field was not really the preferred option for the Texians, what was left? Employing harassing tactics designed to draw the Mexican Army off the main roads and into the woods could not presume to control the enemy's movements entirely. Assuming such tactics were employed by the Texians, the farming and populated areas would still be left vulnerable. In December 1835, the forts in Béxar and Goliad were still considered to be essential to the defense of Texas.

Ideally, the reduction of a fortified position required an attacking force to cross over open ground, thus exposing themselves to enemy fire. One of the most enthusiastic proponents of acquiring a good defensive position may have been James Bowie. Though outnumbered four to one, Bowie scored a most impressive victory in October 1835 near the Mission Nuestra Señora de la Purisma Concepción.

Under the cover of a dense fog, General Cós proceeded against his entrenched enemy with three hundred cavalry and one hundred infantry. Firing from their protected position, the Texian riflemen deterred the Mexicans from getting within musket range. All three charges were repulsed, resulting in approximately seventy-five casualties before Cós withdrew. Bowie lost only one man.

Although he could have been accused of simply fighting for his hometown, Bowie was thinking on a much larger scale. It was Bowie's contention that without taking Béxar, Santa Anna could not conquer Texas.[7] Less than two weeks later, Governor Smith would hear the same logic again from Travis.[8] This perspective conformed with the old military policy which identified Béxar as the essential component in securing the frontier. First, it was designated as such by the Spanish, then the Mexicans, and now the Texians.

Keeping the war out of one's homeland was certainly a concept Crockett could appreciate.[9] The news Georgie Russel had read about while on board the steamboat, the burning of farms and towns by the Mexican Army, was precisely what the Texians wanted to avert. At the Alamo, they believed that the great battle to prevent this kind of destruction could be staged in the general vicinity of Béxar. But until the citizens of Texas arrived, no specific plan of action could be developed. In the meantime, there were the persistent reports that the Mexican Army was on its way. The Alamo only figured into the plans formed by Neill, Bowie, and Travis as a backup in the event the Centralist Army was to arrive before the Texians.[10]

By 1836, the Alamo's days as a mission was only a distant memory. During Cós's brief occupation of the Alamo in the fall of 1835, several significant improvements were made though not enough to impress Jameson. With the exception of approximately twenty artillery pieces positioned on and within its walls, the Alamo was deficient in virtually every characteristic attributable to a fortified structure. The Spanish, who built the complex, were quite capable of constructing military fortifications that could endure sieges involving heavy artillery bombardment. But then again the Alamo, as Jameson well knew, was not designed as a military fortification.

In the event the Mexican Army was to arrive first, the Alamo, despite its imperfections, represented for the experienced yet untutored Colonel Bowie the perfect "strong hold" from which he could employ the same tactics which had worked so well for him in October. This time, however, expecting to once again be confronted by an overwhelmingly superior force, Bowie would augment his defensive position with the largest assortment of artillery that could be found for hundreds of miles. The equally optimistic Jameson, mesmerized by the Alamo's impressive arsenal, predicted they could hold out even if outnumbered ten to one![11] Bowie's idea was never conceived as a delaying action so Houston would have time to build a regular army nor did it require the annihilation of the Mexican Army. Instead, he must have envisioned a war of attrition, occupying the Centralist Army at the Alamo until the citizens rallied and arrived *en masse*, resulting in the eventual withdrawal of an invading army which had been impaired to the point where it was no longer capable of achieving its objectives.

By February 14, it was evident that the situation was already becoming critical. But historically, republicans have placed little value on opinion polls or seeking approval from the masses before making decisions. While such a habit may represent a heightened level of self-confidence and determination, it also suggests a certain degree of arrogance. Many in Texas tended to view the Centralists as less than authentic republicans. Generally more concerned with quality as opposed to sheer quantity, republicans have repeatedly displayed throughout history few signs of intimidation when faced with the prospect of confronting an enemy of vastly superior numbers. Even Dr. Pollard reflected this attitude when he wrote that once the Centralist Army arrived, they would find out just "how republicans can and will fight."[12]

A Reception in the Plaza

It was a short walk from Seguín's house to the Main Plaza where a crowd had gathered near the San Fernando Church. Some just happened to be there as part of their daily routine, but many were members of the Alamo garrison. They had come to welcome this man who had traveled almost a thousand miles, or so it seemed, just to be with them. But just like the curious folks in Little Rock and every other town along the way, they too were eager to get a look at the man who could "whip his weight in wildcats" and "grin a panther out of the highest tree."

It would be reasonable to assume that Crockett gave a speech in Béxar. Though neither Menchaca nor Esparza mentioned anything about a speech, there was a man in the audience that day in the Main Plaza who lived to write about it. Dr. John Sutherland never really intended to write his version of the Alamo story, but finding a popular account flawed, he decided to set about correcting the perceived inaccuracies. Much of what Sutherland related in his manuscript *The Fall of the Alamo* was said to have come from either personal experience or interviews with other participants. From the time when Sutherland left the Alamo to the time he supposedly began work on his manuscript at the age of sixty-eight, almost a quarter of a century had passed. Ironically, it would not be until the one hundredth anniversary of the fall of the

Alamo, or another seventy-six years, before the manuscript would be published.

Whether in Tennessee or Texas, in the absence of a good tree stump to stand upon, a speaker could always count on obtaining a sturdy box from a nearby civic-minded merchant. There being no tree stumps available in the Main Plaza, Sutherland recalled that Crockett was indeed provided with a goods box. Following an extended round of applause, Sutherland noted that once the crowd settled down into what he described as a "profound silence" Crockett proceeded to entertain them with his unique stories and elicit repeated bursts of laughter from the crowd. Crockett reportedly finished the lighter side of his speech with the story of his last congressional campaign, complete with how he told his constituents where they could all go. By this time, the story had proven itself to be a certified crowd pleaser, and it no doubt went over very well here too. But more important, this story now provided a pivotal point, for it brought him to the subject of why he had traveled such a great distance. Sutherland, who made no pretense of quoting Crockett's final statements verbatim, gave the following rendition of his closing remarks: "And fellow citizens, I am among you. I have come to your country, though not, I hope, through any selfish motive whatever. I have come to aid you all that I can in your noble cause. I shall identify myself with your interests, and all the honor that I desire is that of defending as a high private, in common with my fellow-citizens, the liberties of our common country."[13]

The first line attributed to Crockett is a real attention getter. With these opening words, the crowd must have intuitively sensed Crockett's tone suggested a transition to something of a more serious nature. One can imagine the words "I am among you" being followed by a brief yet expressive pause, which lasted just long enough for the audience to realize that he had indeed changed direction. Enunciated deliberately with great effect, the intended meaning of this statement transcends the obvious aspect of his mere physical presence.

Sutherland was convinced Crockett had won the admiration of the overwhelming majority. "It was vintage Crockett," wrote one historian in the 1980s. With these few words "full of false modesty and common-man symbolism," he instantly became the garrison's "natural, democratic leader."[14] There was nothing immodest about this speech. Despite the absence of recognized political liberties, Crockett spoke to the crowd as equals who understood that only a "noble cause" should distract the citizen from his daily pursuits and draw him onto the field of battle. For his part, he would voluntarily accept the responsibility of leadership at a subaltern level without receiving a corresponding designation as such in an official capacity. Crockett was, in effect, telling the volunteers that he looked forward to roughing it in the field, fighting on the front lines with them, going where he was needed, and would be in the right place at the right time. He was prepared to do whatever it took to get the job done.

The 1936 publication of Dr. John Sutherland's *The Fall of the Alamo* remains the only source for the Crockett speech cited above. In the book's foreword, Annie B. Sutherland explained that her grandfather wrote the manuscript for publication in 1860. Following his death in 1867, the manuscript remained in the family's possession until the 1880s when it was delivered to Colonel John S. Ford, who was preparing a book of his own. When Ford died, the collection of *Ford Papers* containing the manuscript was transferred to the University of Texas Library in Austin.

A view of the old San Fernando Church and the Main Plaza from the east. Courtesy of the Daughters of the Republic of Texas Library.

The Sutherland related material can be found in *Volume I* of John S. Ford's *Memoirs*. This also happens to be the same version which was published in book form in 1936. In preparation for the 1936 centennial, Annie Sutherland stated that she requested, and "secured a copy of the manuscript, practically entire, . . ."[15] While she expressed complete confidence that the manuscript was authentic, some historians are not so sure.

Historian Thomas Ricks Lindley is of the opinion that not only does this book contain errors but that those errors are considerable. In fact, Lindley believes something other than a less-than-perfect memory attempting to recall events a quarter of a century old was responsible for the inaccuracies found therein. Despite containing information to which very few would have been privy such as Sutherland's presence at a certain creek crossing on February 28, 1836, Lindley is convinced *The Fall of the Alamo* is a "bogus" product.

Also located at the University of Texas Library in Austin are the *Amelia W. Williams Papers*. This collection includes an unpublished version of Sutherland's *The Fall of the Alamo*, which contains a greatly abbreviated version of the speech. William C. Davis believes this account is a transcript prepared by Williams from what must have been the original. The original has never been located.

Where did all the additional words come from? From notes Sutherland prepared, which have been lost? Or did Ford find the few words in Sutherland's original account worthy of embellishment? If we compare the speech as presented above with what is found in the Williams transcript, Sutherland seems to have remembered very little. As in the published version, Sutherland recalled Crockett telling the crowd about his famous "go to hell" campaign and other "jolly anecdotes." But as for what was actually said, Sutherland only related that Crockett said, "Me and my Tennessee boys, have come to Help Texas as privates, and will try to do our duty."[16] Here, Crockett spoke not only of himself but also of his friends who were still on their way to Béxar. Even more direct than the longer published version, Crockett clearly focused on responsibilities not rights.

Assuming the speech found in the published version of Sutherland's work was an enhancement, it was a very good effort. The explanation Crockett gave in the Nacogdoches banquet hall as to why he had come to Texas was all in fun; his statement to the citizens of San Augustine was not. It is perfectly believable that the speaker who is said to have addressed the crowd in the plaza as "fellow citizens" was the very same man whose speech in Little Rock was dedicated primarily to Texas independence and who required clarification about the character of the "future government"

Dr. John Sutherland may have left the only account of Crockett giving a speech in the Main Plaza. Courtesy of the Texas State Library and Archives Commission.

before signing the Oath of Allegiance. With his speech in the plaza, whatever its precise words, Crockett may very well have reiterated his dedication to the creation of a Republic of Texas. He also committed himself to this garrison stationed on the Texas frontier.

NIGHT OF THE FANDANGO

Upon reaching Washington, Herbert Simms Kimble learned his squad had pushed on without him five days earlier. Not long after his arrival, Kimble recognized a horse belonging to William I. Lewis. He approached John Lott and inquired as to the whereabouts of its owner. Lott explained he had traded his carryall to Lewis in exchange for the horse.[17] Autry had written Martha earlier commenting how he and his traveling companions hoped to purchase a more suitable means of transportation than having to walk all the time. It would appear their wish was finally realized in Washington.

When Crockett told an ailing Noah Smithwick in Bastrop to wait for the other group to come along, he knew exactly who they were, their destination, and their anticipated route. As of February 11, this second group consisting of eight volunteers was still out on the prairies at the home of John Yancy Criswell.[18]

Almost three weeks had passed since Sutherland arrived in Béxar to find the garrison still impoverished. Some volunteers, unable to see how things could possibly improve, had virtually given up. A significant number of volunteers having received no pay nor provisions of any kind were planning to leave the garrison as soon as their term of enlistment expired. The date of expiration just happened to be February 12.

Antonio Menchaca specifically recalled that a party was given in honor of Crockett. As the member of a prominent family, Menchaca secured the best ballroom and assumed the responsibility of inviting "all the principal ladies in the city."[19] With the party still going strong at one o'clock in the morning of the eleventh, a messenger sent by Placido Benavides, the *Alcalde* of Victoria and now employed by the Seguíns as a spy, arrived at the ballroom requesting to speak with Captain Seguín. When informed by the doorman that

Seguín was not present, the messenger then asked to see Menchaca. The letter presented to Menchaca was brief yet disturbing. According to Benavides, Santa Anna was already on the march toward Béxar with thirteen thousand troops! Of these, three thousand were said to be cavalry.

Menchaca wasted no time in sharing this information with Bowie, who in turn decided to notify the Alamo's ranking regular officer. In relating this story, Menchaca made no mention of Neill at all. Since Neill was scheduled to leave the Alamo on the eleventh, command of the garrison was being passed over to Travis who was in attendance. Bowie found this officer on the dance floor, preoccupied with gentlemanly pursuits. When told that Menchaca had just received an extremely important communication from the Río Grande concerning enemy troop movements, Travis responded by saying he was "dancing with the most beautiful lady" in all of Béxar and did not have time to read letters. Needless to say, this was not the reaction Bowie expected. Possibly a little annoyed by the colonel's response, Bowie told Travis in so many words that he *would* excuse himself and *make* time to read *this* letter! The point well taken, Travis politely excused himself.

Making his way back to Menchaca, Travis asked Crockett if he would join them. The contents of the letter were then discussed by Travis, Bowie, and Menchaca in Spanish. Travis estimated it would take an army of that size approximately two weeks to reach Béxar. With that evening marking the fourth day of the march, this would place the expected date of arrival either on or about February 20, well ahead of Houston's projection. In what was possibly his first decision as commander of the Alamo, Travis concluded that since there was plenty of time to prepare, he would return to the dance floor. The party did not break up until 7:00 A.M.[20]

This communication was the most recent in a long line of intelligence reports received by Alamo officers dating back to mid-December when Johnson was first informed that fifteen hundred Mexican soldiers were on their way to reinforce Cós. After Johnson's inauspicious departure from Béxar, Neill downgraded the size of the invasion force to one thousand. A little more than two weeks later, Neill reported that Bowie had been informed by a local priest sympathetic to the republican cause that only "a few hundred cavalry" were destined for Béxar. This news also shifted the main target to the coastal port of Copano and Goliad. But before another week could pass, the Alamo's commanding officer revised the point of attack and the figures again. An informant brought news of the mobilization of two thousand troops along with detailed information concerning the transport of supplies and equipment, all destined for Béxar. Within days, Bowie wrote to the governor explaining that the two thousand were to be joined by another five thousand! It was in this letter that Bowie went on to say "they intend to make a descent on this place in particular, and there is no doubt of it."[21]

The spies employed by Seguín accomplished their assignment. The officers of the Alamo—Johnson, Neill, Bowie, and Travis—were continually being warned of an impending attack well in advance. The early reports, spanning mid-December through January, consistently placed the size of the attack force at between one and two thousand. These seemed to have been variations or revisions concerning Ramírez y Sesma's preparations to reinforce Cós. But by February, the reports invariably disclosed that a much larger attack force, ranging from two thousand upwards, was on its way. This would indicate that Seguín's spies had discovered the change in plans. That change, made in late December, called not only for the recapture of Béxar but of Texas.

Ramón Músquiz, the elected vice governor of the state of Coahuila y Tejas and now the appointed acting governor, lived with his wife in a large stone house located on the southwest corner of the Main Plaza. When the Texians took control of Béxar, they opened their home to soldiers looking for a place to stay. Captain Almeron Dickinson and his wife Susannah, formerly of Hardeman County, Tennessee, readily accepted a special invitation from Mrs. Músquiz. Mrs. Dickinson prepared meals and washed clothes for other boarders, including Sutherland and Crockett.[22] To pay for his room and board, Crockett needed money and once again he was short of cash. On February 13, Crockett traded the promissory note from the sale of his rifles in Nacogdoches to Dr. Horatio Alsbury in exchange for cash.[23] However, events in Béxar during the first few days of Crockett's arrival were far more significant than these personal activities might imply.

Election Time Again!

February 11 marked Travis's first day as commander of the Alamo garrison. Writing the first of many letters from the Alamo on the following day, he pleaded with Governor Smith, like Neill before him, for money, clothing, supplies, and more troops. In addition to being one month since the collapse of the Provisional Government, February 11 was also the day Acting Governor Robinson and the Advisory Committee formally charged Governor Smith with the crimes of libel, embezzlement, and treason against the people of Texas. The combination of the irrepressible tendencies of legislative bodies to expand their sphere of influence and the predictable resistance offered by the executive branch, another political affliction that concerned James Madison, had completely paralyzed government operations in Texas.

On the twelfth, Robinson issued a lengthy public statement wherein he charged Smith with having attempted "to overturn the Republican features of the government, and erect in its stead absolute DESPOTISM . . . His order to the council to dissolve was not only a despotic usurpation of power, but was the most daring insult on the intelligence and moral virtue of a free people that modern times record." It is the "very nature of a Republican Government," continued Robinson, that a legislative body such as the council should represent the interests of the people. Citing the fact that only Congress has the authority to impeach a president, Robinson then asked, "If the Governor is not answerable to the council, to whom is he answerable?" It was Robinson's position that the question ultimately came down to supporting either Henry Smith or the council and true republicanism. Robinson then compared Smith with the likes of Oliver Cromwell, Napoleon, and of course Santa Anna.[24]

We have no idea if Crockett had the opportunity to read Robinson's diatribe, but one would expect him to have recognized in Governor Smith certain traits reminiscent of President Jackson. While Crockett would have stopped short of condoning the governor's highly publicized threat with regards to carrying on by himself, in effect becoming "the government," he may have nonetheless found that Smith had demonstrated a clarity of vision and determination to pursue the appropriate course of action evidently lacking on the part of Robinson and the council.

Upon his arrival in Béxar, Crockett would have begun to learn the details of a chaotic political situation wherein four men were variously acknowledged by separate factions of the population as the legitimate governor. The civil government was irreparably divided and dysfunctional; the militia was virtually nonexistent; the volunteer army was out of control, thoroughly disorganized, and rupturing; and the regular army was little more than a fantasy. He would have learned beyond any possible doubt that Texas was in a rapid descent toward anarchy. In addition, Crockett would have also been informed that the Mexican Army's prime target was definitely Béxar. We may feel relatively comfortable in the belief that Crockett would have looked to the convention as the means by which to restore political order.

According to Sutherland, it was either before or immediately after the meeting at the Seguín residence that Travis approached Crockett with an offer. We have seen in the published version of the plaza speech that Crockett curiously mentioned that he only wanted to serve as a "high private." Was the crowd expecting an announcement? In the Williams transcript, Sutherland stated, "D. Crockett had been requested to take command but refused at the time of Col Travis accepted."[25] The statement's ambiguity is, however, clarified somewhat in the Ford version where it states, "Crockett was immediately offered a command by Col. Travis."[26]

Irrespective of regular army officers, the absence of cooperation from their own government, and the insurmountable odds presented by the approaching Mexican Army, the Alamo leaders had reiterated their resolve on January 26 in the most explicit terms to defend their post. But within six weeks of the garrison's initial proclamation, the specter of majority rule was taking on an entirely different countenance. No longer conducive to any semblance of order, it had become destructive and Neill's departure created an opportunity for the volunteers to exercise their rights. Consequently, Travis may have been anticipating serious trouble long before the arrival of the Mexican Army.

Travis was disenchanted with his assignment from the very beginning. In fact, Travis threatened to resign his commission while en route to Béxar if his orders were not rescinded. The volunteers at the Alamo happened to be the same men he once referred to as a "mob" and whose explosive capabilities he warned should not be mistaken for dependability. If the volunteers, led by Bowie, were to challenge his authority, the regular army could easily lose control of both the garrison and the fort. Not wanting to aggravate an already strained relationship, Travis concurred with the volunteer's assertion that they had every right to elect a commander of their own; however, they thought they were electing an officer to take charge of the entire garrison. The fact that Travis had been sent by the very governor these volunteers supported was totally irrelevant. Crockett's arrival might have afforded Travis a little leverage.

William C. Davis suggested that a group of volunteers approached Crockett and urged him to run against Bowie in the election.[27] Therefore, it is quite possible Crockett may have been approached by both the volunteers and Travis. In the published version, Sutherland simply indicated that Crockett rejected the proposal. But in the Williams transcript, Sutherland said Crockett answered by saying, "I have come to assist Travis as a high Private."[28] Assuming Crockett was cognizant of the promise of civil elections in the future (and this would probably be an accurate assumption), then this was not the shrewdest response he could have given. What Crockett had done was to openly recognize the regular army as the legitimate authority and to make it clear that he intended to go out of his way to cooperate and support Travis.

When not faced with the immediate prospect of battle, citizen soldiers often felt little compulsion to act as if they belonged to a military unit. When left to reach decisions through their own means, soldiers with young minds frequently experience difficulty distinguishing between lawful authority and self-indulgent intruders. Elections often had the unintended effect of emphasizing rights over duties. The central challenge here for leaders is how to channel youthful energy into constructive behavior. Crockett's public acknowledgment of Travis's authority was actually the most responsible thing he could have said.

Concurrent with the democratic expectations of the age, it was widely presumed that if a man possessed leadership ability, this facility would naturally manifest itself with or without the benefit of an education. Noah Smithwick, who served under Bowie's command at Concepción, described him as a "born leader," a man who was "by nature calculated to be a commander of men."[29] Although Bowie commanded the largest number of volunteers in the Alamo, a duly authorized officer in the regular army had left the next highest ranking officer in charge. Since the Auxiliary Volunteers were specifically designed to assist the regulars, it is almost certain that Crockett did not participate in the voting. As for the volunteers who did vote, they gave Bowie an overwhelming victory.

In a letter dated February 12, Travis seemed ready to take on the Mexican Army, which, he claimed, "threatens to exterminate every white man" within Texas. Understanding that substantial reinforcements were needed in order to successfully confront the enemy, Travis concluded by saying that if the enemy arrived at the Alamo first, then the governor would find him "buried beneath its ruins."[30] Yet one more time Travis asked to be reassigned.

Travis's letter of February 13 to the governor has an even darker tone. What were requests the day before became appeals for mercy. Convinced that only regulars were capable of garrisoning a town, Travis asked the governor to send him "some regular troops." Describing his current predicament as "truly awkward & delicate" he berated the governor for having ignored his earlier request to be reassigned. Closing with a sense of desperation, Travis pleaded "allow me to beg that you will give me definite orders—immediately."[31]

Bowie's election called for a celebration, and that of course required the consumption of liquor. Once under the influence, Bowie proceeded to assume the role of garrison commander. Part of the festivities included the release of prisoners.

In a second letter on the thirteenth to Governor Smith, Travis described Bowie's behavior in the most uncomplimentary terms. Attached to Travis's correspondence were legal documents pertaining to the court martial of Private D. H. Barre of the regular army. Included was "the statement of Col. D. Crockett relative to the release of s'd Barre. . . ."[32] This statement from Crockett, no doubt supporting Travis's version of the story, has long since been lost. Adjutant John J. Baugh went into further detail in his letter of the same date with respect to what he described as "this disgraceful business."[33] He stated that under direct orders from Bowie, Barre was extracted from his jail cell by the corporal of the guard amidst the loud cheers of volunteers.

Another garrison member, Sgt. Antonio Fuentes, was also released. Judge Erasmo Seguín ordered his apprehension and incarceration. When Bowie demanded that Fuentes be freed, Seguín refused. Too intoxicated to think straight, Bowie accepted this as a challenge. Reminiscent of the scene which had been played out in Nacogdoches less than two weeks earlier, Bowie gathered all the volunteers loyal to him and took them into the Main Plaza. There, according to Baugh, they "paraded in the square, under Arms, in a tumultuously and disorderly manner, Bowie, himself, and many of his men, being drunk which has been the case ever since he has been in command."[34]

Only back in December, Baugh was one of six captains who had signed a letter protesting the possible intrusion into the operations of the Federal Volunteers by the regular army. Then, too, it was just a couple of years earlier that Crockett had boasted about having participated in a mutiny against General Jackson, only now to back another authoritarian officer and a regular at that. Such a claim enhanced his public image, but this was the real world. Crockett may have been the garrison's "democratic leader," but it was the democracy of a small highly motivated group of citizen soldiers, many of whom, though not always able to maintain a clear focus, still possessed a strong sense of duty. Their leaders, ever cognizant as to the reason why they were there in the first place, were able to provide proper guidance. It is almost certain that Crockett took part in mediating the compromise reached on February 14. That compromise, however fragile, prevented the garrison from breaking up, thereby preserving the only hope of confining the war to the frontier.

The troubled Alamo garrison was an army in waiting—waiting for their fragmented government to straighten itself out, waiting for their comrades to come join them, and waiting for the enemy. Practically every generation has imagined the Americans of 1776 turning out *en masse* to fight for independence against the king of England. But on the Texas frontier, an exasperated Fannin vented his feelings to Acting Governor Robinson, depicting the behavior thus far displayed by the residents of Texas as bordering on "criminal apathy."[35] Five days later, Travis expressed a similar frustration to Governor Smith, complaining that only the horrors of war could motivate them into action.[36] Both officers knew it was getting late. The one measure Travis regretted the governor had not yet taken and the very measure Fannin was now urging the acting governor to implement as soon as possible was what we would call "the draft."

10

Enter the Napoleon of the West

JUST IN TIME

Several weeks after Crockett left Nacogdoches, William F. Gray embarked upon his own journey down the Old San Antonio Road. Like Crockett, Gray checked into Lott's hotel when he arrived in Washington on Saturday, February 13. "It was a frame house, covered with clapboards, a wretchedly made establishment, and a blackguard, rowdy set lounging about." Not having enough beds, most of the guests slept on the floor. For the evening's supper they were served fried pork, "coarse corn bread and miserable coffee."[1] Lott's breakfast, however, proved to be just a little too much for Gray. "Rose early, took a wretched breakfast of the same coarse and dirty materials that we had last night." Gray had no interest in sampling their lunch. "Left Washington at 10 o'clock. Glad to get out of so disgusting a place."[2]

Awful though it may have been, Gray's stop in Washington was not a total disaster. "I was fortunately lodged on a good cot with a decent Tennessean named Kimball, who is looking for land, but says the state of anarchy is such that he is afraid to buy, and is waiting to see the course of things after the meeting of the Convention."[3] Herbert Simms Kimble was one of the capable and respectable individuals who had sworn allegiance to the Provisional Government and to any future government in Texas, but by mid-January he could see that the risky revolutionary movement against the Centralists was clearly taking on all the characteristics of a lost cause.

At this time, Dr. Horatio Alsbury, who was on his way to Nacogdoches where he intended to procure the means to transport his family and belongings to safety before the arrival of the Mexican Army, stopped over in Washington and happened to meet Kimble. When asked about a small group of volunteers on their way to join the army, Alsbury said that yes, he had passed a group in a carryall shortly after departing Béxar. Two weeks later, another man from Béxar arrived in Washington driving the carryall. Kimble approached the driver and asked him how he came into possession of the buggy. The driver claimed to have purchased it from a group of volunteers who arrived in Béxar sometime around February 21.[4]

Based primarily on Sutherland's account, it has generally been accepted that twelve men followed Crockett into the Alamo and subsequently perished there with him.[5] Antonio Menchaca placed the number of Crockett's group at fourteen.[6] Most current Alamo casualty lists contain eleven names from the group that probably made up Crockett's nebulous squad in Nacogdoches.

The first of the two earliest casualty lists can be found in Gray's journal under the date of March 20, 1836. The second list, compiled by John W. Smith and Gerald Navan, appeared four days later in the *Telegraph & Texas Register*. Although it appeared under a later date, the Smith and Navan list may actually be the earlier of the two. Almost without exception, all of the 112 names on the Smith and Navan list can be found on Gray's. There are, on Gray's list, fifteen clusters of names appearing in the exact same order of sequence as on the Smith and Navan list. In many instances, spellings of names were modified for accuracy. Other details such as first names, initials, residences, and places of origin were added. Gray's list contains a total of 154 names including double entries. These combined factors tend to suggest that Gray's list might be an expansion upon the one compiled by Smith and Navan.

Scanning the Smith and Navan list, one quickly comes across the name of "David Crocket," listed third behind Travis and Bowie. Further examination of this list reveals only one name which has even been remotely associated with the Crockett group, that of Dr. John W. Thompson. However, roughly one-fifth of the forty-two additional entries appearing on Gray's list belong to volunteers associated with Crockett. The fact that seven of the names were grouped together could only suggest that whoever supplied these names to Gray knew these men formed a group. When Gray returned to Washington on February 27, Kimble was still in town.

It is highly probable that most of the volunteers belonging to Crockett's squad whose names are found on Gray's list made it as far as Washington. This may in fact be a list of those whom Kimble was able to verify as having left town for Béxar, as he was certainly informed of the squad's departure and destination. He may have therefore assumed they were all killed at the Alamo. The first name on Gray's list, not found on the Smith and Navan compilation, is that of Micajah Autry. Listed in succession several spaces below Autry are the names of Bailey, Cloud, Lewis, Stockton, Thomas, Bowen, and Bayliss.

Having assumed that every member of the squad who left Washington had died at the Alamo, Kimble no doubt believed that as of March 20, the name of Robert Bowen still belonged on the casualty list. Kimble later heard, probably before the month was out, that Bowen had gone as far as the Colorado River and then turned back.[7] This is interesting because the anonymous "Volunteer of 1836" stated that at some point after having passed through Washington, he and another volunteer became ill and were forced to drop out.

Two other names of interest on Gray's list are to be found several spaces below the main cluster of names belonging to those volunteers associated with Crockett. Both William Ray Gilmer (spelled as "Gilmore") and John W. Thompson are listed without their first names. One of the few to have been entered twice by Gray, Thompson's name can also be found amongst the names of other men of his profession exactly as it appears on the Smith and Navan record.

Since Gilmer and Thompson walked from Nacogdoches to Washington, it is conceivable that an arrival date of sometime in early February is a very real possibility. Gilmer stated in his deposition that his company disbanded about a month after its formation. As Gilmer remembered it, he and Thompson parted company at Washington. Contrary to Gilmer's recollections, his group did not dissolve in Washington but instead turned south toward San Felipe de Austin where, on February 9, they purchased twenty-five pairs of brogans along with assorted clothing. Gilmer and Thompson were among those listed as having received clothing.[8] Perhaps John Lott, the Provisional Government's agent in Washington, had by that time received instructions from the acting governor to redirect all volunteers headed for Béxar back to either Goliad or Copano. Because Gilmer and Thompson had long since left town by the time Gray compiled his list, it is also possible that Kimble simply confirmed their departure and assumed they had both gone off to Béxar.

Like Shackford, historian Skipper Steely came to the conclusion that the William Patton who signed the oath in Nacogdoches was Crockett's nephew. Steely, however, does not agree with the assertion that Patton's name belongs on the Alamo casualty list. Steely points out that the Patton family tradition is apparently unaware of William's continuing on with Crockett down to Nacogdoches. Steely does not necessarily agree with all of the details, but he and the family tradition do concur on one important point: William Patton did not die at the Alamo.[9]

Thus far we have only accounted for seven of the possible twelve or fourteen volunteers who might have accompanied Crockett into the Alamo. Though not listed by Gray, it is generally accepted that William K. Fauntleroy, Dr. John Purdy Reynolds, William McDowell, and Joseph G. Washington were also among those who entered the fort on February 23, thereby leaving room for one to three more volunteers. Aside from being in Nacogdoches during the month of January, no trace of J. E. Massie has ever been found. And as for Crockett's friend Ben McCulloch, he definitely did not make it to the Alamo. But if that which Noah Smithwick remembered Crockett telling him about waiting for "another party" of volunteers to pass through Bastrop was intended to be taken literally, the implications would be that Crockett and Thomas might have already been joined by a number of volunteers, men whose names are for the most part lost forever.

The Alamo's most publicized survivor Mrs. Susannah Dickinson gave testimony that a man named Rose was a boarder at the Músquiz house in the days preceding the Mexican Army's entry into Béxar. She believed that James Madison Rose and Crockett were friends. As best as she could recall, Mrs. Dickinson also believed Rose came to Texas with Crockett specifically for the purpose of fighting in the war.[10] The absence of Rose's signature on any version of the oath suggests he was not with Crockett in Nacogdoches during the first two weeks of January. Rose could have caught up with Crockett at some point south of Nacogdoches. Based on her testimony, James Rose, no matter where he may have joined Crockett, should be counted as the twelfth member of the squad.

The final and complete lineup of Crockett's squad of twelve men, identified as both members of this group and Alamo casualties, fits perfectly with the figure provided by Sutherland—perhaps a little too perfectly. Nonetheless, the arrival of the Autry and Cloud faction in the third week of January reunited the squad for the first time since they departed Nacogdoches. In the Archives Division at the Texas State Library in Austin, Thomas Ricks Lindley discovered two affidavits which demonstrates that the Autry and Cloud group may have reached Béxar a few days before Kimble thought they did. Prepared by Captain Patton, the documents confirm that Cloud and Bailey and probably the entire group were assigned to his command shortly after their arrival.[11] Crockett may have assumed responsibility for the group when Patton left the Alamo sometime around February 19. And though they arrived too late to participate in the all-night party honoring Crockett, they made it just in time for the arrival of the Mexican Army.

SELF-DOUBTS AND OTHER CONCERNS

Sam Houston may have lacked formal military schooling, but he was a war hero. He also had the advantage of having served as a lieutenant in the U.S. Army and as major general of the Tennessee Militia. Like Crockett, Houston had little appreciation for either West Point or the product it turned out. "You might as well take dung-hill fowl's eggs," Noah Smithwick quoted Houston as once saying, "and put them in eagle's nests and try to make eagles of them, as to try to make generals of boys who have no capacity, by giving them military training."[12] We might therefore imagine that Houston was not exactly in awe of Fannin.

Spring was fast approaching and the fact that Fannin, a part-time officer in the regular army and a part-time special agent for the council, had four times as many men under his command than the major general of the regular army did not seem to concern the acting governor or his Advisory Committee. One month after the breakup of the Provisional Government, Henry Smith was still acting as governor. Robinson and his committee were still preoccupied with Matamoros.

By early February, the acting governor and his Advisory Committee found themselves reacting to rumors of an impending invasion. In this uncertain environment, the committee's recommendation to redirect troops away from Béxar was hardly necessary. Citizen soldiers marching through Washington on their way to Béxar were few and far between.

In his second letter to Fannin on the thirteenth, Robinson more or less advised him to go ahead with his plans to fortify both Béxar and Goliad. In addition, Robinson suddenly unloaded this on Fannin that "all former orders given by my predecessor, Gen. Houston or myself, are so far countermanded as to render it compatible to now obey any orders you may deem Expedient." And to lend this new directive a little more authority, Robinson signed this letter as "Acting Governor & Commander in Chief of the Army of Texas."[13] Agonizing over the condition of his army and his own predicament, Fannin spent much of the fourteenth writing to the acting governor. Informed through unofficial sources of General Houston's suspension, Fannin had suddenly discovered himself unworthy of the responsibilities being forced upon him. "I do not desire any command, and particularly that of chief. I feel, I know, if you and the council do not, that I am incompetent. . . ."[14]

But when the Advisory Committee analyzed the latest intelligence regarding Santa Anna's plans, they sent another memo to Robinson on February 16 advising the acting governor "that every effort should be made, to sustain the expedition to Matamoros under the command of Col. Fannin. . . ."[15] What the committee did not know was that as far as Fannin was concerned, the expedition was finished.

Late in the third week of February Blas María Herrera, a relative of the Seguíns, reached Béxar with stunning news. Travis, no longer preoccupied with the most beautiful lady in Béxar, was able to devote the necessary time to listen to this latest report. At an officer's meeting, Herrera related how he personally witnessed the crossing of the Río Grande by an army he estimated to number five thousand. This crossing was made only three days earlier thereby placing the

Mexican Army well ahead of schedule, at least as far as that schedule was perceived by the Texians. Herrera further stated that the Dolores Cavalry intended to break off from the main body and sprint toward Béxar.[16] The meeting inexplicably adjourned without reaching a conclusion as to the appropriate course of action.

Even before the Mexican invasion force would have the opportunity to fire the first shot, it appeared as though Santa Anna's publicity campaign with regards to the Centralist Government's decree authorizing the army to execute all prisoners of war was beginning to work. Colonel Jesse Benton, brother of the Missouri senator, writing to a friend from somewhere near Nacogdoches on February 22 noted, "Official information has just reached us that Santa Anna has crossed the Rio Grande and is marching against us with a large army for the purpose of exterminating us." He also noted that a number of "volunteers have consumed our provisions and a great many have left us—just what I expected." In what was beginning to look like a critical situation, Benton concluded, "If we cannot defend the country in any other way, we can do it effectively by adopting the Russian mode of defence against Napoleon in 1812."[17] At the Alamo, no one had any intentions of retreating.

That same day, the man Travis was counting on for reinforcements sat in Goliad waiting either for orders or someone to come and take charge. Again, Fannin tried to convince Robinson that he was not qualified to command. And once again, he requested to be relieved.

The Advisory Committee continued to push their pet project, the Matamoros Expedition, well into the third week of February. Still languishing in a world of their own on the twenty-second, the committee concluded that the enemy was so far from Texas that there was plenty of time to raise, organize, train, and field an army. But rumors of the Mexican Army's advance continued to reach Béxar. Frightened citizens had already begun leaving town as early as the thirteenth. While the arrival of the remainder of Crockett's friends was encouraging, they were small in number and certainly would have reported that traffic on the road to Béxar was fairly light.

Election returns for the municipality of San Augustine had been certified by the appointed judges on February 2. With only a week remaining before the convention, plenty of time had passed if authorities needed to summon Crockett to Washington. Surely, both civic and military leaders in Washington would have known where he could be found. We have no way of knowing if Crockett ever learned of the election results in San Augustine or of his disqualification. Most likely, he simply heard nothing. At some point, he probably accepted the fact that once again things had not turned as he had hoped. Besides, he had another role to play now.

OPENING SHOT

It had been three months since Crockett passed through Little Rock. In the February 19 issue of the *Advocate*, Pike wrote, "Col. Crockett, with 300 men, has gone into the interior, to hunt buffalo, during the cessation of hostilities." This single line serves as an excellent example of how Crockett's name could inspire the distortion of fact to outrageous proportions. After traveling two hundred miles through a sparsely populated region, Crockett's group of followers had increased exponentially from less than ten to three hundred! Yet, with Crockett involved, the story somehow seemed believable.

In the same issue, Pike reported on the recent political developments in Texas including the schism between the governor and the council and that the "election of members to a Convention to form a system of Government, was held on the 1st inst. . . . Among the candidates were the notorious Robert Potter, and Col. Crockett." Crockett's name was also mentioned in another unrelated article. Since the *Advocate* had recently won the Territorial Government's printing contract, the *Gazette* was now threatening to "demolish" their competitor by accusing them of overcharging. Responding to this threat, Pike wrote, "The *Gazette* withholds the outpourings of its wrath upon us, until next week. If the Editor retains his venom too long, he will be, as Crockett said, 'so full of *pison*, that if he bites himself he'll die.'"

Woodruff shot back at Pike in his February 23 issue. "Mr. Pike has constituted himself the 'guardian of the public crib'—and the way he guards it is a 'sin to Crockett.'" While both editors argued over what they agreed were "small matters," there were major developments down in Texas. On the twenty-third, Houston and Forbes triumphantly sealed a treaty with the thirteen tribes, thus guaranteeing their neutrality during the war. Eight miles out of Béxar, the Dolores Cavalry was breaking camp.

Judging from what little documentation we have, it definitely appears that the Texians were caught off guard, barely escaping into the Alamo. Susannah Dickinson would recall her husband pulling a wagon up to the Músquiz house, shouting for her to get in. María de Jesús Delgado Buquor remembered when word came the Dolores Cavalry had been sighted, Travis and Crockett were at her house visiting with her father.[18] The most comprehensive account of the confusion that morning and early afternoon comes from Sutherland. In a mad rush to leave the city, procrastinators were piling whatever belongings they could into their wagons. Shortly after being posted in the bell tower of the San Fernando Church, a sentry began frantically ringing the bells and shouting that he had seen them! Others went up to see for themselves but saw nothing.

Sutherland told how he and John W. Smith took the Laredo Road south out of Béxar to reconnoiter the area. Ascending a slope, they were shocked to have an unobstructed view of the Dolores Cavalry. Attempting to achieve a full gallop in one step on a slippery surface still wet from the previous night's rain, Sutherland's horse lost traction and pitched him into the mud. Once back in the city, Sutherland and Smith were met by Crockett in the empty Main Plaza. Smith went to take care of his family while Sutherland and Crockett headed straight for the Alamo.

Because of all the excitement, Sutherland only became aware of just how badly he had injured his leg when he attempted to dismount after entering the Alamo. Unable to walk on his own, Crockett assisted Sutherland into Travis's office. When Sutherland finished making his report, Travis asked him to ride to Gonzales and warn the citizens. At the first convenient moment, Crockett, who had not yet left the room, approached Travis and said, "Colonel, here I am. Assign me a position, and I and my twelve boys will try to defend it." Sutherland recalled that Crockett was assigned to the "picket wall extending from the end of the barracks, on the south side, to the corner of the Church."[19] The most interesting aspect of this story is that Crockett reported directly to Travis who was the ranking officer in the regular army for his assignment. Once again, this is exactly what the Auxiliary Volunteers were expected to do—work directly with the regular army.

Encountering no resistance upon their entry into Béxar, the Mexican Army simply marched right in. In fact, they had taken the city as easily as Johnson had talked of taking Matamoros, all without firing a shot. Committed to a plan, however flawed, the Alamo garrison was expecting their comrades to join them in Béxar to fight the great decisive battle of the war with Santa Anna on the frontier. Not having received the expected reinforcements, the garrison withdrew into the Alamo just as they had planned in the event the enemy arrived first. Of course, there was no coordinated strategy. As of February 23, the only group of Texians who had any real concept of what they were doing and why had fortified themselves in the Alamo.

After taking control of Béxar, the Mexican Army hung a red flag from the bell tower of the San Fernando Church signaling they had come prepared to carry out the government's policy. In mutual violation of their February 14 agreement, Travis and Bowie sent their own representatives to speak with officers of the Mexican Army. Watching both messengers as they rode back to the Alamo with basically the same response, the garrison could still see the red flag of no quarter waving in the background. The Mexican Army then turned their attention toward the Alamo. Four days after the opening fusillade, Santa Anna wrote to General Vicente Filisola. He alluded to an initial but brief exchange in which "we lost a corporal and a scout, dead, and eight wounded."[20]

In the early days of the republic, Texians talked about Crockett's performance on the first day. According to the story, a Mexican soldier was seen working in the open two hundred yards from the Alamo's walls without any apparent concern for his safety. Acting on his own volition, Crockett applied a "suitable charge into his rifle," took aim, and then fired.[21] The soldier never heard the blast of sound from Crockett's rifle.

The story of Crockett killing a soldier from a distance is without question very old. In fact, Dr. Joseph E. Field heard this story while stationed at Fort Defiance in Goliad and mentioned the incident in his book *Three Years in Texas*, which was published in 1836. Field, who also cited the distance of the shot at two hundred yards, stated that the soldier fell dead on the peninsula of land near the banks of the San Antonio River. Field added that it was the first casualty of the siege.[22]

Continuing in the same letter mentioned above, Santa Anna further informed Filisola that they were "preparing everything for the assault which will take place when at least the first brigade arrives, which is even now sixty leagues away."[23] What is most revealing in his letter is not only that which Santa Anna omits but what he prefers to conceal even from his second-in-command.

THE TWENTY-FIFTH OF FEBRUARY

The problem of who would actually command the Alamo garrison was resolved on the twenty-fourth when Bowie collapsed from pneumonia. Mrs. Juana Alsbury immediately assumed the responsibility of caring for him. Fearing that his illness might be contagious, Bowie later arranged to be moved to another part of the fort. Some fifty years later, Juana remembered Bowie's reassuring words as he was about to be carried out of his quarters: "Sister, do not be afraid. I leave you with Colonel Travis, Colonel Crockett, and other friends. They are gentlemen and will treat you kindly."[24]

On February 25, a messenger from the Alamo reached Goliad. Fannin reacted decisively. When twenty-two-year-old Captain John Sowers Brooks, formerly of the U.S. Army, learned he was to be part of a 320-man force that would set out for the Alamo the following morning, he sat down to write separate letters to his sister and father back home in the United States. While Brooks explained to his sister that he might be killed in this undertaking, he trusted everything would turn out all right. It was, however, the soldier who wrote to his father. "I frankly confess that without the interposition of Providence, we can not rationally anticipate any other result to our Quixotic expedition than total defeat."[25]

The Alamo garrison's predicament placed Fannin in an extremely difficult situation. Writing to Robinson, this time as an officer in the regular army and as an agent for the Provisional Government, Fannin confessed, "I am well aware that my present movement toward Bexar is any thing but a military one—The appeal of Cols. Travis & Bowie cannot however pass unnoticed. . . ."[26] Such a march might have made some sense back on the sixteenth when Fannin was contemplating moving his headquarters to Béxar, but now? Every soldier in this expedition expected to see the Mexican

Cavalry descending upon them at some point along the ninety-five-mile stretch between Goliad and the Alamo.

In what some consider the most patriotic letter in American history, Travis wrote, "I have sustained a continual Bombardment & cannonade for 24 hours. . . ."[27] The courier who carried that letter, Albert Martin, left the Alamo late on the twenty-fourth. The following day, the thundering of artillery from the direction of the Alamo intensified. Martin scribbled a brief message of his own on the back of Travis's letter saying that because of the "very heavy" artillery fire he had heard all day, he suspected that the Alamo had been assaulted. He was right.

Any Texian looking out over the south wall of the Alamo would have realized, certainly no later than the morning of February 25, that they had a very serious problem. Instead of seeing the ideal clear open field, they had a closeup view of the northernmost expanses of La Villita. Without any building or zoning ordinances to restrict haphazard growth, the village had over the years begun to approach the Alamo's main gate. These peculiar battlefield conditions did not go unnoticed by Santa Anna.

It is not entirely clear as to what exactly happened on the twenty-fourth and twenty-fifth, but accounts tend to agree that most of the action was concentrated in the vicinity of the Alamo's south wall. Where the accounts differ is with regards to the degree of intensity. In reading Colonel Almonte's account, we come away with the impression that not much of anything happened on those two days. Almonte noted their artillery opened up on the Alamo in the early hours of the twenty-fourth, killing four and dislodging two artillery pieces, including the eighteen pounder on the southwest corner. In his last sentence under the twenty-fourth, Almonte mentioned that while the military band performed, their artillery lobbed four grenades into the Alamo just to "entertain the enemy."[28]

Mexican artillery resumed firing early on the morning of February 25. Almonte asserted that infantry from both the Matamoros and Ximenez Battalions advanced across the river. As a result of what Almonte described as "random firing," the colonel listed their casualties as two dead and six wounded, which was lighter than those suffered in the initial skirmishing two days earlier.[29] This sense of limited action was not exactly how one noncommissioned officer in the field remembered those two days.

Upon his release as a prisoner of war, Sergeant Francisco Becerra chose to remain in Texas. According to Becerra, things began to move quickly on the twenty-fourth. That day, two companies advanced within firing range of the Alamo's south wall and "30 were killed within a few minutes." Major General Manuel Fernández Castrillón petitioned Santa Anna for permission to withdraw, which was granted. Becerra said that on the following day, "brisk skirmish fighting occurred . . . and losses were inflicted on the Mexican Army."[30] Becerra's description of the twenty-fourth and twenty-fifth suggests action of a much greater intensity than that reported by Almonte, as do the communications from Travis.

From Travis's vantage point behind the walls of the Alamo, the activities were definitely stepped up on February 25. In fact, Travis mentioned in a letter that the Alamo was attacked twice that day. "You have no doubt seen my official report of the action of the 25th ult. in which we repulsed the enemy with considerable loss; on the night of the 25th they made another attempt to charge us in the rear of the fort, but we received them gallantly by a discharge of grape shot and musquertry, and they took to their scrapers. . . ."[31]

The evening attack was not pressed and was only of brief duration. The first attack however, was far more serious. Below is that portion of Travis's "official report" to General Houston pertaining to the morning's attack as it appeared in the April 19 edition of the *Arkansas Gazette.*

To-day at 10:00 o'clock A.M. some two or three hundred Mexicans crossed the river below, and came up under the cover of the houses, until they arrived within point blank shot, when we opened a heavy discharge of grape and canister on them, together with a well directed fire from small arms, which forced them to halt and take shelter in the houses about 90 or 100 yards from our batteries. The action continued to rage for about two hours, when the enemy retreated in confusion, dragging off some of their dead or wounded. During the action the enemy kept up a constant bombardment and discharge of balls, grape and canister. We know, from actual observation, that many of the enemy were killed and wounded—while we, on our part, have not lost a man. Two or three of our men have been slightly scratched by pieces of rock, but not disabled. I take great pleasure in stating, that both officers and men conducted themselves with firmness and bravery. Lieut. Simmons of cavalry, acting as infantry, and Capts. Carey, Dickinson and Blair, of the artillery, rendered essential services, and Charles Despallier and Robert Brown gallantly sallied out and set fire to the houses which afforded the enemy shelter, in the face of the enemy's fire. Indeed the whole of the men, who were brought into action, conducted themselves with such undaunted heroism, that it would be injustice to discriminate. The Hon. David Crockett was seen at all points, animating the men to do their duty.

The artillery, which required the services of a significant percentage of the garrison, had to perform well if the Alamo were to be successfully defended. Though Travis mentioned the names of individuals rating special merit, he contended that it was actually inappropriate or unfair not to specifically mention the name of everyone who participated in the action. The conduct of the last individual mentioned pleased but probably did not surprise Travis. Crockett assumed a leadership role on the morning of February 25, which went well beyond guiding the men of his squad and beyond the confines of the position he may have been assigned to defend. In spite of the fact he was much older than most in the garrison, Crockett demonstrated a spirited willingness to fight on the front lines, to take the same risks as the lowly private, and to be where he was needed most, in this case at the point where the pressure was greatest. It was not the sharp shooting performer of extraordinary individual feats who deserved special merit; it was the charismatic leader, who inspired and motivated others into action, to perform beyond expectations, and prevail against the odds.

To maintain the advantages he had thus far gained as of the twenty-fifth, Santa Anna needed to keep moving. The heavy exchange of artillery fire and the advance of at least several hundred troops almost to the Alamo's main gate on the morning of the twenty-fifth is indicative of a serious assault. In fact, the twenty-fifth was to be the day the Alamo would fall and Santa Anna, the self-ordained "Napoleon of the West," once believed, if only by himself, to be invincible expected to walk right through the front gate.

11

The Dawning of a Republic

THE CONVENTION BEGINS

By the evening of February 25, the burning of La Villita begun
that morning by Charles Despallier and Robert Brown
remained incomplete. In Goliad, Dr. Field heard reports that
the houses near the Alamo had been set on fire. According to his
sources, the arsonists were Captain Dickinson and Crockett.[1] It is
conceivable that Dickinson and Crockett might have actually led
separate groups in this effort.

Along with other civilians, Mrs. Dickinson was quartered in the
church. If Crockett's squad had taken up their position right outside
the front door of the church as Sutherland asserted, Mrs. Dickinson
would have been afforded numerous opportunities to see Crockett
and James Rose on a daily basis. She recalled overhearing one
particular discussion between Rose and her husband about "a
narrow escape Rose had made from a Mexican officer after that first
attack."[2] For Rose to have come that close to a Mexican soldier
before the morning of March 6, it would have been necessary for him
to leave the confines of the fort. Since Rose and Dickinson would not
have had time to discuss much of anything on the morning of the
sixth, "that first attack" must be a reference to the action on the
morning of February 25.

The intensity of the first three days at the Alamo subsided on
Friday, February 26. In the morning there was a brief skirmish
with the Mexican Cavalry. At night, more huts were burned. The

engagement had now settled down into a siege with both sides waiting for reinforcements. For the Mexicans, there were trenches to be dug and harassing tactics, such as false alarms in the middle of the night, to be employed. Until the additional troops and heavy artillery arrived, the shelling of the Alamo by the light field pieces would continue.

By this time, a diluted version of the story that Edward Warren had heard in Nacogdoches seven to eight weeks earlier about Crockett having been killed on the western plains was now circulating throughout the eastern states. On February 26, subscribers to the *Charleston Courier* read, "A letter has been received in Washington, announcing the death of Col. Crockett, soon after his arrival in Texas." No details were given.

When Gray returned to Washington for the convention on the evening of February 27, he found the town to be in a state of "considerable excitement . . . owning to the news from Bexar." Even less impressed by the quality of people hanging around Washington than he was on his first visit, the arrival of a second call for help from Travis on the twenty-eighth moved Gray to remark in his journal, "Some are going, but the *vile rabble* here cannot be moved."[3] Though most Texians were not exactly sure just what they should do, apathy could no longer reign as king. With Mexican troops back on Texas soil and a small group of Texians trapped inside the Alamo, delegates arriving in Washington had little sympathy for reviving the old Mexican Federation.

In Texas, their American heritage notwithstanding, an abridged system of "checks and balances" had done little to prevent the Provisional Government from depreciating into a burlesque of republican tradition. Frustrated by the Provisional Government's pathetic performance, the people of Texas wanted a change in the personnel to run their new government. Of the sixty-four delegates elected, only eight had ever served on the council for any length of time. And none of Governor Smith's enemies would have a role to play at the convention. Acting Governor Robinson was so soundly defeated in his home municipality of Nacogdoches, he received even fewer votes than Houston. But, unlike Houston, no other municipality seemed to want him.

Robinson and Governor Smith, the other principal member of the ineffective Provisional Government, were both scheduled to make appearances at the convention. As part of the transition from the old temporary government to the new, both men were expected to deliver whatever documents they might have in their possession. Robinson arrived first. Though coming in the spirit of cooperation, he was largely ignored. Smith also arrived and was his usual combative self. The people of Texas may have generally favored him over Robinson and the council, but they sensed he was not the right man to lead a new republic.

Convinced that rallying to the aid of the Alamo would prevent the war from reaching the colonies, Governor Smith issued a circular calling upon all Texians to do their duty without delay. In a letter addressed to Houston "Wherever he may be," Acting Governor Robinson asked the general to call upon all able-bodied Texians to report for active duty immediately. All politics aside, Robinson recommended that Houston invoke the name of whichever political authority might elicit the desired response. When Houston finally emerged from seemingly out of nowhere, Gray could not help but notice how differently he was received from all the other delegates. A man of "courtly manners,"[4] he was seen as a capable individual who could form and lead an army.

Within days, news of the February 25 assaults reached New Orleans where it was reported that Santa Anna "demanded a surrender of the fort held by 150 Texans, and on the refusal, he attempted to storm the fort, twice, with his whole force, but was repelled with the loss of 500 men, and the Americans lost none."[5] Though the report was basically correct, some of the figures mentioned, such as Santa Anna already having thirty-five hundred troops in Béxar and the casualties suffered, were overblown. The dissemination of this information had bypassed Washington, momentarily leaving convention delegates unaware that the Alamo had been attacked.

Approximately two-thirds of the convention delegates managed to make it to Washington by March 1. Robert Potter was the only one of the four representatives from Nacogdoches to show up on time. If anyone had an excuse for being late, it would have been the delegation from Old Miller County. Three-fifths of the delegation, including

Collin McKinney, were present for the first meeting. Albert Latimer arrived the following day. Sam Carson was still out on the road.

One of the first topics the convention dealt with was the election of officers. The cautious Herbert Simms Kimble, still waiting to see how things were going to turn out, was selected to serve as secretary of the convention. Perhaps he would now find the answers he sought.

On the second day, the convention turned to dealing with two pressing issues. Several gentlemen appeared before the convention whose status as delegates was in question. Amongst those requesting permission to participate was Jesse Badgett from the Alamo. What man sitting in Convention Hall would have denied equal status to Jesse Badgett as a delegate? Who was going to deny representation to the men in the Alamo? In an all-encompassing move, the convention would eventually settle the matter by declaring that the mere physical presence in Texas of any man meeting the criteria for voting rights automatically guaranteed him full suffrage accorded to citizens.

Also on the second day, committee chair George Childress presented the draft of a formal Declaration of Independence. Representative Houston made a speech urging its adoption. Approval was almost instantaneous. To be certain, much was accomplished in the first two days. Far from the field of action, Texians finally seemed to be moving harmoniously in the same direction. By March 2, the war had acquired a stated political objective—independence from Mexico. As the convention was declaring independence, John Sowers Brooks wrote his mother about the latest from the Alamo. "The Mexicans have made two successive attacks on the Alamo in both of which the gallant little garrison repulsed them with some loss. Probably Davy Crockett 'grinned' them off."[6] That evening, Gray wrote that there was more news from the Alamo:

> An express was this evening received from Col. Travis, stating that on the 25th a demonstration was made on the Alamo by a party of Mexicans of about 300, who, under cover of some old houses, approached within eighty yards of the fort, while a cannonade was kept up from the city. They were beaten off with some loss, and amidst the engagement some Texan soldiers set fire and destroyed

the old houses. Only three Texans were wounded, none killed. Col. Fannin was on the march from Goliad with 350 men for the aid of Travis. This, with the other forces known to be on the way, will by this time make the number in the fort some six or seven hundred. It is believed the Alamo is safe.[7]

And thus ran the logic; as long as the Alamo held on, the convention had nothing to fear.

DIMLY, THROUGH THE HAZE

According to Travis, the Alamo garrison had a total of 150 men when the siege began. Add to that number the 30 men from Gonzales who entered the fort on March 1 and we get a total of 180. The body count taken by Béxar civil authorities on the morning of March 6 totaled exactly 183. But precise figures have always been difficult concerning the Alamo. The first published Alamo casualty list was acknowledged to be incomplete even before it came out. When Amelia Williams began her work in the late 1920s of verifying the garrison's personnel, most lists in existence already comprised between 180 and 188 names. By including 11 additional names labeled as either "probable" or "possible" casualties, Williams as much as admitted that her "verifiable" list of 187 should not be thought of as final. Slightly higher is the list maintained by the Daughters of the Republic of Texas, which currently numbers 189.

At variance with the figure reached by the Béxar authorities are several estimates tallied by other sources. Sutherland calculated the total number of soldiers in the Alamo at 206. Mrs. Dickinson placed the size of the garrison between 210 and 220. Whereas Texans and later historians such as Williams concentrated on confirming the names of approximately 183 defenders, tallies taken by the Mexican Army routinely eclipsed this figure, usually in the 250 range. Their highest count placed the number at 257.

Regarding the size of the garrison in its final configuration, the lack of detailed records will almost certainly prohibit a complete and accurate casualty list from ever being assembled. However, Thomas Ricks Lindley has compiled a list of thirty names which he believes should be added to the Alamo register. Lindley's research has led him to the conclusion that the figures reported by Mexican officers are not contrived but more accurately reflects the actual size of the garrison as of the morning of March 6. To account for most of the difference between the list of verified names and the Mexican figures, Lindley proposes that a second long forgotten group of reinforcements entered the Alamo after March 1. While he writes that the evidence supporting such a theory is far from conclusive and "only portrays the event as if seen through a thick fog," it is nonetheless a possibility well worth examining.[8]

For his study, Lindley has been researching the names of those currently listed as Alamo casualties for clues. From that list, he found the names of fourteen men who had not yet joined the garrison as of February 1. Unfortunately, Lindley has not been able to determine where three of the fourteen men were during that month. In the cases of two others, he has found possible connections with the garrison at Goliad though nothing solid. He has, however, confirmed that eight were members of Fannin's command in February and that two of those were still in Goliad as of the twenty-ninth. This information alone would suggest the possibility of a second group of reinforcements entering the Alamo after March 1. The last name remaining on Lindley's list is that of Dr. John W. Thompson. There has never been an explanation plausible or otherwise as to how or when he reached the Alamo.[9]

That Thompson was killed at the Alamo has never been in question. Thompson's name appeared on the very first Alamo casualty list even though the compilers neither listed nor knew the names of anyone else associated with either Crockett or Gilmer. Gilmer mentioned several of his former comrades confirmed that Thompson had been killed at the Alamo. Considering his last conversation with Thompson, Gilmer saw no reason to doubt what he had been told.[10]

Gilmer stated twice in his Tennessee deposition that Thompson was killed "with Crocket." Regarding their last conversation, Gilmer was quoted as saying, "Thomson said he was going from Washington, as far west as Crocket went—He was going to Crocket, and then with him and he started with that view."[11] It has been previously shown that Thompson did not depart from Washington to join Crockett. So when and under what circumstances did Thompson and Gilmer part company? And since Thompson could not possibly have reached the

Alamo in February with either Crockett or the Autry and Cloud group, when and with whom did he enter the Alamo?

One may recall that Gilmer is the man who also remembered taking a boat ride down the Mississippi along with Crockett and Thompson in the fall of 1835. But in July 1837, two men appeared before the Board of Land Commissioners in Bexar County to bare witness to the fact that they had both seen Crockett in Texas prior to March 2, 1836. One witness was Béxar resident Ambrosio Rodríguez.

Lindley found no evidence in his research to indicate that the second witness, Gonzales resident Dr. Alonzo B. Sweitzer, was even near Béxar during the early months of 1836. Since Crockett went through Bastrop on his way to Béxar, he would have crossed the San Marcos River miles above

Widowed at the Alamo, Mrs. Susannah Dickinson Hannig survived with her infant daughter. Her testimonies regarding the Alamo always seemed somewhat inconsistent. Her account of Crockett entering the Alamo only three days before the end was never taken seriously by historians. Courtesy of the Texas State Library Archives and Commission.

Gonzales. If Crockett did not pass through Gonzales and Sweitzer did not go to Béxar, there seems little possibility given the limited amount of time involved of the two men ever meeting.[12] While the argument could be made that Rodríguez probably saw Crockett in Béxar if not in the Alamo, we have no such explanation for Sweitzer's claim. The strange recollections do not end there.

In late February, three brothers James, Edward, and William Taylor saddled up to ride to the Alamo. Days later at the Cíbolo Creek Crossing, they promised their brother George Taylor that in the event of their deaths, he would be deeded any and all property awarded for services rendered as volunteers in the Gonzales Mounted Rangers. A document was supposedly prepared in the presence of three eyewitnesses, George's six-year-old son J. C., an

One of Travis's messengers, Benjamin Highsmith, returned to report back to his commanding officer, but from his hilltop vantage point overlooking the Alamo, he could see that the fort was completely surrounded. Concluding it would be foolish for him to attempt to reenter the Alamo, Highsmith turned back when he saw Mexican Cavalry approaching. His unusual account of Crockett's entry into the Alamo differed substantially with the popular version. From Early Settlers and Indian Fighters of Southwest Texas *by Andrew Jackson Sowell.*

uncle, and Crockett. What Lindley found so fascinating about this document was the date—March 3, 1836.

In 1890, J. C. Taylor prepared an affidavit wherein he claimed to have personally witnessed the execution of the deed. In his affidavit, J. C. flatly stated, "I saw old Mr. Davy Crockett make his cross mark in the middle of his name after uncle James Taylor wrote his name[.]" J. C. claimed that Crockett was so ill at the time, he was unable to sit up in bed to sign his name.[13] Presumably, we are expected to believe that Crockett, unable to muster up enough strength to sign his name on the third, somehow managed to recover sufficiently to ride forty-plus miles back to the Alamo in time to participate in the final battle, all within seventy-two hours!

Here in the Taylor-Cíbolo Creek deed, we have a definite claim, albeit problematic, that Crockett was seen outside of the Alamo after the siege began. Even if the document is a fake, it is nonetheless strange that anyone would still claim in 1890 to have seen Crockett miles from the Alamo in March 1836. Is it possible that Travis would have sent him out as a messenger while there were others capable of performing this duty? There are the statements of two individuals directly associated with the Alamo which tend to support the theory that Crockett left the fort during the siege. These two statements, though in existence for more than one hundred years, do not fit comfortably into the standard Alamo story and, as a result, have largely been ignored.

In 1876, Mrs. Dickinson told the adjutant general of Texas that three spies entered the Alamo approximately three days before the final attack. Later, in the same interview, she identified one of those spies as Crockett.[14] We might surmise Mrs. Dickinson had the distinct impression Crockett left the Alamo for a specific reason and returned three days before the final assault with two men she knew were also members of the garrison. Judging from her statements, it would appear that she remembered Crockett as having been absent from the fort in terms of days not hours. In light of her claim about Crockett being a spy, we now come to the statement left by another Alamo participant. This explanation not only gives us a plausible idea as to why he might have left the fort but with whom he may have returned.

In 1897, Texas historian Andrew Jackson Sowell interviewed eighty-year-old Benjamin Highsmith. He told Sowell that Crockett entered the Alamo with George C. Kimble, George Washington Cottle, Jacob C. Darst, Galba Fugua, John E. Gaston, Thomas Jackson, Andrew Kent, and Tom Mitchell. Highsmith was well acquainted with Kimble, Cottle, Darst, and Jackson.[15] The problem here is that none of the eight men named by Highsmith were even remotely affiliated with the individuals who formed Crockett's squad in Nacogdoches.

Highsmith, who left either as a messenger sometime around February 18 or during the first days of the siege, almost certainly would have known his friends from Gonzales had not accompanied Crockett into Béxar. It is also highly probable that Highsmith would have been cognizant of the fact that these same friends had not sought refuge within the walls on February 23. Knowing this, why would Highsmith claim that Crockett entered the Alamo with these eight men, none of whom were anywhere near Béxar when the siege began? In addition, Lindley has pointed out that at least seven of the eight men named by Highsmith are generally believed to have entered the Alamo as part of the Gonzales Mounted Rangers on March 1.[16] By linking Crockett's entry into the Alamo with members of the Gonzales Mounted Rangers, Highsmith might have been alluding to his return to the fort.

Lindley has put together a number of fragmented, almost cryptic statements, coming from different sources, which suggest that at some point during the siege Crockett left the Alamo. First, there are the sworn statements of Ambrosio Rodríguez and Dr. Alonzo Sweitzer who both claimed to have seen Crockett in Texas either on or before March 2. According to Sweitzer's account, there are no clear indications as to when or where this contact might have occurred. J. C. Taylor placed Crockett and members of the Gonzales Mounted Rangers at the Cíbolo Creek on the date of March 3. While it has been established that Thompson was in San Felipe de Austin early in the second week of February just as Crockett was entering Béxar, Gilmer would later recall that his friend left the company for the specific purpose of joining the famous frontiersman. Ben Highsmith recalled that Crockett entered the Alamo with a number of men who belonged to the Gonzales Mounted Rangers. And finally, there is the statement from Mrs. Dickinson who claimed Crockett entered the fort three days before the final assault.

THROUGH THE THRESHOLD

While Crockett probably would have been in agreement with the overall strategy of attempting to confine the war to the frontier, it should be recalled that moving into the Alamo was a last resort. Crockett no doubt thought back to 1814 when he watched Creek Warriors barricade themselves inside a house during the Battle of Tallusahatchee, only to have their cover set on fire. He may have also remembered making the forced march to successfully relieve the besieged Fort Talladega.[17] Confining oneself to defending a particular ground has its disadvantages and these experiences, described in his autobiography two decades after the fact, were lessons worth remembering.

If Crockett suspected the withdrawal into the confines of the Alamo to be a move offering no appealing options, he was heard saying as much once inside. Mrs. Dickinson stated she overheard Crockett say on several occasions during the course of the siege, "I think we had better march out and die in the open air. I don't like to be hemmed up."[18] There is, to be certain, frustration expressed in this statement. Yet at the same time, there is also a certain degree of acceptance. From his point of view, the Alamo was clearly an untenable position and unless something dramatic or extraordinary was done to drastically alter the existing disparities, there could only be but one outcome.

Herman Ehrenberg, who was one of the few in Fannin's command to survive the war, claimed Fannin received separate letters from

Travis, Bowie, and Crockett urging him to send reinforcements to the Alamo.[19] If true, this would indicate that Crockett was actively engaged in the attempt to procure reinforcements for the Alamo. However, it is Lindley's contention that Crockett's efforts in this area went far beyond writing letters. Anyone who felt that certain death awaited inside the Alamo was definitely a candidate to go on a mission to procure reinforcements. If we are unable to imagine the inexperienced Travis sending Crockett out to procure reinforcements for the Alamo, perhaps we are better able to imagine Crockett, a man of experience, not asking for permission but telling his commanding officer he was going out!

As of February 25, Crockett was definitely still in the Alamo. Any departure from the fortifications must have occurred between that date and March 2. He would have returned on about the third or fourth but certainly no later than the fifth. And if Crockett did in fact leave the Alamo, his mission may not have taken him any further than the Cíbolo Creek Crossing. Flowing eastward, roughly twenty-five miles north of the Alamo, the Cíbolo Creek makes an abrupt turn and runs south until it intersects with the San Antonio River, which parallels the Old San Antonio-LaBahía Road into Goliad. Lindley asserts it was here at this junction about forty-five miles east of Béxar where the old road crosses the creek, that a small group of Texians including Doctors Sweitzer and Sutherland began congregating on February 28 to wait for Fannin.

In 1987, Lindley discovered the copy of a letter written by Major Robert M. Williamson of Gonzales who was the commanding officer of the Texian Ranging Companies. In fact, what Lindley had actually found was the copy of a translation of Williamson's letter. Lindley theorizes that the original, dated March 1, 1836, was delivered to Travis by James Bonham on March 3 and confiscated three days later by the Mexican Army. After being translated into Spanish, the original was subsequently lost or destroyed. Lindley arranged to have the Spanish version translated into English by Professor Jesús F. de la Teja.[20] Two interesting facts were revealed, one rather startling.

First, Williamson informed Travis that approximately three hundred men led by Colonel John A. Wharton were expected to converge on Gonzales later that evening and another three hundred were on the march from Goliad. Second, Williamson assured Travis of the following: "Sixty men have left this municipality, who in all probability are with you by this date."[21] As for the projected time of arrival, Williamson was correct. What he did not know was that only half had actually reached the Alamo. Lindley believes the second half of the Gonzales group, under the command of Lt. Thomas Jackson, made their way to the Cíbolo Creek Crossing by March 1.[22]

Fannin had dispatched his commissary officer Captain Francis de Sauque to Judge Seguín's *hacienda* to procure provisions. Accompanying Sauque was a small detachment led by Captain John Chenoweth. In addition to the Gonzales Rangers and Captain Juan Seguín's Company, Crockett would have found Daniel Murphy, whose name appears under William Patton's on the Oath of Allegiance, and Dr. John W. Thompson, both of Captain Chenoweth's detachment.

Fannin's move toward the Alamo did not remain much of a secret very long. On February 28, Santa Anna received a report that approximately two hundred troops had departed Goliad for the Alamo. As midnight approached on the twenty-ninth, Ramírez y Sesma quietly left camp with the Dolores Cavalry. Finding no sign of Fannin, the cavalry returned to camp the following day.[23] Fannin then sent word to Sauque and Chenoweth of his decision to abandon his march and return to Fort Defiance. Thinking that Wharton might pass near the Cíbolo Creek Crossing, Fannin wrote, "if informed speedily I will push out 200 and cooperate."[24] Fannin's letter could have reached Cíbolo Creek as early as the morning of March 3.

By this time, Fannin was already aware that General José Urrea and eighty cavalry had mopped up Johnson's detachment of thirty-seven men with no losses at San Patricio. One of the casualties was Albert Pike's former partner at the *Advocate*, Charles E. Rice. Grant was somewhere out on the prairies south of Goliad still harboring dreams of capturing Matamoros and unaware he was being hunted.

On March 2, Urrea found Grant and forty mounted riflemen in an open prairie near a place called Agua Dulce. According to one report, Grant's detachment was "cut to pieces." Several men were taken prisoner, but the rest were killed. Confronting the Mexican Cavalry out in the open whether on foot or on horseback represented for the Texians the absolute worst case scenario.

The addition of almost five hundred troops would have gone a long way toward making the Alamo defensible. But with Fannin back where he started and Wharton's forces still several days march from their destination, the possibility of any reinforcements reaching the Alamo in time was certainly in doubt. Worse yet, such a combined force would be moving on foot. Fannin could conceivably find himself caught out in the open by Ramírez y Sesma's calvary approaching from the west and Urrea's cavalry pursuing them from the southeast. But even if the volunteers who were assembling at the Cíbolo Creek Crossing, which in total did not exceed one hundred, could actually make it into the Alamo, then what? Would it make a difference?

Maybe the thought crossed Crockett's mind while at Cíbolo Creek that he was safe and in the clear. Perhaps, but his return to the Alamo may not have been an academic question or a matter of personal safety. It may have been one of those situations in life where there really was not much to think about.

Assuming this event or something analogous to it actually occurred, we might well imagine that Crockett's reentry into the Alamo could not have been accomplished with the same ease as the entry of the first group of rangers. When George C. Kimble and his group reached the Alamo at 3:00 A.M. on the morning of March 1, the siege lines surrounding the fort had been thinned out by the absence of the Dolores Cavalry. By March 3, the cavalry would have been back on patrol around the Alamo.[25] Any attempt to reinforce the Alamo either on March 3 or thereafter would have almost certainly been confronted by the cavalry, even if the approach was made under the cover of darkness.

Travis's last surviving letter was dated March 3. James Allen, believed to have been the last messenger to leave the Alamo, departed late on the fifth and arrived in Goliad three days later. Whatever information Allen related upon his arrival must have been subjected to the usual distortion process. A survey of letters coming out of Fort Defiance following Allen's arrival indicates an awareness on the part of the rank and file that reinforcements had indeed reached the Alamo. On March 10, letters from Brooks and Joseph B. Tatom only mentioned one group of reinforcements reaching the Alamo. Brooks wrote, "Thirty-two men have cut their way into the Alamo, with some provisions."[26] Tatom informed his sister that the reinforcements numbered "about fifty," which according to his calculations brought the total number of troops in the Alamo to exactly two hundred.[27] There is plenty of room for speculation as to why Fannin did not seem to know anything about reinforcements reaching the Alamo.[28]

The fact that Brooks and Tatom had different figures for the reinforcements would not be anything out of the ordinary. However, it is interesting that Tatom thought the figure was closer to fifty, and Brooks understood that the only group of reinforcements had to fight their way into the Alamo. To further complicate matters, Lindley has discovered another most significant document. Two witnesses stated in an affidavit prepared by Colonel Edwin Morehouse that John T. Ballard was a member of Captain Kimble's Company of Gonzales Mounted Rangers and "having been cut off by the same enemies spies from the Fort Alamo was the cause of his being separated from his immediate officer. . . ."[29] This document certainly implies that a group of reinforcements from Gonzales encountered opposition in their attempt to gain entry into the Alamo. Remember Travis, who is an excellent source of information, stated unequivocally in his letter of the third that the group which entered the fort on the morning of March 1 did so "without molestation."[30] But then, too, the thirty men who entered that morning with Albert Martin and John W. Smith accounts for only half the number Williamson reported had departed Gonzales for the Alamo. Perhaps the second half of Gonzales's reinforcements augmented by assorted volunteers at the Cíbolo Creek Crossing reached the Alamo with Crockett after Travis had written his letter on the third.

If Crockett did in fact make a daring attempt to bring reinforcements into the Alamo, there would have been a small number of people who knew firsthand that such an event had taken place. The overwhelming majority of these people perished on the morning of March 6. Given the lack of firsthand knowledge having been committed to print, there are only the fragments of broken memories. Admitting that hard evidence supporting his theory simply does not exist, Lindley's theory remains at this point conjectural.

One final thought about the possible second group of reinforcements. When Richard Penn Smith was preparing his thoroughly fictitious work, he did so confident that Crockett reached Béxar long before Santa Anna's army. Had Smith been a subscriber to the *Arkansas Gazette*, he might have presented this aspect of his story a little differently. Neatly tucked away amongst the various reports of fact and rumor in his April 12 edition, Woodruff inserted a single yet curious piece of information. "Col. Crockett, with about 50 resolute volunteers, had cut their way into the garrison, through the Mexican troops, only a few days before the fall of San Antonio."

ONE SUNDAY MORNING

In Washington, clerks were instructed to produce five copies of the Declaration of Independence, one of which was to be sent to the Alamo. More than any other group, the soldiers of the Alamo deserved to know that independence had in fact been declared. On March 3, Travis wrote the following to Jesse Grimes:

> Let the Convention go on and make a declaration of independence, and we will then understand, and the world will understand, what we are fighting for. If independence is not declared, I shall lay down my arms, and so will the men under my command. But under the flag of independence, we are ready to peril our lives a hundred times a day, and to drive away the monster who is fighting us under a bloodred flag, threatening to murder all prisoners and make Texas a waste desert.[31]

Sending Travis a copy of the declaration was certainly a thoughtful gesture, but who was going to make the delivery to the Alamo?

It is believed that sometime during the afternoon of the fifth, Santa Anna decided he could wait no more. Why he made such a sudden decision remains something of a mystery, but Dr. Field recalled one rumor in circulation at Fort Defiance. According to the story, Santa Anna decided to go out and make his own reconnaissance at what he believed to be a safe distance. Spotting a most attractive target, Crockett took a shot at him and just barely missed. Santa Anna, ruffled feathers and all, decided right then and there to put an end to this nonsense the very next morning.[32] There would be no climactic barrage to pulverize the enemy position and no breech in the walls by which to gain entry. Ultimately, resistance would be subdued with the bayonet.

Over the course of the siege, the garrison's morale would have fluctuated and peaked with the successes of the twenty-fifth. Thereafter, hope would have begun to diminish a little with each passing day. There would have been a brief resurgence of optimism on occasion, but as it became obvious that the only truly significant reinforcements were for the Mexican Army, all hope would plummet to its nadir. Once a soldier begins to suspect his government is not doing all it can or that the support of his countrymen is nothing more than a product of his imagination, maintaining morale truly becomes a challenge.

For the combat soldier, staged diversions of any type offer indispensable relief from one's reality. Crockett probably told his share of tall tales from the backwoods and the halls of Congress. For her grandchildren, Mrs. Dickinson imitated Crockett's lively performances on his violin during the lulls in activity. Mrs. Susan Sterling recalled for Amelia Williams one story her grandmother used to tell about Crockett's courtyard concerts. Periodically, Crockett would be joined by John McGregor, a native of Scotland, and the owner of a set of bagpipes. As an unrehearsed segment of their jam session Crockett and McGregor engaged in musical contests, each challenging the other to produce the loudest and most dissonant sounds their instruments were capable of making.[33] Inharmonious tones are more often than not viewed as distracting, but at the Alamo they must have been a most welcome distraction.

In addition to soldiers, there were also a number of women and children in the fort. Enrique Esparza remembered that Crockett reserved some of his antics for the children: "Señor Crockett seemed everywhere. He would shoot from the wall or through the portholes. Then he would run back and say something funny. He tried to speak Spanish sometimes. Now and then he would run to the fire we had in the courtyard where we were to make us laugh."[34] Crockett's stories, jokes, and music were only to help alleviate tension, not camouflage reality.

As late as March 3, Travis was still convinced that Béxar could be the site of the "great and decisive battle ground" of the war,[35] but it would have required more than a Herculean effort on the part of the

Texians to lift the siege. Some two or three thousand enemy troops arrived on March 3. The Texians' hope that their fight at the Alamo would hold the line until their comrades arrived to halt the Mexican Army's advance, thus confining the war to the frontier, was becoming increasingly improbable. It was beginning to appear that within days, the Mexican Army would again be on the move to wage war upon the very people the men of the Alamo sought to protect.

As to why their countrymen had not rallied to the "standard," that was a question each individual soldier had to deal with as a matter of faith. And yet no matter how much faith the Alamo soldiers might have placed in their fellow Texians, the feeling or suspicion that they had been abandoned could never have been completely suppressed. More than anyone else, the men of the Alamo had reason to think of Texas as a lost cause. If their adopted country did not care about them, they had certainly demonstrated how much they cared about their new country!

At the convention, all available information indicated the Mexican Army was bogged down at the Alamo, 150 miles to the southwest. Fannin, who had left Goliad for the Alamo almost seven days earlier, must surely be there by now. With the Alamo reinforced, Santa Anna was going nowhere. And all over the country, Texians were mobilizing for war.

On Friday, March 4, Houston's nomination for the position of commander-in-chief of the army was opposed, not surprisingly, by the tireless Robert Potter. At the close of Friday's session, it was decided to take the weekend off. After all, as long as the Alamo held on, the convention and Texas were safe.

Distant flashes on the horizon illuminated the Sunday morning sky as the reverberation of the Alamo's thunder rumbled across the prairies. Too far away to see or hear any of what was happening at the Alamo, it was about this time that members of the convention were awakened and called to an emergency session: Travis's letter of the third had just arrived. Delegates as well as townsfolk gathered in and around Convention Hall to hear the letter read aloud. This was when the convention first became aware of the fact that Fannin never made it to the Alamo. In the ensuing confusion, Potter proposed the convention promptly adjourn and without further delay go to the aid of the Alamo. This proposal was met with what must have seemed like the unanimous approval of everyone present. At what might have been the convention's most crucial moment, Houston rose to speak and urged the delegates to remain and complete what needed to be done. As the commander-in-chief, he would assemble the forces of Texas and take the field.

Even by the time Travis's letter was being read, it was all over at the Alamo. Santa Anna gave civil authorities the job of locating for him the bodies of three men. The positive identification of these three bodies was important enough for him to mention in his official battle report to the secretary of war: "Among the dead are the first and second enemy commanders, Bowie and Travis. Colonels they were. Of the same rank was Crockett."[36]

Among the citizens who entered the fort that morning to assist the wounded were Señor Candelaria, husband of the famous Madam Candelaria, and Eulalia Yorba. Although Eulalia never found the words adequate to express her experience, she could never erase from her memory the scenes of horror she saw inside the Alamo. That morning, Eulalia noticed the body of someone she recognized. "I remember seeing poor old Colonel Davy Crockett as he lay dead by the side of a dying man, whose bloody and powder-stained face I was washing." She recalled that Crockett's shirt and coat were so saturated with blood, its original color was no longer discernible.[37]

Santa Anna gave specific orders for the disposing of the bodies of the rebel force. The Alameda, the eastern road from Béxar flanked on both sides by rows of cottonwood trees, was selected as the cremation site. Two funeral pyres were built, one on each side of the road. The bodies were placed in alternating layers on wood cut from a nearby forest and then drenched with flammable liquids. At five in the afternoon, the work of extermination entered its final phase. Nothing was to remain of the rebels.

12

In Remembrance

CONCLUSIONS: AN ACCOUNTING

B y the time Travis's comment about two hundred artillery shells pounding the Alamo had circulated amongst the rank and file at Goliad, the figure had literally exploded! This and other awe-inspiring news enticed private John Cross to believe that the Mexican Army was suffering severe losses on a daily basis.[1] In what he imagined to be the heroic effort still going on at the Alamo, Evan M. Thomas wrote: "Davy Crockett and James Bowie are fighting like Tigers 200 Americans are in the fort against 5,000 troops and Santa Ana at the head the fort is the strongest in the world they have thrown 2,000 bums and not kild a single American but 3 wounded 1,800 mexicans are Laying on the field Dead[.]"[2]

Beginning on the twelfth and continuing through the four-teenth, Gray wrote, "No intelligence yet from the Alamo." On the thirteenth, he added, "The anxiety begins to be intense."[3] But once the destruction of the Alamo garrison was finally confirmed beyond all reasonable doubt on the fifteenth, Gray noted that the overall conduct of convention members descended to an undigni-fied level. Rumor spread amongst the delegates that the Mexican Cavalry had crossed the Colorado River unopposed. Houston, who had promised to place himself and his army between the enemy and the convention, was said to be in full retreat. After hurriedly creating a new political state on March 17, the convention hastily finished. "The members are now dispersing in all directions, with haste and in confusion. A general panic seems to have seized them," Gray observed.[4]

Evacuating Washington in company with Jesse Badgett and Herbert Simms Kimble, Gray indicated that Kimble had seen enough. He was going home, "disgusted with Texas."[5] Gray, Badgett, and Kimble were at Groce's Landing when Travis's slave, Joe, was interviewed by members of the New Provisional Government on March 20. Gray quoted Joe as saying, "Crockett and a few of his friends were found together, with twenty-four of the enemy dead around them."[6] The next day, Badgett caught the Old San Antonio Road north into Nacogdoches.

On March 24, Gail Borden of the *Telegraph & Texas Register* referred to the Alamo as "the Thermopylae of Texas." With all of Texas in a state of panic, Borden described the deaths of Travis and Bowie in heroic terms, but in a brief eulogy to Crockett he resorted to transfigurative language. According to one report which preceded Badgett into Nacogdoches, the entire Alamo garrison had surrendered and was then murdered! But when Badgett left Nacogdoches for Jonesboro on March 25, local citizens could only think of the Alamo in terms of Greek martyrdom. A town meeting held the following day resulted in a resolution which proclaimed, "Thermopylae is no longer without parallel." They added, "David Crocket (now rendered immortal in Glory) had fortified himself with sixteen guns well charged, and a monument of slain foes encompasses his lifeless body."[7]

Within days of Edward Warren's New Year's Day letter materializing in the March 19 edition of the *Bangor Advertiser*,[8] newspapers across the United States were soon scrambling to correct reports of Crockett's death printed a month earlier. The *Morning Courier and New York Enquirer*, which initially expressed doubt as to the validity of the story, happily reported that Crockett was "still alive and grinning."[9] Readers in Charleston first learned about "fort Alamo" on the twenty-sixth when the *Courier* published a somewhat distorted report of the February 25 assault. General Cós had presumably led four thousand soldiers against the Alamo, but "was completely defeated and routed, with the loss of 500 of his best troops," after which he promptly retreated from Texas. While forming the foundation for public perception of a great victory at the Alamo, this electrifying report would soon be superseded by news that was utterly shocking. Three days later, the *Courier* printed the latest news from out west: "*Davy Crockett not dead.*—We are happy to state, on the authority of a letter from Tennessee, that the report of the death of the eccentric Davy Crockett, is not true. 'He started (says the letter) on a hunting expedition to the Rocky Mountains, and then dropped down into Texas; but we expect him home early in the spring.'"

As the above report was circulating throughout the United States, several New Orleans newspapers ran stories announcing that an execution had taken place at the Alamo. As news of the Alamo made its way to the U.S. border, much of the information was altered or embellished. Historian Bill Groneman has pointed out that despite wild variations in the details, the reports agreed that all of the fort's defenders were killed.[10]

On April 7, a letter was written on board a Mississippi River schooner loaded with Texas refugees fleeing from the advancing Mexican Army. While updating his recipient of the recent news, the writer mentioned the destruction of the Alamo garrison. "Davy Crockett was among the number. He had fully sustained his great character for intrepidity during an unsuccessful attempt of the enemy to storm the Alamo, just one week before the massacre."[11]

Again, on April 7, a Miller County resident wrote to Albert Pike in Little Rock. After announcing, "the Hon. David Crockett is no more," the letter stated that he had killed twenty-three Mexican soldiers. It went on to state that "after the massacre he was found with the breech of his gun broke off, and it grasped by the muzzle in his left hand, and his butcher knife in his right. Both told a tale of death—for they were bathed in the blood of his enemies."[12] By now, Crockett's name had become inseparably associated with a tragic event that was in the process of being classified as one of the great heroic fights in history.

Woodruff's April 12 edition was the first newspaper in Little Rock to provide residents with details of the disaster. Much of the information appearing on the front page was derived from the New Orleans newspapers. However, Badgett's arrival in Little Rock on the tenth gave Woodruff an edge over Pike. Woodruff quickly interviewed Badgett, the substance of that conversation appearing on page two of the *Gazette's* publication under the headline "Latest From Texas." While rectifying errors which appeared in previous reports, Badgett told Woodruff that after Travis was killed, command fell to Captain Baugh. Following Baugh's demise in the second hour of fighting, Badgett explained that command then descended to Crockett, "who likewise soon fell." While this transfer of authority could never have been substantiated, Badgett's account certainly informed Little Rock readers how Texians viewed Crockett's ranking in the Alamo chain of command.

IMAGES OF OUR OWN REFLECTIONS

Responding to the dramatic news about Crockett and the Alamo, Carey and Hart saw an opportunity to unload their overstock of the tedious *Tour* book, thus contributing to correct the misconception that the backwoodsman needed to be caged. It was, however, *Exploits*, which along with the *Narrative* provided the literary basis for securing the kind of balance Crockett had desired for his public image. Historian William Bedford Clark theorized that Richard Penn Smith had molded the David of history, the most popular figure amongst a small group of "disparate adventurers" who had been "elevated to the status of martyrs to the cause of Texas independence and United States expansionism," into the "sanitized" Col. David Crockett of *Exploits*, a gentleman of the forest and an image which would eventually serve as a model for the popular western.[13]

Before the 1830s were over, the Crockett legend had taken a headfirst dive into what historian Daniel J. Boorstin called "the great democratic world of print."[14] The image of the barbaric and some-times cannibalistic Crockett as celebrated in the *Davy Crockett Almanacs* gained ascendancy in the 1840s, while James Hackett carried on with his stage show portraying the boisterous but good-natured Colonel Nimrod Wildfire well into the 1850s. Hackett may have looked a little older, but Wildfire, frozen in time like a cellu-loid image, never matured. Everyone probably suspected that Wildfire would have gone to the Alamo if given the opportunity; everyone knew that Crockett actually did.

The authority of the written word was again reinforced by the moving image when in 1874, Frank Mayo gave his first performance

Elizabeth Crockett was eventually able to fulfill David's wish when she moved to Texas with their son, Robert Patton Crockett. Above is the authorization to draw on the designated special account for payment due to Mrs. Crockett for services rendered by her husband. The authorization was signed by state auditor, John Milton Swisher. Courtesy of the Texas State Library Archives and Commission.

in the play "Davy Crockett; Or, Be Sure You're Right, Then Go Ahead." For that particular generation of Americans, Mayo was Davy Crockett. This version of Crockett shared many of the traits possessed by Wildfire, except he was obviously more domesticated. Only on rare occasion would Crockett's public image ever again descend to the depths of barbarism.

As the baby boom generation watched Disney's version of Crockett, America was in the early stages of an ideological transformation. A new generation of social scientists were discovering that good societies are really created by the infinite anonymous masses of common people and not by great leaders. Labor unions denounced Crockett as an individualist, a man who did not belong in the lonely crowd, and thus an inappropriate image for the adulation of American children. By the mid-1960s, America was struggling to maintain a correlation between reality and the old values. Ideologically motivated to rewrite history with an expanding democratic flare, we began to discover a need to apologize for our past. To disparage Washington, Jefferson, or some other constituent in the American pantheon of heroes as a hypocrite or worse was one thing, but after the assaults on Crockett's personal character by the aristocratic Vernon L. Parrington and the liberal reactionaries of the mid-1950s, some historians must have recognized the potential for embarrassment by being too critical of the historical man. As Arthur M. Schlesinger Jr. pointed out, Crockett may have been a "phony," but he was nonetheless "authentically of the people."[15]

Eyewitness accounts of Crockett's execution at the Alamo resurfaced at a time when contrarian theories, often masked with conceited hostility, were paraded as forbidden truth before an America developing a guilt-ridden conscience. The Alamo was supposedly the one battle, which perhaps more than any other, exemplified America's dedication to the concept of liberty. But no matter how much we may rationalize the disparity in the odds at the moment of capitulation or the undeniably perfectly reasonable acceptance of the Mexican officer's humanitarian gesture, the story of Crockett's surrender and execution suggests the absence of the kind of tenacious resistance we expect from the *King of the Wild Frontier*.

Like Walter Blair, Richard Boyd Hauck found the mutations of the legendary Davy Crockett far more interesting than the historical David Crockett. Vigorously promoting the theory which Shackford had fought so hard to discredit, Hauck contended that the Crockett who actually lived and died is unknowable to us. Separated by space and time, it is Davy who constitutes for us the essential reality. A dynamic pliable abstraction, Davy is a Jungian archetype onto which is projected the popular values and desires of each generation.[16] As both the antihero and the hero, Davy has the capacity "to be nearly all things to all people."[17] In a culture governed by a presumed law of moral relativity, one image is just as valid as the next.

Denying that the "new perspectives" embraced any of the features associated with debunking, Hauck blamed the disciplined minds of Shackford and Folmsbee for the denigration of the legendary Crockett.[18] Within the quantum-like framework of post-modern thought, Hauck could think of the historical Crockett as a common man who possessed an uncommon style, a self-reliant "fierce individualist" whose sense of moral virtue prevented him from becoming a successful politician. To him, Crockett's individualism was driven by an almost juvenile impulse, the main purpose of which was to simply defy authority.[19] Paul Andrew Hutton concurred, declaring that Crockett "was just too independent, and too honest to be a congressman, much less president."[20] But whereas Hauck stressed Crockett's "militant individualism," Hutton emphasized Crockett's relevance as a symbol of egalitarianism.

When asked by the *Texas Monthly* to write an article about Crockett during what many nostalgically view as the high tide of political conservatism, Hutton was a little apprehensive: "How could I write an article that would prove appealing in a cynical age of media hype that produced wretched, violent heroes like Rambo? The essential decency of the real Crockett, as well as the Davy of my youth, would never play in 1986. Davy was too unburdened by psychosis and overburdened with decency, too hateful of violence and loving of peace, and far too caring for the underprivileged to sell as a hero in the era of Reagan. He was a truly admirable human being, well worth our admiration."[21] The extravagant accolades went unnoticed by those who thought Hutton had gone too far when he staunchly defended the story of Crockett's surrender and execution. While affirming that he nonetheless died heroically, Hutton argued that the real Crockett could not possibly have been killed in a manner such as imagined by those who watched Fess Parker in that closing scene. According to Hutton, it would have been out of character.[22] In the apparent attempt to endow Crockett with certain Gandhi-like sensitivities, Hutton clearly overstated his case here. The Alamo was a tough place to be for anyone with such an intense aversion to violence.

Crockett's "essential decency" may very well have been more believable during the Eisenhower Era. But conventional wisdom now contends that an entire generation of American children had been duped by Disney into believing Crockett went to Texas to fight for freedom. We should know and understand that heroes are not born but manufactured and marketed just like any other product. With the emphasis placed here on the individual, we may rest assured that at the Alamo, Crockett "fell in defense of his vision of freedom."[23] Greater than the sum of his egalitarian merits, he was and is for the pop culture mind set a celebration of the self.

There was a time when Crockett was seen as a natural proponent for the liberal ideology embodied in Jacksonian Democracy. In recent years however, it was the conservative element which has moved so aggressively to safeguard Crockett's heroic image as though he were a religious icon. Adherents of the "new perspectives" conceded that Crockett was a hero, however, they believed that the traditionalists had reached the correct conclusion for all wrong reasons.[24] But what Hauck and especially Hutton seemed to be saying is that as one of the pioneers who explored the spiritual frontier of democracy, post-modern liberals have every reason to reclaim Crockett as one of their own. Mark Derr, for example, insisted that Crockett was not merely representative of the common people, he was the "'original' common man."[25] Hutton was even more emphatic, asserting that having fought for "human rights," particularly those of the "underprivileged and dispossessed," Crockett "represented the pure spirit of American democracy. . . ."[26] The fact that Crockett continues to be portrayed as symbolic of the "common man" should only serve to facilitate the transition. Yet there remains that one hurdle which forever frustrates and confounds the postmodern democratization of the Crockett image, and that is reconciling the apparent inconsistency of his political record as a human rights activist and his voluntary participation in the Texas Revolution.

IN THE LIKENESS OF IMAGES PAST

Possibly inspired by Rousseau's proclamation that human beings are born in a natural state of freedom, the traditional view is to see Crockett as a child of nature, a mythical descendant of Adamic inno-cence who, uncorrupted by the demoralizing influences of society, matured into adulthood free of the neurotic disorders symptomatic of urban dwellers. Reviewing *Exploits* in 1839, a London magazine concluded that Crockett could only have been a product of both the western frontier of America and democracy,[27] in effect, freedom and equality. It is now generally agreed that social environment and particularly cultural conditioning have a profound impact on an individual's development. While Tocqueville postulated that the ultimate effect of democracy was to isolate each individual from his class, family, and friends, Crockett lived his entire life knowing next to nothing about his family's history. The twentieth century's expansive maelstrom of radical environmentalism left no room for Crockett's biological parents or his ancestors. Having grown up deprived of the influences Featherstonhaugh and Jefferson considered absolutely essential to the formation of good character, many who knew Crockett personally were left with the unmistakable impression that he never lived up to his potential. In reality, Crockett's place of birth and the socially and economically deprived environment into which he was born and matured did little to prepare him for his entry into society or the career he ultimately pursued.

We live in an epoch of liberalism. Its influence is pervasive. Currently dominating the commercial high ground of pop culture, postmodern liberalism glorifies the perceived rights of the individual above all else and promises that the maximization of freedom will amply suffice as a substitute for moral virtue. There is a scene in the movie *The Alamo* where John Wayne's Crockett confesses to Travis that he likes the sound of the word "republic." Almost as if anticipating the philosophy of Harold J. Laski, Crockett proceeded to define a republic as a place where the individual is basically free from social restraint or coercion. People, he explained, were at liberty to say what they thought and go where they wanted, intoxicated or not. Of course, the audience, already familiar with the Crockett legend, expected Wayne's character to do more than simply respond to natural impulses. Not surprisingly, in a social environment where the individual is imagined to be supreme, the corresponding rights of other individuals invariably tend to rank a distant second. The public's well-being does not necessarily even rate consideration.

The American pioneer has frequently been perceived by the popular imagination as a rugged individualist. However, Daniel J. Boorstin maintained that the settlement of the frontiers was actually forged by groups and not solitary individuals. Boorstin pointed out that the individuals who led these groups were not simply men of individual accomplishment but men with an extraordinary ability to organize, manage, and persuade people to work together under extremely difficult circumstances. Boorstin cited two examples of pioneer leadership. The first was Daniel Boone, and the second, despite his faults, was "Davy Crockett."[28]

The Texas Revolution, as with any war, provided certain individuals with unparalleled opportunities to exert their leadership abilities. Travis's respect for the man was obvious, but in 1902 an elderly Enrique Esparza described the extent of Crockett's role at the Alamo by saying, "He was always at the head."[29] Five years later, Enrique elaborated further: "Crockett seemed to be the leading spirit. He was everywhere. He went to every exposed point and personally directed the fighting. Travis was chief in command, but he depended more upon the judgement of Crockett and that brave man's intrepidity than upon his own."[30] Even if we were to assume that the words attributed to Esparza, words which bordered on hero worship, had been coaxed or tampered with, this is nonetheless a statement which has the credibility of realism in a world where only a small percentage of the global population possesses true leadership abilities. If Crockett did, in fact, assume command of a fractured garrison in those final chaotic moments, it is exactly what would have been expected of him.

Addressing the government of the Republic of Texas on April 26, 1836, Colonel William H. Wharton spoke of those who had died "in defence of the great principle of human liberty" at the Alamo. Restricting himself by respectfully paying homage to each of the garrison's four most prominent leaders, Wharton spoke of Crockett, a man whom he admittedly knew only by reputation: "Of Col. David Crocket, it is unnecessary here to speak. He was known, at least by character, to all of us. Suffice it to say, that although the world has been often amused with his innocent eccentricities, no one has ever denied to him, the character of a firm and honest man—qualities which would cancel ten thousand faults if he has them."[31] It was obvious to Wharton that the popular stories depicting Crockett as a free spirited, irresponsible individual were absurd. Wharton's audience understood that men whose panoramic vision of the world was limited to what affected their personal and immediate concerns do not, as a general rule, suddenly convert themselves into responsible citizens. Crockett was not seen as worthy of their respect because he was imperfect like everyone else but because he had his republican priorities in proper order.

During a resurgence in the late nineteenth century of stories depicting Crockett as a primitive, Dr. S. H. Stout of Texas felt compelled to write an article refuting these perceptions. Gathering information in preparation for his article, Dr. Stout wrote to Captain William L. Foster, asking for his recollections of the man. William's father was Ephraim Hubbard Foster, a former governor and senator of Tennessee, and a personal friend of Crockett's.

> I remember David Crockett well and always with pleasure. He was very often a guest of my father, always a pleasant, courteous and interesting man, who, though uneducated in books, was a man of fine instincts and intellect, and entertained a laudable ambition to make his mark in the world. He was a man of a high sense of honor, of good morals, not intemperate in drinking, nor a gambler. I never saw him attired in a garb that could be regarded as differing from that worn by gentlemen of his day—never in a coon skin cap or hunting shirt.[32]

Foster knew the Crockett who went to Texas was a gentleman.

Reinterpreting Crockett's expedition to Texas for late twentieth century Americans, historian Stephen L. Hardin synthesized ideals from the old and new ways of thinking. Hardin explained that Crockett "traveled hundreds of miles from his home to fight—and if necessary die—for the promise of a new life for himself and his family. Those were, in themselves, the actions of a heroic gentleman."[33] In a social climate where motives limited to the individual's personal interests can be interpreted as heroic, Hardin still managed to elevate Crockett's motives beyond the totally self-indulgent. The ideal of being "other directed," a quality past generations of Americans had come to expect from their heroes, is totally absent here.

Throughout western society, gentlemanly behavior has always suggested adherence to a higher, more rigid standard of conduct than what is expected of the majority. With the "rise of the common man," there came virtue in mediocrity. Though hardly a candidate for sainthood, David Crockett was never too honest to be a congressman or a president of the United States. But if Crockett is to be seen as the "pure spirit of democracy" by those of us who have found reassurance in the fact that George Washington could tell a lie, we might feel inclined to emphasize that he was a man and like any other man he had doubts, made less than perfect decisions, and did not always behave in accordance with his own principles. And yet, Hauck suspected that like Benjamin Franklin, an authentic product of the Enlightenment and another imperfect individual whose personal exploits have received plenty of publicity, the real Crockett "generally" placed the public good ahead of his personal interests.[34] Such behavior has never been nor can it now be considered typical of the majority of people.

THERMOPYLAE AND BEYOND

In 1834, Crockett visited the battlefield at Bunker Hill. Reflecting upon the blessings of liberty, Crockett said, "I resolved on that holy ground, as I had done elsewhere, to go for my country, always and everywhere." After quoting this passage from *Tour*, one historian noted a century later that Crockett did indeed remain true to that pledge.[35] But did he really? Had not Crockett given up on the United States? So, how should Americans understand Crockett's patriotism?

As details of events in Texas reached the United States in April 1836, the Alamo instantly acquired an aura of mythical proportions in the mind of the American public. Almost since the beginning of the siege, Texians equated the Alamo with Thermopylae. In fact, it was Travis who suggested the analogy. Once besieged by Mexican forces, he began concluding his correspondences from the Alamo with the closing, *"Victory or Death."* Any Spartan would have understood.

Upon learning the tragic news from Béxar, General Houston reached back to the classical age of heroes when he wrote, "The conduct of our brave men in the Alamo was only equalled by Spartan valor."[36] Denoting unfailing devotion, the word "Spartan" has always been synonymous with patriotism. In Sparta, children were rigorously trained to be totally devoted to their city-state. At Thermopylae, Spartans died in defense of Sparta and all of Greece.

The American flag did not fly at the Alamo during the famous siege, but in a sense it may as well have. Travis's most famous letter was not only addressed "To The People of Texas," but to "all Americans in the world." As more details of what actually happened became available to him, Houston improved upon the ideal of "Spartan valor" by writing, "There was not a man in the Alamo, but what, in his death, honored the proud name of an American."[37] Houston understood that according to American ideals, patriotism meant more than just being loyal to your home and the land of your parents; it meant being devoted to certain abstract political and philosophical principles. As we have seen, it was Houston who called upon Americans in the United States to come to Texas and defend the constitutional rights of the inhabitants, and when it appeared that the Texians were losing focus it was Houston who insisted the war must remain a war based on principles. Viewed within this context, a war based on principles, Crockett's involvement with the Texas Revolution should really not be all that surprising.

When Crockett started on his journey to Texas, his immediate concerns were personal. Those concerns soon expanded. When Crockett took the Oath of Allegiance, he voluntarily entered into a social contract with fellow citizens, who, in order to form a new political association for the expressed purpose of securing their rights to liberty, were willing to relinquish their freedom to do as they pleased. One could hardly categorize this as the act of a self-interested person.

Crockett's objection to the imprecise wording of the oath was not empty melodrama. His self-designated rank of "high private," a ranking unknown to the world perhaps, but one which demonstrated an awareness of his own limitations, also acknowledged the necessity for hierarchy. Despite Crockett's past tirades against West Point and the regular military, he supported Travis, the properly designated military authority, against the populist will of the volunteers. Better than anyone else, Crockett, who was there as he said to do his duty, knew the Alamo was no place for ordinary "individualism" or any of its more "militant" manifestations.

It was only with the approach of the Mexican Army that Richard Penn Smith permitted Crockett the luxury of dating his entries so he could at least pretend that the end product had once been a journal. Though he did not have access to Travis's letter of March 3, Smith correctly speculated that liberty remained very much on Crockett's mind. Under the date of March 2, Smith made it appear as if Crockett knew the Constitutional Convention was meeting that very day "to frame our Declaration of Independence." In a barrage replete with Aristotelian disdain, the writer expressed his contempt for individual liberty coupled with unlimited latitude. "Such independence," he wrote, "is the worst of tyranny." On March 5, he had Crockett make one final, dramatic entry. With no more time for writing and bombs bursting all around him, he hurriedly scrawled, "Go ahead! Liberty and independence forever!"[38]

David Crockett's "vision of freedom" was one of political liberty. A number of thinkers down through the ages, beginning with Aristotle, have thought of political liberty as a distinctly unique form of freedom which cannot be understood in terms of individualism, but only from within the framework of a republican community. Originally published during the apex of Jacksonian Democracy, Smith's portrayal of Colonel David Crockett as the ultimate freedom fighter lent relevancy to *Exploits*. Such a description of the man today would be much too small in scope and much too superficial to reflect the David of history. *Exploits* was a work of deception, but it was a deception which its real author knew had to be reflective of its subject.

It would appear to some that without proper guidance, even Americans can lose the facility to understand why their patriots were once considered heroic. Political Science scholar Walter Berns has pointed out that the average person simply is "not naturally inclined to be a patriotic citizen." And in fact, Berns went even further by asserting that the average person "is not *naturally* inclined to be a citizen of any sort."[39] Patriotism, Berns concluded, must be "cultivated" through a sustained curriculum in our nation's schools.[40] Somehow, and somewhere along the way, Crockett managed to acquire an elevated sense of public-spiritedness and patriotism. Clearly, Smith felt the Crockett worth remembering was not the individual who had his moment of transcendental self-realization in the Arkansas wilderness, but the David of history who dedicated himself, fought and subsequently died, to establish a better republic for Texas.

Given the level of priority society has presently assigned to individual rights and equality, there really is not very much for the postmodern liberal mind to find admirable about Crockett in Texas. It was, after all, upon the "altar of manifest destiny" that Crockett supposedly suffered martyrdom.[41] Scholars of the new paradigm may be correct to assert the projected image of the Davy of legend can be used to gauge the mind-set of the people. But should we realistically expect the "new perspectives" to tell us anything about the historical Crockett? In the runaway universe of postmodern liberalism—where the mere utterance of the word "democracy" with its expansive assortment of vulgarities and excesses, all of which tends to evoke paradisiacal visions amongst its devotees—there can be little in the way of expectations.

REMEMBER

Although skeptical of the motives which had propelled the Texas Revolution, Colonel Edward Stiff traveled to the struggling Republic of Texas in 1839. During his tour, he visited the newly established community of Houston, a city named after a hero for whom he had no respect. To his surprise, the city had named streets in honor of Travis and Fannin, but nothing for "honest Davy Crockett." It appeared to him that Texas had already forgotten.[42] Today, Houston does have a street named for Crockett, and Texas did not forget.

In Clarksville, there is a street named in memory of the real Crockett who passed just north of their town. A roadside marker, located within the present-day Clarksville city limits, designates the former home site of William Becknell and specifically mentions Crockett's visit. Further west, just off Clarksville Street in Paris, stands the Crockett Jr. High School near the grounds where tradition contends he made camp. Not too far from Lake Davy Crockett lies Honey Grove, which has no doubts about from whom it received its name. Crockett Park is located about a half mile west of the downtown district on land donated by Samuel Erwin.

Visitors to the Sterne-Hoya House in Nacogdoches, now a Texas Historic Landmark, are informed that Crockett did indeed sleep at the former home of Nicholas Adolphus and Eva Rosine Sterne. Nacogdoches also boasts of being the place where Crockett formally dedicated himself to the future Republic of Texas. On the campus of Stephen F. Austin University, there stands a replica of the Old Stone Fort where Crockett is said to have signed the Oath of Allegiance.

The David Crockett Oak Tree in 1938. Courtesy of Eliza Bishop.

Leaving Nacogdoches on Highway 21 through the pine trees of the east Texas hill country, the visitor passes through the Neches District of the Davy Crockett National Forest. About sixty-five miles down the road from Nacogdoches is the city of Crockett, Texas.

Andrew Edwards Gossett made certain that the city of Crockett was incorporated as the seat of Houston County in 1837, but as the Centennial Celebration of 1936 approached, residents realized they lacked something tangible linking them to the days of the revolution. Then someone discovered the David Crockett Oak Tree. This, it was said, was the very tree out of which Crockett shot a raccoon, thereby increasing his collection of coonskin caps. The David Crockett Spring, located on Highway 21 at the southwest end of the city in the parking lot of an old gas station adjacent to a railroad overpass was a site designed for visitors. Modestly decorated with a water fountain and a painted backdrop featuring Crockett in a serene pastoral setting, this was not the spot where Crockett camped. The actual location of the spring and Crockett's campsite was about a quarter mile to the north on Pease Street next to the cemetery. Today, the spring from which Crockett drew water has long since been paved over, and the David Crockett Oak Tree is gone.[43] Still, leading residents take pride in the fact that their community is named after an honorable man and encompasses the ground on which he slept.

Further south, on the grounds of the old town, stands the Star of the Republic Museum in the Washington-on-the-Brazos State Historical Park. Visitors are informed that Crockett passed through the site of the Constitutional Convention on his way to the Alamo. Whether one looks for David or Davy, his trail eventually leads us to the Alamo.

Having envisioned Texas as another chance to build a republic along the lines of what America's Founders had intended, David Crockett can only be viewed as the "natural, democratic leader" amongst republicans for whom freedom and political liberty meant responsibility. Confident in their own abilities, the revolutionaries of Texas considered the conservative centralist form of republicanism as a system ill-suited for men of their talents. Fulfilling the requirement that republicans must be ornery,[44] the men of the Alamo garrison appraised certain values to be worth fighting for, worth killing for, and worth risking their lives for. The Republic of Texas would have been better off had they survived the war.

On February 25, 1837, ashes, charred bones, shreds of uniforms, and buttons were collected from the funeral pyres and placed in a small casket draped in the flag of the Republic of Texas. At four in the afternoon, a procession of civil authorities and military personnel made their way from the San Fernando Church to the site of the pyres. There, Colonel Juan Seguín spoke of the "spirit of liberty" which acknowledged their "brothers, Travis, Bowie, Crockett, and others," men whose conduct in the face of tyranny merited a place "in the pages of history." He described how the bodies of these heroes had been bound and dragged to the spot where they were standing and burned. Seguín then appealed to the audience to remember their "worthy companions" and to dedicate themselves to the cause of Texas liberty.[45]

Gail Borden regretted he did not have all the names of those who fought and died at the Alamo, so as he said, "that we might publish them, and thus consecrate to future ages the memory of our heroes who perished at the Thermopylae of Texas."[46] To that end, the marble Cenotaph was erected in 1939. At the Cenotaph's base are four prominent reliefs. The name chiseled beneath the image representing Crockett is that of "David" not the more familiar "Davy." Today, the Cenotaph stands silently in the Alamo Plaza so that we might remember those citizen soldiers who fought and died to build a better republic, those soldiers for whom there are no graves.

Crockett's adventures in the woods do not form the most meaningful facet of his life's story. What really matters to us is his relationship to civil society and to our culture. Embarking upon his final journey with an unusually high sense of awareness of the rules of conduct and a consistency of behavior expected only of leading citizens, David Crockett exhibited what the ancient Greeks called *arete*, a superior quality of character they believed to be possessed by too few people. And it is precisely this quality that formed the very core of the dominant Davy Crockett legend, as publicized by Smith, perpetuated by Rourke, and made a virtual reality by Disney—that of an individual born without title or social and economic advantage who grew up into a basically honest man of high standards and who more often than not, behaved in accordance with those principles and put the welfare of the "public thing" ahead of his own personal interests.

No matter how this story is told, we end up with the David of history and the most enduring image of the legendary Davy which best represents him, fighting at the Alamo fully anticipating that the Constitutional Convention would declare Texas independent and create a new republic. As one of the few men who acted boldly at a critical juncture, he reminds us that in the real world there is good and bad, right and wrong, and that we can have blood on our hands and still remain decent. During his last journey, Crockett conducted himself in a manner which revealed that his ideals were republican rather than democratic, and his character, more noble than common. Crockett's final journey not only epitomizes his entire life, but it represents one of those rare episodes when actual conduct begins to approximate the ideal.

List of Abbreviations

DRT   Daughters of the Republic of Texas Library, San Antonio

SARA   Southwest Arkansas Regional Archives, Old Washington Historic State Park, Washington, Arkansas

SHC -UNC   Southern Historical Collection, University of North Carolina, Chapel Hill

TXSL   Texas State Library and Archives Commission, Austin

CAH-UT   Center for American History, University of Texas, Austin

Notes

INTRODUCTION

1. *Arkansas Advocate*, December 16, 1836.

2. Arthur M. Schlesinger Jr., *The Age of Jackson* (Boston: Little, Brown and Co., 1953), 116.

3. James A. Shackford, *David Crockett, The Man and the Legend* (Westport, Conn., 1981), ix.

4. Ibid.

5. Ibid., vii, 250–52.

6. Richard Boyd Hauck, "The Man in the Buckskin Hunting Shirt," in Lofaro, *Davy Crockett: The Man, the Legend, the Legacy, 1786–1986* (Knoxville, Tenn.: University of Tennessee Press, 1985), 7.

7. Paul Andrew Hutton, "Davy Crockett, Still King of the Wild Frontier, And a Hell of a Nice Guy Besides," *Texas Monthly*, (November 1986), 244.

8. Paul Andrew Hutton, "An Exposition on Hero Worship," in Lofaro, *Crockett at Two Hundred, New Perspectives on the Man and the Myth* (Knoxville, Tenn.: University of Tennessee Press, 1989), 37.

9. Richard Boyd Hauck, "The Real Davy Crocketts, Creative Autobiography and the Invention of his Legend," in Lofaro *Crockett at Two Hundred*, 189.

10. Hauck, "The Man in the Buckskin Hunting Shirt," 17.

11. Hutton, "Davy Crockett, Still King of the Wild Frontier," 246.

12. Richard Boyd Hauck, "Making It All Up, Davy Crockett in the Theater," in Lofaro, *Davy Crockett: The Man, the Legend, the Legacy, 1786–1986*, 103.

13. Margaret J. King, "The Recycled Hero: Walt Disney's Davy Crockett," in Lofaro, *Davy Crockett: The Man, the Legend, the Legacy*, 144, 151.

14. Richard Shenkman, *Legends, Lies & Cherished Myths of American History* (New York: William Morrow and Co., Inc., 1988), 114.

15. Peter Jennings and Todd Brewster, *The Century* (New York: Doubleday, 1998), 339.

16. Richard Boyd Hauck, *Davy Crockett: A Handbook* (Lincoln: University of Nebraska Press, 1982), xxi.

17. Hutton, "Exposition on Hero Worship," in Lofaro, *Crockett at Two Hundred*, 37.

1. A REPUBLIC IN SEQUENCE

1. George Wilson Pierson, *Tocqueville in America* (Gloucester, Mass.: Peter Smith, 1969), 385–86.

2. Ibid., 386.

3. James A. Shackford and Stanley J. Folmsbee, eds., *A Narrative of the Life of David Crockett of the State of Tennessee, by David Crockett* (Knoxville, Tenn.: University of Tennessee Press, 1973), 43.

4. Ibid., 49.

5. Ibid., 135.

6. Pierson, *Tocqueville in America,* 349.

7. Ibid., 386.

8. M. J. Heale, "The Role of the Frontier in Jacksonian Politics: David Crockett and the Myth of the Self-Made Man," *The Western Historical Quarterly,* (October 1973), 406.

9. Ben Perley Poore, *Perley's Reminiscences of Sixty Years in the National Metropolis,* vol. 1, (Philadelphia: Hubbard Brothers Publishers, 1886), 181.

10. Ibid., 181.

11. Shackford and Folmsbee, *A Narrative,* 168–69.

12. Ibid., 5.

13. Ibid., 11.

14. Shackford, *David Crockett, The Man and the Legend,* 112.

15. Emma Inman Williams, Jackson to Samuel Hays, April 23, 1831, *Historic Madison, The Story of Jackson and Madison County Tennessee,* (Jackson, Tenn.: Madison County Historical Society, 1946), 403.

16. Ibid., Crockett to Col. T. J. Tobyns, May 27, 1834, 424.

17. Ibid., Crockett to John Ash, December 27, 1834, 426.

18. Schlesinger Jr., *The Age of Jackson,* 110.

19. Shackford, *David Crockett, The Man and the Legend,* 162.

20. Robert V. Remini, *Andrew Jackson and the Course of the American Empire, 1767–1821* (New York: Harper & Row Publishers, 1977), 1.

21. Shackford, *David Crockett, The Man and the Legend,* 174..

22. John Spencer Basset, ed., Andrew Jackson to James K. Polk, May 12, 1835, *Correspondence of Andrew Jackson,* vol. 5, *1833–38,* (Washington, D.C.: Carnegie Institute of Washington, 1931), 346.

23. Ibid., Jackson to Felix Grundy, October 5, 1835, 371.

24. Shackford, *David Crockett, The Man and the Legend,* 204.

25. *Arkansas Advocate,* July 10, 1835.

26. *Jackson Sun,* July 26, 1985.

27. Ibid.

28. Skipper Steely, *Forty-Seven Years,* 1988, 310, SARA.

29. *Sunday Express* found in David Crockett File, DRT.

30. Williams, *Historic Madison,* 80.

31. Newspaper interview with Mrs. Matilda Fields, found in David Crockett File, DRT.

32. Shackford, *David Crockett, The Man and the Legend*, 205–6.

33. Interview with Mrs. Matilda Fields, David Crockett File, DRT.

2. THE JOURNEY BEGINS

1. Constance Rourke, *Davy Crockett* (New York: Harcourt, Brace and World, Inc., 1934), 179.

2. David Crockett, *Davy Crockett's Own Story, As written by himself,* (Stamford, Conn.: Longmeadow Press, 1992), 242. A recent product combining the *Narrative, Tour,* and *Exploits.*

3. Shackford, *David Crockett, The Man and the Legend*, 210.

4. Ibid., 211.

5. Jeff Long, *Duel of Eagles* (New York: William Morrow and Co., Inc., 1990), 100.

6. Ibid., 100; Hauck, "The Man in the Buckskin Hunting Shirt," 17.

7. Walter Lord, *A Time To Stand* (New York: Harper & Brothers, 1961), 52.

8. William C. Davis, *Three Roads to the Alamo* (New York: HarperCollins, 1998), 407.

9. Shackford, *David Crockett, The Man and the Legend*, 308.

10. Amelia W. Williams and Eugene C. Barker, eds., Houston to James Prentiss, April 20 & 24, 1834, *The Writings of Sam Houston, 1813–63,* vol. 1, (Austin, Tex., and New York: Jenkins Publishing and Pemberton Press, 1970), 289–91.

11. Newspaper interview with Mrs. Matilda Fields, David Crockett File, DRT.

12. Samuel C. Reid Jr., *The Scouting Expeditions of McCulloch's Texas Rangers* (1847; reprint, Freeport, N.Y.: Books for Libraries Press, 1970), 24.

13. Gary S. Zaboly, "Crockett Goes to Texas: A Newspaper Chronology," *Journal of the Alamo Battlefield Association I* (Summer 1995), 6.

14. Basset, Jackson to Andrew J. Hutchings, October 31, 1835, *Correspondence of Andrew Jackson,* vol. 5, *1833–38,* 374.

15. A. W. Neville, *The Red River Valley: Then and Now* (Paris, Tex.: North Texas Publishing Company, 1948), 11–12.

16. Reid Jr., *The Scouting Expeditions of McCulloch's Texas Rangers,* 24.

17. Newspaper interview with Mrs. Matilda Fields, David Crockett File, DRT.

18. Newspaper article about Elizabeth and David Crockett, David Crockett File, DRT.

19. Walter Blair, *Horse Sense in American Humor: From Benjamin Franklin to Ogden Nash* (New York: Russell & Russell, 1942), 50.

20. Rourke, *Davy Crockett,* 151.

21. Lord, *A Time to Stand,* 52.

22. Robert Patton Crockett to Smith Rudd, June 15, 1880, Manuscripts Department, Lilly Library, Indiana University. Robert was reading an early combination of the *Narrative, Tour,* and *Exploits* books.

23. Steely, *Forty-Seven Years,* 306, SARA.

24. Rourke, *Davy Crockett,* 150–51.

25. Ardis Edwards Burton, *Walt Disney Legends of Davy Crockett,* (Racine, Wisc.: Whitman Publishing Company, 1955), 131–32.

26. Williams and Barker, *The Writings of Sam Houston, 1813–63,* vol. 1, 302.

27. Atlas Jones to Calvin Jones, November 13, 1835, SHC-UNC.

28. Calvin Jones to Edmund D. Jarvis, December 2, 1835, SHC-UNC.

29. James D. Davis, *History of the City of Memphis* (Memphis, Tenn.: Hite, Crumpton, and Kelly, 1873), 142.

30. Ibid., 143.

31. Ibid.

32. Ibid., 144.

33. Ibid., 145.

3. ACROSS THE AMERICAN NILE

1. Lord, *A Time to Stand,* 50.

2. Ibid., 52–53.

3. Davis, *History of the City of Memphis,* 139–40.

4. *Arkansas Gazette,* November 17, 1835.

5. George William Featherstonhaugh, *Excursion Through the Slave States* (New York: Harper & Brothers, 1844), 96.

6. Fred W. Allsopp, *Albert Pike: A Biography* (Little Rock, Ark.: Parke-Harper Company, 1928), 116.

7. *Arkansas Gazette,* "Sunday Magazine," May 15, 1955.

8. Blair, *Horse Sense in American Humor,* 43.

9. William F. Pope, *Early Days In Arkansas* (Little Rock, Ark.: Frederick W. Allsopp, 1895), 183–84.

10. Ibid., 185.

11. Albert Pike, *Autobiography of General Albert Pike* (Washington D.C.: Library of the Supreme Council, A & ASR, n.p.), 79.

12. James R. Masterson, *Arkansas Folklore: The Arkansas Traveler, Davey Crockett, and Other Legends,* (Little Rock, Ark.: Rose Publishing, 1974), 316.

13. Pope, *Early Days In Arkansas,* 185.

14. *Arkansas Gazette,* May 15, 1955.

15. *Arkansas Gazette,* November 17, 1835.

16. *Arkansas Advocate,* September 11, 1835.

17. Pope, *Early Days In Arkansas,* 185.

18. Poore, *Perley's Reminiscences of Sixty Years in the National Metropolis,* vol. 1, 152.

19. Masterson, *Arkansas Folklore,* 28.

20. Crockett, *Davy Crockett's Own Story, As written by himself,* 255–58.

21. Vance Randolph, *Ozark Mountain Folks* (New York: Vanguard Press, 1932), 140–41.

22. Rourke, *Davy Crockett*, 157–58.

23. Vance Randolph, *We Always Lie to Strangers: Tall Tales from the Ozarks* (Westport, Conn.: Greenwood Press, 1951), 160.

24. Avantus Green, *With This We Challenge* (Little Rock, Ark.: n.p., 1945), 61.

25. *Arkansas Gazette*, May 15, 1955.

26. Zaboly, "Crockett Goes to Texas: A Newspaper Chronology," 9.

27. Shackford and Folmsbee, *A Narrative*, 89.

28. Pope, *Early Days In Arkansas*, 184.

29. *Arkansas Advocate*, July 10, 1835.

30. Ibid., August 14, 1835.

31. Ibid., November 13, 1835.

32. Zaboly, "Crockett Goes to Texas: A Newspaper Chronology," 6.

33. Ibid., 10, 18. Zaboly quoted the *Arkansas Advocate* as saying that Crockett and his group were "armed cap-a-pie. . . ." In an endnote on page 18, Zaboly explained that it means "From head to foot."

4. THE THRESHOLD UNFOLDS

1. *Arkansas Gazette*, November 17, 1835.

2. *Arkansas Advocate*, November 20, 1835.

3. Crockett, *Davy Crockett's Own Story, As written by himself*, 270.

4. James W. Nichols, "Adventures of an Old Texas Ranger," *The Texas Monthly* (December 1891), 342.

5. *The Star*, June 26, 1936, David Crockett File, DRT.

6. Featherstonhaugh, *Excursion Through the Slave States*, 119.

7. Ibid., 120.

8. Shackford, *David Crockett, The Man and the Legend*, 212–13.

9. Rick Tice, *Dooley's Ferry—Historic Transit Highway, Texas Gazette*, (1976), SARA.

10. Steely, *Forty-Seven Years*, 306–7, SARA.

11. Pat B. Clark, *The History of Clarksville and Old Red River County, Texas*, (Dallas: Mathis, Van Nort and Company, 1937), 4.

12. Claude V. Hall, "Early Days in Red River County," (June, 1931). *Northeast Texas Historical Articles About Its Beginnings*, (Paris, Tex.: Wright Press, 1984), 18–19, 23.

13. *Honey Grove Signal-Citizen*, March 20, 1931.

14. Ibid.

15. Clark, *The History of Clarksville*, 4–7.

16. Larry Beachum, *William Becknell, Father of the Santa Fe Trade* (El Paso: Texas Western Press, 1982), 84.

17. Clark, *The History of Clarksville*, 4–5.

18. *Dallas Morning News*, January 6, 1894.

19. Ibid.

20. Clark, *The History of Clarksville*, 4.

21. *The Independent*, August 31, 1883.

22. Clark, *The History of Clarksville*, 4.

23. Ibid., 7.

24. *Dallas Morning News*, January 6, 1894.

25. Steely, *Forty-Seven Years*, 318, SARA.

26. *The San Antonio Light*, David Crockett File, DRT.

27. Hall, "Early Days in Red River County," 19.

28. *Honey Grove Signal-Citizen*, March 20, 1931; Steely, *Forty-Seven Years*, 319, SARA.

29. Ibid.

30. Clark, *The History of Clarksville*, 5.

31. William C. Binkley, ed., *Official Correspondence of the Texan Revolution*, vol. 1, *1835–36* (New York: D. Appleton-Century Co., 1936), 231.

32. Wallace O. Chariton, ed., *100 Days in Texas: The Alamo Letters* (Plano, Tex.: Wordware Publishing, 1990), 22.

33. *The San Antonio Light*, David Crockett File, DRT.

34. Ibid.

35. *The Independent*, August 31, 1883.

36. Zaboly, "Crockett Goes to Texas: A Newspaper Chronology," 6.

37. Ibid., 10.

38. Ibid.

39. Neville, *The Red River Valley*, 11.

40. *Honey Grove Signal-Citizen*, March 20, 1931.

41. Clark, *The History of Clarksville*, 5.

42. David Crockett to Wiley and Margaret Flowers, January 9, 1836. David Crockett File, DRT.

43. *Honey Grove Signal-Citizen*, March 20, 1931; Stanley J. Folmsbee and Anna Grace Catron, *David Crockett In Texas*, East Tennessee Historical Society, (Knoxville, Tenn.: No. 30, 1958), 52. Carolyn S. Scott was fairly certain that Crockett was referring to the Bois d'Arc Creek when her findings were printed in 1931. Probably unaware of Scott's research, Folmsbee and Catron merely suggested that this is what Crockett meant.

44. Bright Ray, *Legends of the Red River Valley* (San Antonio, Tex.: The Naylor Company, 1941), 111–15.

45. *The Independent*, August 31, 1883.

46. Steely, *Forty-Seven Years*, 310, SARA.

47. W. A. Carter, *History of Fannin County, Texas* (Bonham, Tex.: Fannin County Historical Commission, 1885), 40–41.

48. *The Independent*, August 31, 1883; Clark, *The History of Clarksville*, 5.

49. Steely, *Forty-Seven Years*, 308, SARA; Neville, *The Red River Valley*, 12.

50. Rourke, *Davy Crockett*, 167–69.

51. Clark, *The History of Clarksville*, 20.

52. Ibid., 20.

53. *Path For Dooley's Ferry Road Was Started by Wild Animals*, PLF. # 195, SARA.

54. Featherstonhaugh, *Excursion Through the Slave States*, 124.

55. Ibid., 122.

56. Ibid., 167.

57. Ibid., 123.

58. Ibid., 62.

59. *Niles' Weekly Register*, August 27, 1836.

60. Ibid.

5. A CALLING ON SONG

1. Samuel Eliot Morison, Henry Steele Commager, and William E. Leuchtenburg, *A Concise History of the American Republic*, vol. 1, (New York: Oxford University Press, 1983), 237.

2. Z. N. Morrell, *Flowers and Fruits from the Wilderness* (Boston: Gould and Lincoln, 1872), 26.

3. Ibid., 29–30.

4. Zaboly, "Crockett Goes to Texas: A Newspaper Chronology," 16.

5. Chariton, *100 Days in Texas*, 8.

6. Ibid.

7. Ibid.

8. Eugene C. Barker, "The Texan Revolutionary Army," *The Quarterly of the Texas State Historical Association*, (April 1906), 228.

9. Fannin to Henry Smith, November 30, 1835, in Binkley, *Official Correspondence*, vol. 1, 146–48.

10. Travis to Governor and Council, December 3, 1835, in Binkley, *Official Correspondence*, vol. 1, 163.

11. Williams and Barker, *The Writings of Sam Houston, 1813–63*, vol. 1, 317–18.

12. Johnson to Wyatt Hanks and J. D. Clements, December 24, 1835, in Binkley, *Official Correspondence*, vol. 1, 235–36.

13. To Genl. F. W. Johnson, December 25, 1835, in Binkley, *Official Correspondence*, vol. 1, 237.

14. Johnson to Wyatt Hanks and J. D. Clements, December 24, 1835, in Binkley, *Official Correspondence*, vol. 1, 235–36.

15. *Telegraph and Texas Register*, January 23, 1836.

16. Ibid.

17. Johnson to Council, January 3, 1836, in Binkley, *Official Correspondence*, vol. 1, 267.

18. Daniel Cloud to I. B. Cloud, December 26, 1835, in Chariton, 73.

19. Daniel Cloud to Friend, December 25, 1835, in Chariton, 67.

20. Micajah Autry to Martha Autry, January 13, 1836, Adele Looscan, "Micajah Autry, A Soldier of the Alamo," *The Quarterly of the Texas State Historical Association*, vol. 14, *1911*. (Austin, Tex.) 319.

21. Affadavit of Hugh F. Rose, Erasmus T. Rose, and Samuel J. Rose, Texas General Land Office.

22. Amos Andrew Parker, *Trip to the West and Texas*. Originally published in 1835 (New York: Arno Press, 1973), 120.

23. William F. Gray, *From Virginia to Texas, 1835: Diary of Col. Wm. F. Gray, Giving Details of His Journey to Texas and Return in 1835–1836 and Second Journey to Texas in 1837*. Originally published in 1909; reprint (Houston, Tex.: Fletcher Young Publishing Co., 1965), 91–92.

24. Morrell, *Flowers And Fruits From the Wilderness*, 31.

25. Ibid., 35–37.

26. Ibid., 39.

27. Ibid., 41.

28. John H. Jenkins, ed., *The General's Tight Pants: Edward Warren's Texas Tour of 1836* (Austin, Tex.: The Pemberton Press, 1976), 5.

29. Ibid.

30. Long, *Duel of Eagles*, 107, 109.

31. Garry Wills, *John Wayne's America: The Politics of Celebrity* (New York: Simon & Schuster, 1997), 209, 211–13.

32. Louis Wiltz Kemp, *The Signers of the Texas Declaration of Independence* (Salado, Tex.: Anson Jones Press, 1944), 375.

33. *Niles' Weekly Register*, April 9, 1836.

6. RETURN TO CIVILIZATION

1. Statement of C. A. Sterne, October 27, 1924, Robert Bruce Blake Research Collection, vol. 62, 334.

2. Chariton, *100 Days*, 21–22.

3. James Gaines to James W. Robinson, January 9, 1836, in Binkley, *Official Correspondence*, vol. 1, 282.

4. George Louis Crocket, *Two Centuries in East Texas: A History of San Augustine County and Surrounding Territory from 1685* (San Augustine, Tex.: Christ Episcopal Church, 1932), 89.

5. Ibid., 179.

6. Ibid., 89.

7. Ibid., 121–22.

8. *Galveston News*, January 9, 1898.

9. *Morning Courier and New York Enquirer, Extra*, March 26, 1836.

10. Gaines to Robinson, January 9, 1836, in Binkley, *Official Correspondence*, vol. 1, 284.

11. David Crockett to Wiley and Margaret Flowers, January 9, 1836, David Crockett File, DRT.

12. Shackford, *David Crockett, The Man and the Legend*, 109.

13. Houston to Governor Smith, January 6, 1836, in Chariton, 107.

14. Ibid., 107.

15. John Henry Brown, Governor Smith to Council, January 9, 1836, *Life and Times of Henry Smith: The First American Governor of Texas* (Austin, Tex.: The Steck Company, 1935), 186–88.

16. Ibid., Smith to Robinson, January 10, 1836, 192.

17. Ibid., Smith to Council, January 9, 1836, 187, 189–90.

18. Chariton, *100 Days,* 147.

19. Charles Adams Gulick Jr., Winnie Allen, Katherine Elliott, and Harriet Smither, eds., *The Papers of Mirabeau Buonaparte Lamar,* vol. 1, (Austin, Tex.: Pemberton Press, 1968), 296

20. *Muster Rolls of the Texas Revolution,* DRT, 126. The oath on p. 125 states "for the Government of the Army of Texas."

21. Rourke, *Davy Crockett,* 174.

22. Shackford, *David Crockett, The Man and the Legend,* 219.

23. Ibid.

24. Ibid., 219.

25. Forbes to Robinson, January 12, 1836, Gulick Jr., *Lamar Papers,* vol. 1, 296.

26. Ibid.

27. *Muster Rolls of the Texas Revolution,* DRT, 124–27.

28. Originally published in the *Telegraph and Texas Register* on April 28, 1838, and reprinted in *Niles' Weekly Register,* June 23, 1838.

29. Eugene C. Barker, "Notes On Early Texas Newspapers, 1819–1836," *Southwestern Historical Quarterly,* vol. 21, (July, 1917), 143.

30. William Kennedy, *Texas: The Rise, Progress, and Prospects of the Republic of Texas* (Ft. Worth, Tex.: Molyneaux, 1925), 556.

31. Binkley, *Official Correspondence, Vol. I,* 269.

32. Davis, *Three Roads to the Alamo,* 695.

33. Shackford, *David Crockett, The Man and the Legend,* 219.

34. Folmsbee and Catron, *David Crockett In Texas,* 52.

35. Lon Tinkle, *Thirteen Days to Glory,* (College Station, Tex.: Texas A&M University Press, 1985), 134; Lord, *A Time to Stand,* 53–54.

36. Mark Derr, *The Frontiersman: The Real Life and the Many Legends of Davy Crockett* (New York: William Morrow and Company, Inc., 1993), 229.

37. Davis, *Three Roads to the Alamo,* 414.

38. Ibid., 415.

39. Ibid., 410.

40. Peter Harper File, Audited Military Claims, TXSL.

41. *Niles' Weekly Register,* June 23, 1838.

42. Ibid.

43. Rourke, *Davy Crockett,* 174.

44. Lord, *A Time to Stand,* 54.

45. Davis, *Three Roads to the Alamo,* 415–16.

46. *Muster Rolls of the Texas Revolution*, 127, DRT.

47. William R. Everdell, *The End of Kings: A History of Republics and Republicans* (Chicago: University of Chicago Press, 1983), 6.

48. Amartya Sen, "Democracy as a Universal Value," *American Educator*, (Summer 2000), 20.

49. Everdell, *The End of Kings*, 8.

50. Ibid., 6; Adams to Roger Sherman, July 17, 1789, Quoted from: Adams Charles Francis, [ed.], *The Works of John Adams, Second President of the United States* (Freeport, N.Y.: Books For Libraries Press, 1969), 428.

51. David Crockett to Wiley and Margaret Flowers, January 9, 1836, David Crockett File, DRT.

52. Burton, *Walt Disney Legends of Davy Crockett*, 137–38.

7. DOWN THE KING'S ROAD

1. *Muster Rolls of the Texas Revolution*, 125, DRT.

2. Herbert Simms Kimble letter, September 5, 1836, William Irving Lewis File, DRT.

3. Davis, *Three Roads to the Alamo*, 413.

4. *Muster Rolls of the Texas Revolution*, 126, DRT.

5. Affidavit of William Ray Gilmer, Texas General Land Office, Austin, Texas.

6. Amelia Williams, "A Critical Study of the Siege of the Alamo and of the Personnel of Its Defenders," *The Southwestern Historical Quarterly*, vol. 37, No. 4, Chap. 5, (April 1934), 281.

7. Micajah Autry to Martha Autry, January 13, 1836, Looscan, "Micajah Autry," 320.

8. James M. Day, compiler, *The Texas Almanac, 1857–1873: A Compendium of Texas History* (Waco, Tex.: Texian Press, 1967), 174.

9. *Austin City Gazette*, April 14, 1841.

10. Williams, *A Critical Study*, vol. 37, No. 3, Chap. 4, (January 1934), 167.

11. Crockett, *Davy Crockett's Own Story, As written by himself*, 299.

12. Rourke, *Davy Crockett*, 169.

13. Ibid., 179.

14. Daniel Cloud to Friend, December 25, 1835, in Chariton, 69.

15. Long, *Duel of Eagles*, 109, 129.

16. Ibid., 129–31.

17. Ibid., 128.

18. Ibid., 129.

19. Micajah Autry to Martha Autry, January 13, 1836, Looscan, "Micajah Autry," 319.

20. Forbes to Robinson, January 12, 1836, Gulick Jr., *Lamar Papers*, vol. 1, 296.

21. Micajah Autry to Martha Autry, January 13, 1836, Looscan, "Micajah Autry," 319.

22. Williams, *A Critical Study*, vol. 37, No. 3, Chap. 4, 167.

23. Ibid., vol. 37, No. 4, Chap. 5, (April 1934), 250–51.

24. Ibid., vol. 37, No. 3, Chap. 4, (January 1934), 165.

25. Ibid., vol. 37, No. 3, Chap. 4, (January 1934), 165, vol. 7, No. 4, Chap. 5, (April 1934), 264.

26. Affidavit concerning Achilles L. Harrison by Dr. William P. Smith, April 24, 1836, TXSL

27. Audited Military Claims, Republic of Texas, TXSL.

28. Ibid.

29. John H. Jenkins, ed., *The Papers of the Texas Revolution, 1835–36,* vol. 4, (Austin: Presidial Press, 1973), 66.

30. Crockett, *Davy Crockett's Own Story, As written by himself,* 318. The article, printed by the *New York Sun,* appeared in the May 10, 1836 issue. This article can be found in Zaboly, "Crockett Goes to Texas: A Newspaper Chronology," 14.

31. David Crockett to Wiley and Margaret Flowers, January 9, 1836. David Crockett File, DRT.

32. John Henry Brown, *Indian Wars & Pioneers of Texas,* L. E. Daniell, Pub., (1904; reprint, Austin, Tex., State House Press, 1988), 299.

33. Micajah Autry to Martha Autry, January 13, 1836, Looscan, "Micajah Autry," 319.

34. Ibid., 319.

35. Derr, *The Frontiersman,* 240; Davis, *Three Roads to the Alamo,* 415.

36. Neill to Governor and Council, January 8, 1836, in Binkley, *Official Correspondence,* vol. 1, 278.

37. Edward Warren to Uncle, February 1, 1836, Jenkins, *The General's Tight Pants,* 10.

38. Parker, *Trip to the West and Texas,* 122–23.

39. Evangeline Gossett Newcomer, *The Family of Gossett,* (Pico, Calif.: John M. McCoy, 1954), 165–66.

40. Frank Mulder Gossett, *Andrew Edwards Gossett: Citizen-Civil Officer-Soldier-Founder of City of Crockett, 1812–1890.* Frank Mulder Gossett File, Crockett Public Library, Crockett, Texas, 1969, 2–3.

41. *East Texas Vacation Guide,* Complied by Tourist Department East Texas Chamber of Commerce, (Longview, Tex., 1988), 61–62. *Crockett and Houston County,* Crockett Chamber of Commerce, (Crockett, Tex., n.d.).

42. *History of Houston County: 1687–1979.* Complied and edited by History Book Committee of Houston County Historical Commission, (Tulsa, Okla.: Heritage Publishing Company, 1979), 10.

43. Fannin to Robinson, January 21, 1836, in Binkley, *Official Correspondence,* vol. 1, 322.

44. *Proclamation,* January 19, 1836, Gulick Jr., *Lamar Papers,* vol. 1, 300–01.

45. Parker, *Trip to the West and Texas,* 129.

46. Gray, *From Virginia to Texas, 1835*, 103.

47. Herbert Simms Kimble letter, September 5, 1836, William Irving Lewis File, DRT.

48. David Crockett File, Audited Military Claims, TXSL.

49. Ibid.

50. Neill to Houston, January 14, 1836, in Binkley, *Official Correspondence*, vol. 1, 295.

51. Hauck, "The Real Davy Crocketts," in *Crockett at Two Hundred*, 189.

8. IN NO PARTICULAR HURRY

1. Nathan Mitchell, *Life of Nathan Mitchell*, n.p., 12–13, CAH-UT.

2. Ibid., 12.

3. John Milton Swisher, *The Swisher Memoirs* (San Antonio, Tex.: The Sigmund Press, 1932), 18.

4. Ibid., 19.

5. Ibid.

6. Ibid.

7. Ibid., 21.

8. Ibid., 21–22.

9. Gulick Jr., *Lamar Papers*, vol. 1, 93–94.

10. Ibid., 93–94.

11. Ibid., 94.

12. Johnson to Council, January 30, 1836, in Binkley, *Official Correspondence*, vol. 1, 366.

13. Williams and Barker, Houston to Henry Smith, January 30, 1836, *The Writings of Sam Houston, 1813–63*, vol. 1, 348.

14. Ibid., 350–51.

15. Ibid., 352.

16. Ibid., 353.

17. Ibid., 354.

18. Binkley, *Official Correspondence*, vol. 1, 372.

19. Neill to Governor and Council, January 23, 1836, in Binkley, *Official Correspondence*, vol. 1, 328.

20. Binkley, *Official Correspondence*, vol. 1, 372.

21. Johnson to Council, January 30, 1836, in Binkley, *Official Correspondence*, vol. 1, 367.

22. Council to the People of Texas, December 10, 1835, in Chariton, 22.

23. Gray, *From Virginia to Texas, 1835*, 92.

24. Ibid., 90.

25. Pollard to Henry Smith, February 13, 1836, in Binkley, *Official Correspondence*, vol. 2, 423–24.

26. Kemp, *The Signers of the Texas Declaration of Independence*, 233.

27. Ibid., 178.

28. Certificate of Election Returns, Municipality of San Augustine, Texas, February 2, 1836, TSLA.

29. Long, *Duel of Eagles*, 128.

30. Hauck, "The Real Davy Crocketts," in *Crockett at Two Hundred,* 189; Hutton, "Davy Crockett, Still King of the Wild Frontier," 245.

31. Derr, *The Frontiersman,* 240; Davis, *Three Roads to the Alamo,* 416.

32. Officers at Bexár to the Convention, in Binkley, *Official Correspondence,* vol. 1, 394.

33. Volunteers at Refugio to the Convention, in Binkley, *Official Correspondence,* vol. 2, 430.

34. Officers at Bexár to the Convention, in Binkley, *Official Correspondence,* vol. 1, 394.

35. Gray, *From Virginia to Texas, 1835,* 90.

36. Herman Ehrenberg, *With Milam And Fannin: Adventures of a German Boy in Texas' Revolution* (Dallas: Tardy Publishing Co., 1935), 21.

37. Ibid., 22.

38. Andrew Jackson Sowell, *Early Settlers and Indian Fighters of Southwest Texas . . . Facts Gathered from Survivors of Frontier Days* (Austin: Ben C. Jones & Co., 1900), 46–47.

39. Noah Smithwick, *The Evolution of a State; or, Recollections of Old Texas Days* (Austin: University of Texas Press, 1983), 117.

40. Ibid.

41. Charles Richard Williams, ed., *Diary and Letters of Rutherford Birchard Hayes,* vol. 1, *1834–60,* 261.

42. Ehrenberg, *With Milam And Fannin,* 25.

9. FANDANGO IN SAN ANTONE

1. Andrew Forest Muir, ed., *Texas In 1837: An Anonymous Contemporary Narrative* (Austin: University of Texas Press, 1958), 94.

2. Binkley, *Official Correspondence,* vol. 1, 395.

3. Green B. Jameson to Henry Smith, February 11, 1836, Binkley, *Official Correspondence,* vol. 2, 410.

4. Davis, *Three Roads to the Alamo,* 718.

5. Antonio Menchaca, *Memoirs* (San Antonio: Yanaguana Society Publications II, 1937), 22.

6. Howard R. Driggs and Sarah S. King, *Rise of the Lone Star: A Story of Texas Told by Its Pioneers* (New York: Frederick Stokes Co., 1936), 220.

7. Bowie to Henry Smith, February 2, 1836, in Binkley, *Official Correspondence,* vol. 1, 382.

8. Travis to Henry Smith, February 13, 1836, in Binkley, *Official Correspondence,* vol. 2, 420.

9. Shackford and Folmsbee, *A Narrative,* 72–73.

10. Green B. Jameson to Sam Houston, January 18, 1836, in Chariton, 155.

11. Ibid.

12. Pollard to Henry Smith, February 13, 1836, in Binkley, *Official Correspondence,* vol. 2, 424.

13. John Sutherland, *The Fall of the Alamo* (San Antonio: The Naylor Company, 1936), 11–12.

14. Hutton, "Davy Crockett, Still King of the Wild Frontier," 245.

15. Sutherland, *The Fall of the Alamo*, viii.

16. Davis, *Three Roads to the Alamo*, 516, 718–19.

17. Herbert Simms Kimble letter, September 5, 1836, William Irving Lewis File, DRT.

18. Chariton, *100 Days*, 222.

19. Menchaca, *Memoirs*, 22.

20. Ibid., 22–23.

21. Bowie to Henry Smith, February 2, 1836, in Binkley, *Official Correspondence*, vol. 1, 383.

22. Charles Ramsdell, *San Antonio: A Historical and Pictorial Guide* (Austin: University of Texas Press, 1959), 76.

23. David Crockett File, Audited Military Claims, TXSL.

24. *Proclamation, By The Acting Governor of the Provisional Government of Texas*, February 12, 1836, Gulick Jr., *Lamar Papers*, vol. 1, 324-329.

25. Davis, *Three Roads to the Alamo*, 719.

26. Ibid., 719–20.

27. Ibid., 720.

28. Ibid., 519.

29. Smithwick, *The Evolution of a State*, 114, 138.

30. Travis to Henry Smith, February 12, 1836, in Binkley, *Official Correspondence*, vol. 2, 416–17.

31. Travis to Henry Smith, February 13, 1836, in Binkley, *Official Correspondence*, vol. 2, 419–20.

32. Travis to Henry Smith, February 13, 1836, in Binkley, *Official Correspondence*, vol. 2, 421.

33. Baugh to Henry Smith, February 13, 1836, in Binkley, *Official Correspondence*, vol. 2, 423.

34. Ibid., 422.

35. Fannin to Robinson February 7, 1836, in Binkley, *Official Correspondence*, vol. 2, 402.

36. Travis to Henry Smith, February 12, 1836, in Binkley, *Official Correspondence*, vol. 2, 416.

10. Enter the Napoleon of the West

1. Gray, *From Virginia to Texas, 1835*, 107.

2. Ibid., 108.

3. Ibid., 107.

4. Herbert Simms Kimble letter, September 5, 1836, William Irving Lewis File, DRT.

5. Sutherland, *The Fall of the Alamo*, 11–12.

6. Menchaca, *Memoirs*, 22.

7. Herbert Simms Kimble letter, September 5, 1836, William Irving Lewis File, DRT.

8. Jenkins, *The Papers of the Texas Revolution, 1835–36*, vol. 4, 297–98.

9. Steely, *Forty-Seven Years*, 310, SARA.

10. C. Richard King, *Susannah Dickinson, Messenger of the Alamo*, (Austin, Tex.: School Creek Publishers, 1976), 76.

11. "Documents of the Texas Revolution," *The Alamo Journal*, February 1995, 9.

12. Smithwick, *The Evolution of a State*, 140.

13. Gulick Jr., Robinson to Fannin, February 13, 1836, *Lamar Papers*, vol. 1, 331.

14. Fannin to Robinson, February 14, 1836, in Chariton, 232.

15. Advisory Committee to J. W. Robinson, February 15, 1836, in Binkley, *Official Correspondence*, vol. 2, 433.

16. Sutherland, *The Fall of the Alamo*, 13–14.

17. Jesse Benton to a friend, February 22, 1836, in Chariton, 249–50.

18. Timothy M. Matovina, ed., *The Alamo Remembered: Tejano Accounts and Perspectives* (Austin: University of Texas Press, 1995), 90–91.

19. Sutherland, *The Fall of the Alamo*, 20.

20. Santa Anna to Don Vincente Filisola, February 27, 1836, in Chariton, 279.

21. Muir, *Texas In 1837*, 113.

22. Joseph E. Field, *Three Years In Texas* (Austin: Steck Co., 1935), 17.

23. Santa Anna to Don Vincente Filisola, February 27, 1836, in Chariton, 280.

24. Matovina, *The Alamo Remembered*, 45.

25. John Sowers Brooks to Father, in Chariton, 274.

26. Fannin to J. W. Robinson, February 25, 1836, Gulick Jr., *Lamar Papers*, vol. 1, 339.

27. Travis, *To The People of Texas and all Americans in the World*, February 24, 1836; Chariton, *100 Days*, 267.

28. "The Private Journal of Juan Nepomuceno Almonte," *The Southwestern Historical Quarterly*, vol. 48, (Austin: n.p., July 1944), 17.

29. Ibid., 17–18.

30. Francisco Becerra, *A Mexican Sergeant's Recollections of the Alamo and San Jacinto* as told to John S. Ford in 1875 (Austin: Jenkins Publishing Co., 1980), 19.

31. Travis to Jesse Grimes, March 3, 1836, in Chariton, 306.

11. THE DAWNING OF A REPUBLIC

1. Field, *Three Years In Texas*, 17.

2. King, *Susannah Dickinson, Messenger of the Alamo*, 77.

3. Gray, *From Virginia to Texas, 1835*, 120.

4. Ibid., 121.

5. "Texas Forever!!," in Chariton, 288.

6. John Sowers Brooks to Mother, March 2, 1836, in Chariton, 299.

7. Gray, *From Virginia to Texas, 1835,* 123–24.

8. Thomas Ricks Lindley, "A Correct List of Alamo Patriots," *The Alamo Journal,* (December 1993), 7; Thomas Ricks Lindley, "Davy Crockett: The Alamo's High Private," *Alamo Journal,* (December 1988), 3–11.

9. Ibid., 7.

10. Affidavit of William Ray Gilmer, Texas General Land Office.

11. Ibid.

12. Lindley, "Davy Crockett: The Alamo's High Private," 8.

13. Ibid., 7.

14. Affidavit of Susannah Hannig to Adjutant General of Texas, September 23, 1876, DRT.

15. Sowell, *Early Settlers and Indian Fighters of Southwest Texas,* 9–10.

16. Lindley, "Davy Crockett: The Alamo's High Private," 6.

17. Shackford and Folmsbee, *A Narrative,* 90.

18. J. M. Morphis, *History of Texas* (New York: United States Publishing Company, 1875), 175.

19. Ehrenberg, *With Milam And Fannin,* 155.

20. Thomas Ricks Lindley, "James Butler Bonham, October 17, 1835–March 6, 1836," *The Alamo Journal* (August 1988), 5, 10.

21. Ibid., 5.

22. Lindley, "A Correct List of Alamo Patriots," 6.

23. "The Private Journal of Juan Nepomuceno Almonte," *The Southwestern Historical Quarterly,* 19.

24. Fannin to Francis De Saugue, March 1, 1836, in Binkley, *Official Correspondence,* vol. 2, 475.

25. "The Private Journal of Juan Nepomuceno Almonte," *The Southwestern Historical Quarterly,* 19.

26. John S. Brooks to Father, March 10, 1836, in Chariton, 356.

27. Joseph B. Tatom to Sister, March 10, 1836, in Chariton, 357.

28. Fannin to General Mexia, March 11, 1836, in Chariton, 360.

29. Thomas Ricks Lindley, "Appendix to a Correct List of Alamo Patriots," *The Alamo Journal,* (March 1996), 12.

30. Travis to the President of the Convention, March 3, 1836, in Chariton, 304.

31. Travis to Jesse Grimes, March 3, 1836, in Chariton, 306.

32. Field, *Three Years,* 57.

33. Williams, *A Critical Study,* vol. 37, No. 4, Chap. 5, (April 1934), 271.

34. Driggs and King, *Rise of the Lone Star,* 223.

35. Travis to the President of the Convention, March 3, 1836, in Chariton, 305.

36. Miguel A. Sánchez Lamego, *The Siege and Taking of the Alamo* (Santa Fe, N. Mex.: Blue Feather Press for the Press of the Territorian, 1968), 36.

37. Matovina, *The Alamo Remembered,* 57.

12. In Remembrance

1. John Cross to Brother and Sister, March 9, 1836, in Chariton, 353.
2. Evan M. Thomas to Father, March 10, 1836, Ibid., 354–55.
3. Gray, *From Virginia to Texas, 1835*, 130.
4. Ibid., 134.
5. Ibid., 148.
6. Ibid., 137.
7. "Proclamation of Nacogdoches Meeting," *Arkansas Gazette*, May 3, 1836.
8. Zaboly, "Crockett Goes to Texas: A Newspaper Chronology," 12–13.
9. *Morning Courier and New-York Enquirer EXTRA*, March 26, 1836.
10. Bill Groneman, *Defense of A Legend: Crockett and the de la Peña Diary* (Plano, Tex.: Wordware Publishing, 1994), 82–83.
11. *Charleston Observer*, April 30, 1836.
12. *Arkansas Advocate*, April 22, 1836.
13. William Bedford Clark, "Col. Crockett's Exploits and Adventures in Texas: Death and Transfiguration," *Studies in American Humor I* (June 1982), 66–67.
14. Daniel J. Boorstin, *The Americans: The National Experience* (New York: Random House, 1965), 328.
15. Schlesinger Jr., *The Age of Jackson*, 278.
16. Hauck, "The Real Davy Crocketts," in *Crockett at Two Hundred*, 181.
17. Michael A. Lofaro, "The Hidden 'Hero' of the Nashville Crockett Almanacs," in Lofaro, *Davy Crockett: The Man, the Legend, the Legacy, 1786–1986*, 47.
18. Hauck, "The Real Davy Crocketts," in *Crockett at Two Hundred*, 179, 181.
19. Hauck, *Davy Crocket: A Handbook*, 41.
20. Hutton, "Davy Crockett, Still King of the Wild Frontier," 130.
21. Hutton, "An Exposition on Hero Worship," in *Crockett at Two Hundred*, 27.
22. Hutton, "Davy Crockett, Still King of the Wild Frontier," 246.
23. Ibid., 248.
24. Hutton, "An Exposition on Hero Worship," in *Crockett at Two Hundred*.
25. Derr, *The Frontiersman*, 269.
26. Hutton, "Davy Crockett, Still King of the Wild Frontier," 248; Hutton, "An Exposition on Hero Worship," in *Crockett at Two Hundred*, 37.
27. M. J. Heale, "The Role of the Frontier in Jacksonian Politics," 422.
28. Boorstin, *The Americans: The National Experience*, 57–58, 61.
29. Matovina, *The Alamo Remembered*, 69.
30. *San Antonio Express*, May 12, 1907.
31. *Address of the Honorable Wm. H. Wharton*, Gulick Jr., *Lamar Papers*, vol. 1, 363–64.

32. Dr. S. H. Stout, "David Crockett," *The American Historical Magazine*, vol. 7, (January 1902), 18–19.

33. Stephen L. Hardin, "Gallery: David Crockett," *Military Illustrated*, #23 (February–March 1990), 35.

34. Hauck, "The Real Davy Crocketts," in *Crockett at Two Hundred*, 183.

35. P. L. Franklin, "Col. Crockett Visits Boston," *National Republic*, (December 1929), 31.

36. Houston to James Collinsworth, March 13, 1836, in Chariton, 364.

37. Houston to James Collinsworth, March 17, 1836; in Chariton, 378.

38. Crockett, *Davy Crockett's Own Story, As written by himself*, 371–373.

39. Walter Berns, *Making Patriots*, (Chicago: University of Chicago Press, 2001), 18.

40. Ibid., 11, 134.

41. Hutton, "Davy Crockett, Still King of the Wild Frontier," 246.

42. Edward Stiff, *The Texas Emigrant*. Originally published in 1840 (Waco, Tex.: Texian Press, 1968), 315.

43. Author's conversation with Eliza Bishop of the Houston County Historical Commission, (Crockett, Tex.).

44. Everdell, *The End of Kings*, 306.

45. *Telegraph and Texas Register*, April 4, 1837.

46. *Telegraph and Texas Register*, March 24, 1836.

Bibliography

PRIMARY MATERIALS
Books
Adams, Charles Francis, ed. *The Works of John Adams, Second President of the United States.* Vol. 6. Freeport, New York: Books for Libraries Press, 1969.

Bassett, John Spencer, ed. *Correspondence of Andrew Jackson.* Vol. 5, 1833–38. Washington, D.C.: Carnegie Institute of Washington, 1931.

Becerra, Francisco. *A Mexican Sergeant's Recollections of the Alamo and San Jacinto . . . as Told to John S. Ford in 1875.* Austin: Jenkins Publishing Co., 1980.

Binkley, William C., ed. *Official Correspondence of the Texan Revolution, 1835–1836.* 2 vols. New York: D. Appleton-Century Co., 1936.

Chariton, Wallace O., ed. *100 Days in Texas: The Alamo Letters.* Plano, Tex.: Wordware Publishing, 1990.

Daughters of the Republic of Texas. *Muster Rolls of the Texas Revolution.* Austin: Office of the Custodian General, 1988.

Davis, James D. *History of the City of Memphis.* Memphis, Tenn.: Hite, Crumpton, and Kelly, 1873.

Day, James M., comp. and ed. *The Texas Almanac, 1857–1873: A Compendium of Texas History.* Waco, Tex.: Texian Press, 1967.

Ehrenberg, Herman. *With Milam and Fannin: Adventures of a German Boy in Texas' Revolution.* Translated by Charlotte Churchill. Edited by Henry Smith. Dallas: Tardy Publishing Co., 1935.

Featherstonhaugh, G. W., *Excursion Through the Slave States.* New York: Harper & Brothers, 1844.

Field, Joseph E. *Three Years in Texas, Including a View of the Texan Revolution, and an Account of the Principal Battles, Together With Descriptions of the Soil, Commercial and Agricultural Advantages, etc. 1836*; reprint, Austin: Steck Co., 1935.

Gray, William Fairfax. *From Virginia to Texas, 1835: Diary of Col. Wm. F. Gray, Giving Details of His Journey to Texas and Return in 1835–1836 and Second Journey to Texas in 1837.* Originally published in 1909; reprint, Houston: Fletcher Young Publishing Co., 1965.

Gulick, Charles A., Jr., and others, eds. *The Papers of Mirabeau Buonaparte Lamar.* 6 vols. Austin: Pemberton Press, 1968.

Jenkins, John H., ed. *The General's Tight Pants: Edward Warren's Texas Tour of 1836.* Austin: The Pemberton Press, 1976.

Jenkins, John H., ed. *The Papers of the Texas Revolution, 1835–1836.* 10 vols. Austin: Presidial Press, 1973.

Matovina, Timothy M., ed. *The Alamo Remembered: Tejano Accounts and Perspectives.* Austin: University of Texas Press, 1995.

Menchaca, Antonio. *Memoirs.* San Antonio: Yanaguana Society Publications II, 1937.

Morphis, J. M. *History of Texas From Its Discovery and Settlement, With A Description of its Principal Cities and Counties, and the Agricultural, Mineral, and Material Resources of the State.* New York: United States Publishing Company, 1875.

Morrell, Z. N. *Flowers and Fruits from the Wilderness.* Boston: Gould and Lincoln, 1872.

Muir, Andrew Forest, ed. *Texas In 1837: An Anonymous, Contemporary Narrative.* Austin: University of Texas Press, 1958.

Parker, Amos Andrew. *Trip to the West and Texas.* Originally published in 1835, reprint, New York: Arno Press, 1973.

Paulding, James Kirke. *The Lion of the West; Retitled the Kentuckian, or A Trip to New York: A Farce in Two Acts.* Revised by John Augustus Stone and William Bayle Bernard. Edited by James N. Tidwell. Stanford, Calif.: Stanford University Press, 1954.

Pope, William F. *Early Days In Arkansas.* Little Rock: Frederick W. Allsopp, 1895.

Poore, Ben Perley. *Perley's Reminiscences of Sixty Years in the National Metropolis.* Vol. 1. Philadelphia: Hubbard Brothers Publishers, 1886.

Reid, Samuel C., Jr. *The Scouting Expeditions of McCulloch's Texas Rangers.* Originally published in 1847; reprint, Freeport, N.Y.: Books For Libraries Press, 1970.

Shackford, James A. and Stanley J. Folmsbee, eds., *A Narrative of the Life of David Crockett of the State of Tennessee, by David Crockett.* Philadelphia: Carey & Hart, 1834; reprint, Knoxville, Tenn.: University of Tennessee Press, 1973.

Smithwick, Noah. *The Evolution of a State; or, Recollections of Old Texas Days.* Compiled by Nanna Smithwick Donaldson, 1900; reprint, Austin: University of Texas Press, 1983.

Sowell, Andrew Jackson. *Early Settlers and Indian Fighters of Southwest Texas . . . Facts Gathered from Survivors of Frontier Days.* Austin: Ben C. Jones & Co., 1900.

Stiff, Edward. *The Texas Emigrant.* Originally published in 1840. Waco: The Texian Press, 1968.

Sutherland, John. *The Fall of the Alamo.* San Antonio: The Naylor Company, 1936.

Swisher, John M. *The Swisher Memoirs.* San Antonio: The Sigmund Press, 1932.

Williams, Amelia W. and Eugene C. Barker, eds. *The Writings of Sam Houston, 1813–1863,* Austin and New York: Jenkins Publishing and Pemberton Press, 1970.

Williams, Charles Richard, ed. *Diary and Letters of Rutherford Birchard Hayes.* Vol. 1, 1834–60. Columbus, Ohio: The Ohio State Archaeological and Historical Society, 1922.

Articles

Almonte, Juan Nepomuceno. "The Private Journal of Juan Nepomuceno Almonte." *Southwestern Historical Quarterly* 48 (July 1944): 10–32.

Nichols, James Wilson. "Adventures of An Old Texas Ranger." *The Texas Monthly* 1 (December 1891): 340–343.

Stout, Dr. S. H. "David Crockett." *The American Historical Magazine* 7, no. 1 (January 1902): 3–21.

Newpapers

Arkansas Advocate, Little Rock.

Arkansas Gazette, Little Rock.

Austin City Gazette, Austin, Texas.

Charleston Courier, Charleston, South Carolina.

Charleston Observer, Charleston, South Carolina.

Morning Courier and New York Enquirer, New York.

Niles Weekly Register, Baltimore, Maryland.

Telegraph and Texas Register, San Felipe de Austin and Columbia, Texas.

Documents

Atlas Jones to Calvin Jones, November 13, 1835, SHC-UNC.

Calvin Jones to Edmund D. Jarvis, December 2, 1835, SHC-UNC.

David Crockett to Wiley and Margaret Flowers, January 9, 1836, David Crockett File, DRT.

Herbert Simms Kimble letter, September 5, 1836, William Irving Lewis File, DRT.

Bill of Sale. Two rifles sold by Crockett to Thomas J. Rusk, TSLA.

Promissory note issued by David Crockett to John Lott, TSLA.

Promissory note issued by B. Archer M. Thomas of Crockett's Company to John Lott, TSLA.

Certificate of Election Returns Municipality of San Augustine, TSLA.

Promissory note issued by David Crockett to Dr. Horatio Alsbury, TSLA.

Certification by Dr. William Smith concerning Achilles L. Harrison, TSLA.

Certification of Public Debt of the Late Republic of Texas Owed to the heirs of David Crockett, TSLA.

April 12, 1859. Affidavit of Captain William Ray Gilmer relative to Dr. John W. Thompson. General Land Office of the State of Texas.

September 23, 1876. Affidavit of Mrs. Susan Hannig. Adjutant General's Letters Concerning the Alamo Massacre, DRT.

Houston Memo. Confirming the service and discharge of Lt. Peter Harper. Audited Claims. Republic Claims Files. Claim #540. Reel #41. Library and Archives Commission, Texas.

Rudd Manuscripts, Robert Patton Crockett to Smith Rudd, June 15, 1880. Manuscripts Department, Lilly Library, Indiana University, Bloomington, Indiana.

Statement of C. A. Sterne, October 24, 1924, taken by Kate Hunter, Robert Bruce Blake Research Collection, Volume LXII, Special Collections, R. W. Steen Library, Stephen F. Austin University, Nacogdoches, Texas.

October 24, 1853. Affadavit of Hugh F. Rose, Erasmus T. Rose, and Samuel J. Rose relative to James Madison Rose, General Land Officer of the State of Texas.

Manuscripts

Mitchell, Nathan. *Life of Nathan Mitchell* CAH- UT.

Pike, Albert. *Autobiography of General Albert Pike,* Washington D.C., Library of the Supreme Council, A. & A. S. R.

SECONDARY MATERIALS

Books

Allsopp, Fred W. *Albert Pike: A Biography.* Little Rock: Parke-Harper Company, 1928.

Barker, Eugene C. *Mexico and Texas, 1821–1835: University of Texas Research Lectures on the Causes of the Texas Revolution.* Dallas: P. L. Turner Co., Publishers, 1928.

Beachum, Larry M. *William Becknell: Father of the Santa Fe Trade.* El Paso: Texas Western Press, 1982.

Berns, Walter. *Making Patriots.* Chicago: University of Chicago Press, 2001.

Binkley, William C. *The Texas Revolution.* Louisiana State University, 1952.

Blair, Walter. *Horse Sense in American Humor: From Benjamin Franklin to Ogden Nash.* New York: Russell & Russell, 1942.

Boorstin, Daniel J. *The Americans: The National Experience.* New York: Random House, 1965.

Brown, John Henry. *Life and Times of Henry Smith: The First American Governor of Texas.* Reprint: Austin: The Steck Company, 1935.

Brown, John Henry. *Indian Wars & Pioneers of Texas.* Austin: L. E. Daniel, Pub., 1904; reprint, Austin, Tex.: State House Press, 1988.

Burton, Ardis Edwards. *Walt Disney Legends of Davy Crockett.* Racine, Wisc.: Whitman Publishing Company, 1955.

Carter, W. A. *History of Fannin County, Texas.* Bonham, Tex.: Fannin County Historical Commission, 1885.

Clark, Pat B. *The History of Clarksville and Old Red River County, Texas.* Dallas: Mathis, Van Nort and Company, 1937.

Crocket, George Louis. *Two Centuries in East Texas: A History of San Augustine County and Surrounding Territory from 1685.* San Augustine, Tex.: Christ Episcopal Church, 1932.

Crockett, David. *Davy Crockett's Own Story, As written by himself.* Stamford, Conn.: Longmeadow Press, 1992.

Davis, William C. *Three Roads to the Alamo.* New York: HarperCollins, 1998.

Derr, Mark. *The Frontiersman: The Real Life and the Many Legends of Davy Crockett.* New York: William Morrow and Company, Inc., 1993.

Driggs, Howard R. and Sarah S. King. *Rise of the Lone Star: A Story of Texas Told by Its Pioneers.* New York: Frederick Stokes Co., 1936.

Everdell, William R. *The End of Kings: A History of Republics and Republicans.* Chicago: University of Chicago Press, 1983.

Green, Avantus. *With This We Challenge.* Little Rock: n.p., 1945.

Groneman, Bill. *Defense of a Legend: Crockett and the de la Peña Diary.* Plano, Tex.: Republic of Texas Press, 1994.

Hauck, Richard Boyd. *Davy Crockett: A Handbook.* Lincoln: University of Nebraska Press, 1982.

History Book Committee of Houston County Historical Commission, *History of Houston County, Texas: 1687–1979.* Tulsa, Okla.: Heritage Publishing Company, 1979.

Jennings, Peter and Todd Brewster. *The Century.* New York: Doubleday, 1998.

Kemp, Louis Wiltz. *The Signers of the Texas Declaration of Independence.* Salado: Anson Jones Press, 1944.

Kennedy, William. *Texas: The Rise, Progress, and Prospects of the Republic of Texas.* London, 1841. Reprint: Ft. Worth: Molyneaux Craftsman, 1925.

King, C. Richard. *Susannah Dickinson, Messenger of the Alamo.* Austin: Shoal Creek Publishers, 1976.

Lamego, Miguel A. Sánchez. *The Siege and Taking of the Alamo.* Translated by Consuelo Velasco. Santa Fe: Blue Feather Press for the Press of the Territorian, 1968.

Lofaro, Michael A., ed. *Davy Crockett: The Man, the Legend, the Legacy, 1786–1986.* Knoxville, Tenn.: University of Tennessee Press, 1985.

Lofaro, Michael, A. and Joe Cummings, eds. *Crockett at Two Hundred: New Perspectives on the Man and the Myth.* Knoxville, Tenn.: University of Tennessee Press, 1989.

Long, Jeff. *Duel of Eagles,* New York: William Morrow, 1990.

Lord, Walter. *A Time To Stand.* New York: Harper & Brothers, 1961.

Masterson, James R. *Arkansas Folklore: The Arkansas Traveler, Davey Crockett, and Other Legends.* Little Rock: Rose Publishing, 1974.

Medearis, Mary. *Washington, Arkansas: History on the Southwest Trail.* Hope, Ark.: Etter Printing Company, 1976.

Morison, Samuel Eliot, Henry Steele Commager, and William E. Leuchtenburg. *A Concise History of the American Republic.* Vol. 1, to 1877. New York: Oxford University Press, 1983.

Morrison, William Brown. *Military Posts and Camps in Oklahoma.* Oklahoma City: Harlow Publishing, 1936.

Newcomer, Evangeline Gossett. *The Family of Gossett.* Pico, Calif.: John M. McCoy, 1954.

Neville, A. W. *The Red River Valley: Then and Now.* Paris, Tex.: North Texas Publishing Company, 1948.

Pierson, George Wilson. *Tocqueville In America.* Gloucester, Mass.: Peter Smith, 1969.

Ramsdell, Charles. *San Antonio: A Historical and Pictorial Guide.* Austin: University of Texas Press, 1959.

Randolph, Vance. *Ozark Mountain Folk.* New York: Vanguard Press, 1932.

Randolph, Vance. *We Always Lie To Strangers: Tall Tales from The Ozarks.* Westport, Conn.: Greenwood Press, 1951.

Ray, Bright. *Legends of the Red River Valley.* San Antonio: The Naylor Company, 1941.

Remini, Robert V. *Andrew Jackson and the Course of the American Empire, 1767–1821.* New York: Harper & Row Publishers, 1977.

Rourke, Constance. *Davy Crockett.* New York: Harcourt, Brace and World, Inc., 1934.

Schlesinger, Arthur M., Jr. *The Age of Jackson.* Boston: Little, Brown and Co., 1953.

Shackford, James Atkins. *David Crockett: The Man and the Legend.* Originally published in 1956; reprint, Westport, Conn.: Greenwood Press Publishers, 1981.

Shenkman, Richard. *Legends, Lies & Cherished Myths of American History.* New York: William Morrow and Company, Inc. 1988.

Tinkle, Lon. *Thirteen Days to Glory.* College Station, Tex.: Texas A & M University Press, 1985.

Williams, Emma Inman. *Historic Madison: The Story of Jackson, and Madison County, Tennessee, from Prehistoric Moundbuilders to 1917.* Jackson, Tenn.: Madison County Historical Society, 1946.

Williams, Samuel Cole, L.L.D. *Beginnings of West Tennessee: In the Land of the Chickasaws.* Johnson City, Tenn.: The Watauga Press, 1930.

Wills, Garry. *John Wayne's America: The Politics of Celebrity.* New York: Simon & Schuster, 1997.

Yoakum, Henderson King. *History of Texas from its First Settlement in 1655 to its Annexation to the United States in 1846.* 2 vols. New York: Redfield, 1855.

Articles

Barker, Eugene C. "Declaration of Causes for Taking Up Arms against Mexico." *Quarterly of the Texas State Historical Association* 15 (January 1912): 173–85.

Barker, Eugene C. "The Texan Revolutionary Army." *Quarterly of the Texas State Historical Association* (April 1906): 227–61.

Barker, Eugene C. "Notes On Early Texas Newspapers, 1819–1836." *Texas State Historical Association* (July 1917): 127–44.

Clark, William Bedford. "Col. Crockett's Exploits and Adventures in Texas: Death and Transfiguration." *Studies in American Humor* 1 (June 1982): 66–76.

Folmsbee, Stanley J. and Anna Grace Catron. "David Crockett In Texas." *East Tennessee Historical Society* no. 30 (1958): 48–74.

Franklin, P. L. "Col. Crockett Visits Boston." *National Republic* (December 1929): 30–31, 45.

Hall, Claude V. "Early Days in Red River County." In *Northeast Texas: Historical Articles About It's Beginnings* 1. Paris, Tex.: Wright Press, 1984. Originally published in *East Texas State Teachers College Bulletin* 14 (June 1931).

Hardin, Stephen L. "Gallery: David Crockett." *Military Illustrated* 23 (February/March 1990): 28–35.

Heale, M. J. "The Role of the Frontier in Jacksonian Politics: David Crockett and the Myth of the Self-Made Man." *Western Historical Quarterly* 4 (1973): 405–23.

Hutton, Paul Andrew. "Davy Crockett, Still King of the Wild Frontier, And a Hell of a Nice Guy Besides." *Texas Monthly* (November 1986): 122–31, 244–48.

Lindley, Thomas Ricks. "James Butler Bonham, October 17, 1835–March 6, 1836." *The Alamo Journal* 62 (August 1988): 3–11.

Lindley, Thomas Ricks. "Davy Crockett: The Alamo's High Private." *The Alamo Journal* 64 (December 1988): 3–11.

Lindley, Thomas Ricks. "A Correct List of Alamo Patriots." *The Alamo Journal* 89 (December 1993): 3–7.

Lindley, Thomas Ricks. "Documents of the Texian Revolution." *The Alamo Journal* 95 (February 1995): 9.

Lindley, Thomas Ricks. "Appendix to a Correct List of Alamo Patriots." *The Alamo Journal* 100 (March 1996): 12–13.

Looscan, Adele B. "Micajah Autry, A Soldier of the Alamo." *Quarterly of the Texas State Historical Association* 14 (1911): 315–24.

Pohl, James W. and Stephen L. Hardin. "The Military History of the Texas Revolution: An Overview." *Texas State Historical Association* 89 (January 1986): 269–308.

Ross, Margaret Smith. "Davy Crockett in Arkansas." *Arkansas Gazette Sunday Magazine* (May 15, 1955).

Sen, Amartya. "Democracy As A Universal Value." *American Educator* (Summer 2000): 16–22, 50–52.

Tice, Rick. "Dooley's Ferry—Historic Transit Highway." *Texas Gazette* (1976), SARA.

Williams, Amelia. "A Critical Study of the Siege of the Alamo and the Personnel of Its Defenders." *Southwestern Historical Quarterly* 36–37 (1933–34): 36 no. 4 (April 1933): 251–87; 37 no. 1 (July 1933): 1–44;

37 no. 2 (October 1933): 79–115; 37 no. 3 (January 1934): 157–84; 37 no. 4 (April 1934): 237–312.

Zaboly, Gary S. "Crockett Goes to Texas: A Newspaper Chronology." *Journal of the Alamo Battlefield Association I* (Summer 1995): 5–18.

Path for Dooley's Ferry Road Was Started by Wild Animals, SARA.

Manuscripts

Gossett, Frank Mulder. *Andrew Edwards Gossett, Citizen-Civil Officer-Soldier-Founder of City of Crockett, 1812–1890.* Frank Mulder Gossett File, John H. Wootters-Crockett Public Library, Crockett, Tex.

Steely, Skipper, *Forty-Seven Years*, 1988, SARA.

Newspaper Articles

Article of Elizabeth and David Crockett. David Crockett File, DRT, n.p, n.d.

"Crockett's Camp." *The Independent*, Honey Grove, Tex., 31 August 1883.

"Davy Crockett's Kinsmen In Texas." *Dallas Morning News*, 7 July 1925.

"Enrique Esparza, Alamo's Only Survivor, Who Claims to Have Been There During the Seige, Tells the Story of the Fall." *San Antonio Express*, San Antonio, Tex., 12 & 19 May 1907.

"Famed Blevins House, Built of Hewn Logs, Never was Tavern." *The Star*, David Crockett File, DRT, 26 June 1936.

"Monumental Confusion: Where in the Sam Hill did Davy Crockett tell the world to get off?" *Jackson Sun*, Jackson, Tenn., 26 July 1985.

"More Facts About David Crockett's Route." *Honey Grove Signal-Citizen*, 20 March 1931.

"Mrs. Elizabeth White." *Galveston News*, Galveston, Tex., 9 January 1898.

"Mrs. Ibbie Gordon." *Dallas Morning News*, 6 January 1894.

"Pioneer Woman Recalls Days of Alamo When Davy Crockett Took the Shortcut." *San Antonio Light*, n.d.

The Courier. Article on Mrs. Matilda Fields, David Crockett File, DRT.

Sunday Express. William Alexander Ridgway article, David Crockett File, DRT.

Vacation Guides

East Texas Vacation Guide. Complied by Tourist Department East Texas Chamber of Commerce, Longview, Tex., 1988.

Crockett and Houston County. Crockett Chamber of Commerce, Crockett, Tex., n.d.

Index